HENRY JAMES AND THE IMAGINATION OF PLEASURE

Tessa Hadley examines how Henry James progressively disentangled himself from the moralising frame through which English-language novels in the nineteenth century had imagined sexual passion. Hadley argues that his relationship with the European novel tradition was crucial, helping him to leave behind a way of seeing in which only 'bad' women could be sexual. She reads James's transitional fictions of the 1890s as explorations of how disabling and distorting ideals of women's goodness and purity were learned and perpetuated within English and American cultural processes. These explorations, Hadley argues, liberated James to write the great heterosexual love affairs of the late novels, with their emphasis on the power of pleasure and play: themes which are central to James's ambitious enterprise to represent the privileges and the pains of turn-of-the-century leisure-class society.

TESSA HADLEY is Lecturer in English and Creative Studies at Bath Spa University College. Her novel, *Accidents in the Home* is published in 2002 by Jonathan Cape.

HENRY JAMES AND THE IMAGINATION OF PLEASURE

TESSA HADLEY

CAMBRIDGE
UNIVERSITY PRESS

PUBLISHED BY THE PRESS SYNDICATE OF THE UNIVERSITY OF CAMBRIDGE
The Pitt Building, Trumpington Street, Cambridge, United Kingdom

CAMBRIDGE UNIVERSITY PRESS
The Edinburgh Building, Cambridge CB2 2RU, UK
40 West 20th Street, New York, NY 10011-4211, USA
477 Williamstown Road, Port Melbourne, VIC 3207, Australia
Ruiz de Alarcón 13, 28014 Madrid, Spain
Dock House, The Waterfront, Cape Town 8001, South Africa

http://www.cambridge.org

© Tessa Hadley 2002

First published 2002

Printed in the United Kingdom at the University Press, Cambridge

Typeface Baskerville Monotype 11/12.5 pt.   *System* LATEX 2ε [TB]

A catalogue record for this book is available from the British Library.

Library of Congress Cataloguing in Publication data
Hadley, Tessa.
Henry James and the imagination of pleasure / by Tessa Hadley.
p.   cm.
Includes bibliographical references and index.
ISBN 0-521-81169-4
1. James, Henry, 1843–1916 – Criticism and interpretation.   2. Imagination in literature.
3. Pleasure in literature.   I. Title.
PS2127.I4 H33   2002
813′.4 – dc21   2001037826

ISBN 0 521 81169 4 hardback

*To Eric and Wilbur, who were at
the beginning.*

Contents

Acknowledgements

Colleagues and friends at Bath Spa University College have been generous with their time and their help while I was writing this book: thanks in particular to Gavin Cologne-Brookes, Paul Edwards, Richard Francis, David Timms. Thanks, too, to the Humanities Faculty for giving me relief from teaching so that I could concentrate my efforts. Thanks to Jean Gooder whose suggestions were always inspiring. Eric Hadley gave me good advice, amongst other things.

Parts of chapter 2 appeared in an essay on *What Maisie Knew* in *English*, Autumn 1997: thanks to the English Association for permission to reprint this material.

Introduction

There has been a quiet revolution: new readings in the last ten years
or so have overturned our perceptions of the erotic in Henry James's
fictions. For all the variations in emphasis and the differences in tone,
new ways of explicitly addressing the homoerotic in his writing have
made themselves quickly at home in our awareness. They seem indeed
to have taken up space that was ready and waiting for them. We had
needed ways of including something that had been missing from our
account of the work (although if we had read the letters it could hardly
have been missing from our imagining of James's life); we needed a critical vocabulary to encompass the whole passional range of this writer
whose register of passionate feeling was distinctively not delimited by the
conventions of the heterosexual pursuit. Whether we now choose to discuss a James deeply preoccupied with homosexual secrets and 'panics',
as Eve Kosovsky-Sedgwick does; or a serene James remarkably 'exempt
from alarm, anxiety and remorse' about his 'queerness', as Hugh Stevens
does; or whatever other account we choose to give ourselves of what this
passional force means and does inside the writing, the debate has been
changed, and all the fictions are illuminated from a slightly different
place from now onwards.[1]

Inevitably, readings of a homoerotic James have complicated an older
and very persistent account of him as an unsexual writer, prudish and
allergic to things of the flesh. With new confidence, critics are finding in
the work evidence of an imagination deeply stirred by and responsive
to the energies of the erotic (Ross Posnock in particular is eloquent on
James's 'capacious affective life' and the need to 'dislodge the critical debate from its fixation on renunciation'[2]). The readings of James's novels
that follow grow out of this shift in perspective. They concentrate on the
centrality of heterosexual love stories in the *oeuvre* and on James's deep
and sympathetic treatment of women: and yet that concentration is not
unconnected to the new homoerotic perspectives on the writing. It is

James's freedom from 'definitional frames' of hetero- and homosexuality that gives him his special purchase on the whole urgent business of gender definition and gender identity in his society, and makes all the more poignant and complex his rendering of the entanglements of his men and women in love.[3]

The readings that follow will develop an account of an evolution in James's attitudes to sexuality – and to women's sexuality in particular – out of a fairly conventional propriety in the earlier work, through the seismic shifts of perception in the writing of the 1890s, to the liberated rich imaginings of pleasure in the late novels. Perhaps part of the reason why so much criticism for so long insisted upon an unsexual James (or, in a slightly different version, upon a James squeamishly appalled and fascinated by sex[4]) is that James's novels of his middle period do indeed seem to be structured inside a moral framework inherited from his great Victorian predecessors, in which the power of sexuality can only exert itself obliquely and destructively, from the shadowy margins of the work.[5] In *The Portrait of a Lady*, the framework Isabel is trapped inside (taken over almost wholesale from *Daniel Deronda*, as if James wanted to set himself George Eliot's puzzle) is conceived entirely as an Apollonian conflict of ideals: she needs to be good, and she needs to be free, and she can't be both. The Dionysiac 'comet in the sky' or 'hot wind of the desert' (these formulas come from the 1905 revisions) only touch Isabel momentarily and distractingly when Caspar kisses her: and it is from the power of the Dionysiac that she takes flight at the end, back into her dilemma.

In the novels and stories of the 1890s, James seems to be thinking himself round and beyond the terms of Isabel's dilemma and Isabel's renunciation. He is unpicking them, so to speak, and unmaking their terms, exploring their origins in the complicated double binds of a particular ideal of womanhood. Part of that unpicking and unmaking involves outing the sexual facts from the shadows: insisting upon, rather than taking flight from, the reality of what Osmond did with Madame Merle, the driven promiscuousness of Maisie's parents, the dingy dissimulations over whether Sir Claude has been in Mrs Beale's bedroom, the all-but-spoken unspeakableness between Peter Quint and Miss Jessel, Lord Petherton transferring his predatory attentions from the aunt to the niece. The foreground of these transitional works in James's *oeuvre* is busy with improprieties: all of them rendered, however, with some considerable distaste. *What Maisie Knew* and 'The Turn of the Screw' in particular, whose subject is the legacy for the imagination of a guilty Victorian propriety, are themselves uncomfortable in a rather Victorian way, only able to imagine innocence for an unsexual child. There is indeed a squeamishness in James's fascination with soiled secrets in these stories; a distaste at adult sexuality (less so, perhaps, in *The Awkward Age,* which seems more forgiving, more generously reconciled to the susceptibilities of its protagonists).

But James changes his mind.[6] In *The Ambassadors,* in fact, he rehearses exactly that story, the story of a man changing his mind about propriety and sexuality. Strether not only finally has to stop prevaricating and face the reality of the relationship between the lovers: he also, having held off in his Woollett reticence from even admitting to their physical embraces, allows himself to begin to enjoy imagining them ('he found himself supposing innumerable and wonderful things', 468[7]). Imagining them he envies them, he feels acutely his fifty-five years and his missed opportunities. Having come to Paris to rescue a young man entangled in a love affair which was distracting him from his real purposes, he ends up exhorting him to make the love affair his purpose ('Let Rome into Tiber melt . . .'). This is not only a novel which registers the *power* of sexuality (*The Portrait of a Lady* does that, Osmond and Madame Merle's affair dragging all those brighter lives in its dark tides): it also registers its pleasures.

Strether's story is the story of James's *oeuvre:* from his beginnings in a moralised English-language novel tradition, James makes something like Strether's journey to voluptuous imaginings of pleasure. Any reader who had only heard from critics about James's sexlessness, James's resignation and renunciation, James's interest in alienated observers from life's margins, must have been astonished by opening *The Ambassadors* or *The Wings of the Dove* or *The Golden Bowl,* with their ripe worldliness, the passionate and sexual love affairs at their centres, and James's obvious infatuation with the glamour and glitter and stylishness of these beautiful young scions of a *fin-de-siècle* leisure class.

James's attitude does not end, of course, with infatuation, but it is perhaps enlightening to begin there. In re-inscribing James into 'responsibility', as recent criticism has quite rightly wanted to do, with regard to the great issues of his era – class, race, nation – there is always a danger that the work will be made to do penance, as it were, for its pleasures; that readings will suggest a James whose attitude towards the world in his books is essentially disapproving and denunciatory. The interesting question, and the one that will be taken up in what follows, is whether it is possible to offer a reading of the work which yields a writer at once responsible toward the large ethical implications of his class, his privilege and his age, and at the same time deeply responsive to the possibilities of pleasure that age and leisure class afford. Posnock, for one, is interested in a 'strikingly different Henry James . . . one who is more like Walt Whitman than Henry Adams in opening himself to incessant stimuli and relaxing the anxious Victorian ethos of strenuous masculinity'.[8]

There is a way of making out the whole history of James's *oeuvre* in the light of that great release of ripe worldliness in the late novels. Far from reading the development into the late style as a progressive retreat into the ivory tower of art, it is possible to think of the late style with its difficulties, its lofty aristocratic ironies, its rhetorical display, as the way James found for writing himself out of that common-sensical middle-class middle-ground which the English-language novel had made its own: a middle-ground which had always been profoundly ill at ease with worldliness, with glamour, and with sex. In the transitional novels of the late 1890s James wrestled with his writing: with his narrative forms, bent upon displacing that middle-ground proneness to judgemental omniscience; and with his material, as he explored to their very source the ideals of feminine innocence and decency and chastity which haunt *What Maisie Knew*, 'The Turn of the Screw' and *The Awkward Age*. As he uncovered the sources of those ideals in a distorting patterning of gender in his culture, progressively he liberated himself to step over the boundaries of the middle ground into the open space outside; to make the journey Strether makes in *The Ambassadors* from a nervous conventional propriety to a grown-up reconciliation with, and honouring of, the sensual side of life.

Inseparable from that journey in the *oeuvre* is the evolution of the late style. J. M. Coetzee in an aside calls James 'the outstanding exception' to the following generalisation about the novel form:

The traditional novel is wedded to an ideal of realism that includes not only the representation of the ordinary speech of ordinary people, but the imitation, in its own narration, of a sober, middle-class manner. The poetics of the novel are anticlassical: with exceptions, it does not go in for the aristocratic mode of irony.[9]

James's late narratives are anything but sober. They break all the rules of that 'formal realism' which Ian Watt considers virtually co-extensive with the English novel, with its 'pursuit of verisimilitude', its pretence of being no more than a 'transcription of real life'.[10] And rather than reading this 'aristocratic irony' of the late style as representing James's retreat from the middle ground of common humanity, we might try to read it instead as his escape from the middle-ground constraints of the English-language novel, from a moralising propriety, from a proneness to sententiousness, from a deep suspicion of pleasure, from a sexual puritanism entangled with ideals of feminine innocence and chastity.

If James virtually 'invents' an aristocratic irony for his late style, it can only have a tenuous and oblique relationship with the 'real' style of any 'real' late nineteenth-century aristocracy. Something in his phrasing and vocabulary and exaggeratedly inflated poise mimics the flair and drawl and slang we might think of as aristocratic; he borrows from the louche arch talk of a smart set whose *moeurs* and attitudes can still be distinguished from those of a 'respectable' middle class. Such a smart set certainly had not been much written about in nineteenth-century English novels (Trollope's ruling class sound so bourgeois); it was not a significant presence in English letters. Unlike the works of the eighteenth-century ironists (Gibbon, Swift, Hume) whose 'aristocratic' style Coetzee contrasts with the novelists in his essay, James's ironies cannot be confidently addressed to an audience of peers, cannot depend upon 'a bond among the élite who can decode its inverted operations'.[11] If James has taken refuge in 'aristocratic' ironies it is not in order to recover the security of a supportive élite. There is finally something self-consciously *quixotic* about James's sustained high style; perhaps his 'aristocratic' is as invented as Don Quixote's 'romance', with its impossibly exaggerated refinement? And like Cervantes, perhaps James is making full play of the ironic conjunction of a high style with novelistic realism? Thomas Mann writes about Cervantes's self-criticising Spanishness: 'it looks as into a mirror at its own grandezza, its idealism, its lofty impracticality, its unmarketable high-mindedness – is this not strange?'[12]

It would be impossible to discuss issues of passion and propriety in the late nineteenth-century novel without addressing the difference between the English-language tradition and the European one. English-language fiction was still governed on both sides of the Atlantic by a fierce convention of propriety: no matter if one learns that even George Lewes (Prince Consort to the creator of *Adam Bede* and *The Mill on the Floss*) told scurrilous anecdotes in (male) company after dinner, it was not permissible to represent that reality of English social life in fiction. The episode in

The Awkward Age, where newly married, sexually teasing Aggie captures
and sits on an 'improper' French novel so that she can be pulled off
again by a Lord Petherton unconvincingly concerned for her 'morals',
is James's ironic rehearsal of the English convention that European
novels were improper and forbidden. A man may own a French novel
(Vanderbank does); he may lend it to a married woman (he lends
it to Mrs Brookenham); but she must find it 'disgusting' and should
on no account let it fall into the hands of her unmarried daughter
(Mrs Brookenham makes sure Nanda sees it and reads it, so that she
is spoiled for marrying Van).[13] As late as 1890 Edmund Gosse, intro-
ducing his *International Library* series, felt bound to apologise for it with
something of the hot-under-the-collar rectitude of a housemaster initiating a discussion of the birds and the bees:

> Life is now treated in fiction by every race but our own with singular can-
> dour . . . the [Continental] novelists have determined to disdain nothing and
> to repudiate nothing which is common to humanity; much is freely dis-
> cussed . . . which our race is apt to treat with a much more gingerly discretion.
> It is not difficult, however, we believe – it is certainly not impossible – to discard
> all which may justly give offence, and yet to offer to an English public . . . many
> masterpieces of European fiction.[14]

This disjunction between the English language and European fiction
traditions was something that James himself was always intrigued by,
bothered by; in his critical essays, even from the decades when the material of his own novels fitted unexceptionably inside the parameters of
an English propriety, James the reader and critic kept returning to those
other possibilities outside. The writer who loved Balzac and admired
Flaubert had to answer satisfactorily for himself why he could not write
about, say, adultery and prostitution in his own novels; and he had to ask
himself whether he would want to if he could.

From his first experiences of living alone in Paris in 1876, French
culture – its *moeurs*, its talk, its literature – had suggested itself to the young
James as an essential counterpoint to his own Anglo-Saxon background.
His letters home that year (he was in his early thirties) were full of a
slightly uneasy playfulness, teasing and upsetting his family and friends
with glimpses of Gallic frivolity and wickedness. His brother William
wrote to him to warn him to give up his 'French tricks' in his letters: his
bons mots and rhetorically stylish constructions were antipathetic to the
James family atmosphere, whose sense of humour savoured more of the
schoolroom than the salon.[15]

Henry wrote to Thomas Perry that he had heard Zola characterise Gustave Droz's writing as *'merde à la vanille'*.

Why the Flaubert circle don't like him [Droz] is their own affair. I don't care . . . I send you by post Zola's own last – *merde au naturel*. Simply hideous.[16]

James bristled with defensive critical dissent, but he bristled with consciousness, too, at the forbidden word used so casually and cleverly. Although William's and Henry's letters to one another were preoccupied with their bowel movements to a degree unique, probably, in collected letters, the word *merde* or its English equivalent had never been put on paper between them. Initiated, James would not simply shrink and think New England thoughts: he tried the note out for himself.

To W. D. Howells he wrote:

They are all charming talkers – though as editor of the austere *Atlantic* it would startle you to hear some of their projected subjects. The other day Edmond de Goncourt (the best of them) said he had been lately working very well on his novel – he had got into an episode that greatly interested him and into which he was going very far. *Flaubert*: 'What is it?' *E de G*: 'A whore-house *de province*'.[17]

Howells – 'editor of the austere *Atlantic*' – wrote back to thank God he was not a Frenchman.

James wrote home about the emancipated young girl of the Faubourg Saint-Germain who asked him what he thought of incest as the subject for a novel; and about the Turgenev–Viardot gossip. And years later in a letter to Edmund Gosse he recalled one more story; this one presumably he kept to himself at the time:

the memory of a Sunday afternoon at Flaubert's in the winter of 75–76, when Maupassant, still *inédit*, but always 'round', regaled me with a fantastic tale, irreproducible here, of the relations between two Englishmen, each other, and their monkey! A picture the details of which have faded for me, but not the lurid impression.[18]

Along with brothels and incest, there must have been plenty of mention in the Flaubert *cénacle* of homosexuality; we have no idea how much of an initiation – linguistic, imaginative – this might have been for James.

James in Paris in 1876 was not of course only interested in 'naughty' stories. There is a wealth of other material in the letters home, more the sort of thing the young American abroad was supposed to be getting out of Paris: the contemplation of beauty and the culture of the mind. But there are, strikingly, enough stories from 'Babylon' (as James teasingly called it in his letters) to suggest a shock of contact for a sensibility neither immune to suggestion nor simply comfortably assimilative. James is nothing like, say, his Chad in *The Ambassadors;* Chad is prompt to avail himself of the opportunity to exchange New World constraint for Old World licence, but that is all. When the time comes for him to return to Woollett Chad will change worlds back again, unscathed.

It is not the exchange of values that interests James, the mere substituting of one set for the other; but the contradictory co-existence of opposed values. Howells's austerity and Zola's indecency exist in the same world: what is unspeakable in one language is casual conversation in another. James writes to Howells that 'you and he [Zola] don't see the same things – you have a wholly different consciousness – *you* see a totally different side of a different race'.[19] This flexibility of language, that can say in one place what is unspeakable in another, is what Mikhail Bakhtin calls its 'heteroglossia':

Actual social life and historical becoming create within an abstractly unitary national language a multitude of concrete worlds, a multitude of bounded verbal-ideological and social belief systems; within these various systems . . . are elements of language filled with various semantic and axiological content and each with its own different sound.[20]

It does not matter that for our purposes here these different 'verbal-ideological' systems are not in fact within one 'national language'. James's position in Paris, between languages, trying to communicate blasé Parisian sophistications to New England decencies, is in Bakhtin's account the very type of the novelist's interest in and relationship to heteroglossia:

All languages of heteroglossia . . . are specific points of view on the world, forms for conceptualizing the world in words, specific world views, each characterized by its own objects, meanings and values. As such they all may be juxtaposed to one another, mutually supplement one another, contradict one another and be interrelated dialogically. As such they encounter one another and co-exist in the consciousness of real people – first and foremost, in the creative consciousness of people who write novels.[21]

The disjunction between the *moeurs* of the French and the New England intelligentsia, and between the English-language and French novel traditions, was not simply a matter of the naming or the silencing of taboo subjects. The whore-house and the *merde* were signs of a profound difference of attitude in the French novel: sexual impropriety was to be named along with every other reality because it was *there,* because representation for Flaubert, Zola, Maupassant came dragging after it none of the clumsy apparatus of moralisation. James writes about the Flaubert *cénacle* in an essay on Turgenev years later:

What was discussed in that little smoke-clouded room was chiefly questions of taste, questions of art and form; and the speakers, for the most part, were, in aesthetic matters, radicals of the deepest dye. It would have been late in the day to propose among them any discussion of the relation of art to morality, any question of the degree in which a novel might or might not concern itself with the teaching of a lesson. They had settled these preliminaries long ago, and it would have been primitive and incongruous to refer to them.[22]

We may suspect that the young James rather wanted to ask that 'primitive and incongruous' question about the teaching of 'lessons', and that he found the extravagant certainty and impenetrable consensus of the little group infuriatingly narrowly focused (there is plenty of irony at their self-importance in that 'radicals of the deepest dye'). But what the older James is recording, looking back, is not so much a moment of conversion to what the French writers believe as a moment of liberation from being certain at all; his encounter with precisely their certainty and their consensus gave him a new purchase from outside on the moralising frame of his own English-language fiction.[23] It is possible to write within a quite different frame, and to write well; and before the moralist can condemn he has to answer the sheer persuasiveness of the work of a Maupassant, say, whose sensual, visual, intelligent power sits 'like a lion in the path':[24]

this little group, with its truly infernal intelligence of art, form, manner − its intense artistic life . . . and in spite of their ferocious pessimism and their handling of unclean things, they are at least serious and honest.[25]

and:

We are accustomed to think, we of the English faith, that a cynic is a living advertisement of his errors . . . It is easy to exclaim that if he judges life only from the point of view of the senses, many are the noble and exquisite things that he must leave out. What he leaves out has no claim to get itself considered till after we have done justice to what he takes in.[26]

The juxtaposition of these two different fictional frames of reference becomes a recurrent theme in James's criticism of the 1880s and 1890s. The English tradition asks questions in novels about what is 'good' and what is 'right' (or – at worst – imposes answers to those questions). The European novel asks whether what it writes convinces, whether it feels like life, whether it tells the truth about how life feels (but a dimension is missing – what is 'good', what is 'right'?). Again, James's position outside the two frames stimulates him, keeps him interrogating, doubting.

He argues in a number of essays, but at length in his 1888 essay on Maupassant and his 1902 essay on Italian novelist Mathilde Serao, that the explanation for the convention of propriety governing English fiction at the end of the century lies in how thoroughly through its history the English novel had been in the control of women: not only frequently and successfully written by them, but also hugely and significantly read by them.[27] In a culture (such as that represented in *The Awkward Age*) where certain kinds of information were conventionally proscribed for women, the consequences of such female participation in the novels' making had to be significant:

if the element of compromise – compromise with fifty of the 'facts of life' – be the common feature of the novel in English speech, so it is mainly indebted for this character to the sex comparatively without a feeling for logic . . . Nothing is at any rate more natural than to trace a connection between our general mildness, as it may be conveniently called, and the fact that we are likewise so generally feminine.[28]

Again, this is not simply a matter of the proscription of certain taboo subjects. The obligatory innocence, or excision of unsuitable subject matters from the material of fiction, tended, James argued, to result in an overall moralising 'optimism':

No doubt there is in our literature an immense amount of conventional blinking, and it may be questioned whether pessimistic representation in M. Maupassant's manner does not follow his particular original more closely than our perpetual quest of pleasantness (does not Mr Rider Haggard make even his African carnage pleasant?) adheres to the lines of the world we ourselves know . . . It must never be forgotten that the optimism of that [English] literature is partly the optimism of women and spinsters; in other words the optimism of ignorance as well as delicacy.[29]

James writes ambivalently about that optimism. Straddling the disjunction between fictional possibilities, he can see the English-language version as naive and vulnerable beside the better-informed cynicism of, say, a Maupassant; or even (in the case, say, of African carnage) as saccharine mendacity. From both these possibilities he wants to dissociate himself, and the 'honesty' of the French realists and naturalists (in spite of their 'pessimism and handling of unclean things') fills him sometimes full of disgust for the 'soap and water' of English fictional propriety.[30]

His complaints, however, are always counterweighed with positive emphasis on strong 'feminine' qualities in English fiction: its 'piety, in the civil and domestic sense'.[31] In English, he suggests, it has been the women writers rather than the men who have written for the 'grown-ups':

The female mind has in fact throughout the competition carried off the prize in the familiar game, known to us all from childhood's hour, of playing at 'grown-up'; finding thus its opportunity, with no small acuteness, in the more and more marked tendency of the mind of the other gender to revert, alike in the grave and the gay, to those simplicities which there would appear to be some warrant for pronouncing puerile. It is the ladies in a word who have lately done most to remind us of man's relations with himself, that is with woman. His relations with the pistol, the pirate, the police, the wild and the tame beast – are these not prevailingly what the gentlemen have given us?[32]

James's sense of the essential deep seriousness of women's narrow focus in their subject matter – their writing turns inward, upon relationships and the personal, not outward to the world – counterbalances interestingly the problem of women's 'ignorance'. A certain masculine bravado may even get in the way of seriousness; his point here is obviously aimed at Rider Haggard and Stevenson rather than the French novelists, but that wariness of the *élan* of male adventure (the French adventure is more likely to be sexual than colonial or on horseback), and that sympathy for the feminine and inward-turning, will persist in James even into the very improper last novels.

James even suggests in his Serao essay that the future freedom of the English novel may depend on that very tradition of its femininity which has so constrained it:

the novel will surely not become less free in proportion as the condition of women becomes more easy. It is more or less in deference to their constant concern with it that we have seen it, among ourselves, pick its steps so carefully; but there are indications that the future may reserve for us the surprise of having to thank the very class whose supposed sensibilities so oppressed us for teaching it not only a longer stride, but a healthy indifference to an occasional splash.[33]

The 'constant concern' and the careful picking of steps imply the inhibiting propriety of the women, which has limited what the English novel has been able to do; but they imply too the concentration and commitment – precisely, the carefulness – with which the women have worked, within their frame. The frame, James understands, is cultural and imposed, not intrinsic (their 'supposed sensibilities'; and 'the novel will . . . not become less free in proportion as the condition of women becomes more easy'). And it may be the very carefulness they have painfully learned which will in the future qualify the women writers to liberate the novel from 'oppressions' just as they will have liberated themselves.[34]

The optimism of English literature has been the 'optimism of ignorance *as well as delicacy*'. We might choose to read that 'delicacy' as mere residue of the moralism James is progressively shedding as he grows farther from his roots in Hawthorne and George Eliot and nearer to the filial homage to Balzac of his 1905 American lecture.[35] On the other hand, the chapters following will explore the possibility that 'delicacy', the female-centredness of the English tradition, persisted as a value for James even into the late fictions; the possibility that what interested him, again, was not the exchange of one system for another, but a perch between, a fictional medium in which both possibilities, a feminine-optimistic and a masculine-cynical, could be made real and co-existent, and neither of them offered as exhaustive.

James's prophecy was not fulfilled: it was Joyce and Lawrence who were to 'teach' the novel to make its 'splash' in forbidden waters; and the modernist period was to bring to an end the long predominance of women writers in the English-language novel tradition. On the other hand, while the great male modernists pursued their dizzying intellectual adventures, ruthlessly radical, contemptuously anti-bourgeois and anti-domestic, it was Jean Rhys and Elizabeth Bowen, Willa Cather and Katharine Mansfield who stubbornly and carefully nurtured the quieter traditions of English fiction, and kept alive, not exactly its old 'optimism', but at least its intimacy with the ordinary and everyday, its movement of inward-turning self-awareness, and its concentration on relationships, on 'man's relations with himself, that is with woman'.[36]

James asserts an extraordinary thing when he suggests in the essay on Serao that 'man's relations with himself' *are* his relations 'with woman'. (It would be tempting to say that one cannot imagine Flaubert making such a remark: but there is that mystifying '*Madame Bovary, c'est moi*', in reference to a novel which seems to expend all its energies in defining a femaleness essentially and in every way unlike the dissecting intelligent maleness of its author.[37]) In the light of the recent recovery in criticism of the power of the homoerotic in his writing, James's phrase seems even more compressedly and paradoxically suggestive. The woman represents for man some aspect of himself that he cannot know without knowing her; or, it is only in relation to her otherness that he can come into relation with himself. In coming into relation with himself, the man *becomes*, syntactically at least, the woman *(Madame Bovary, c'est moi).*

Behind that complex representation of two sexes at once inseparable and utterly separate, there lie two kinds of history: an individual's psychic history of gendered self and otherness, and also a cultural history, of perceptions of gender, and of all those learned patterns for the 'relations' between man and woman. Implicit in James's sentence, for example, is the pattern in which a woman is called a man's 'best self', or 'better half'; and implicit too are all those novels where the man returns from his adventures 'with the pistol, the pirate, the police, the wild and the tame beast' to lose himself or find himself at last in the embrace of his Intended (that's all the name she ever gets in Conrad's *Heart of Darkness*: and in Conrad needless to say he never makes it back). Those histories – the particulars of the patterns of relations in a given era, and how those patterns express or thwart the drive of self-definition through and against a man–woman polarity – are James's great subject; and the centrality of that male–female polarisation is not displaced when we reposition James outside the heterosexual perspective.[38]

This may be an *oeuvre* shot through with a passionate perception of the desirability of its men; but it is not an *oeuvre* in which women are marginalised, or redundant, or simply used to dissimulate to an unsuspecting public a deeper, exclusively homoerotic dynamic. Its girls and women are not disguised boys or men. The homoerotic in these novels never replaces or stands in for the charge of the heteroerotic; James's imagination was erotically polymorphic. The power, the plight, and the particular history of women have a fundamental importance in his work, and the heterosexual problematic is its fundamental puzzle: puzzling because the two sexes are constructed to stand opposed and unlike and yet co-dependent. The 'difference', the differentiation of gender in culture is the very subject of the work; James's own ambiguously gendered position places him in distinction from but attraction to *both* differentiated genders in their heterosexual circlings and strugglings and play.

Hugh Stevens in his book on *Henry James and Sexuality* gives an account of how he began to write on 'representations of femininity' in James and then became concerned instead with the 'representation of same-sex desire in his writing': he makes tentative connections between both kinds of representations, seeing in both how they express a 'fascination with the marginal, with alterity'.[39] Certainly one wants to make out a James who chooses to write about, but not out of, the centres of power inside his culture. His novels and stories are nuanced, probing, unsettling explorations of how notions of femaleness are shaped and enforced within a late nineteenth-century leisure class; they describe a system of gender differentiation inequitable in its very foundations, and forms and ideals of femaleness which deliver individual women over into the grip of painful contradictions and into powerlessness.

One of James's subjects is the complex evolution of that system over the generations: his treatment of Isabel's *impasse* in *The Portrait of a Lady* is in a sense the starting place for his exploration of the heterosexual problematic inside a precise cultural history. The English-language novel had always made much of its material and gained much of its energy from the spirit and independent-mindedness of its heroines; from their *resistance* to what presses on them, so to speak (from Clarissa to Maggie Tulliver via Elizabeth Bennet, the disconcerting Becky Sharp, Jane Eyre, and numerous others). No doubt the novel also nurtured in its reading public a high valuation of that spirit and that independent-mindedness. At the same time, in order for their resistance to be poignant and admirable, to be real, the pressure upon these heroines had to be given an unanswerable force, had to be the very frame within which their stories exist. The English novel in the nineteenth century had made its space within the parameters of certain conventions of femininity and feminine goodness; and its stories had mostly been of women struggling for accommodation of their spirit and their independence within those conventions.

In Isabel Archer James makes this struggle reach its logical *impasse*. Isabel, who has always put the highest value upon her personal freedom, is trapped in a loveless marriage to a man who attacks and erodes that freedom. Nothing holds her in the marriage but convention; all the arguments Caspar Goodwood makes to persuade her to leave her husband are, to our modern ears, unanswerable. But convention in *The Portrait of a Lady* is never *merely* convention; it is rendered as grown in to the very structures of Isabel's imagination, entangled with the roots of her idea of herself. And not only Isabel; what James represents in Isabel is a whole literary ideal of chaste womanhood, an ideal that has deeply succumbed to the poignant sacrificial aesthetic of Isabel's contradiction. A whole literature is hooked, so to speak, on the heady gesture with which Isabel will *refuse* and the way she will turn her heavy movement of submission into a thwarted negative assertion, a dignity, a piece of pride. It is beautiful, and its aesthetic is more ancient than the novel; it borrows something, for example, from Hermione's gesture of wronged submission in *The Winter's Tale*. Shakespeare's turning Hermione into a statue both underlines for us that her gesture is part of an available formal female rhetoric, and warns of the power of that rhetoric to drain away vitality and warmth. Of course Hermione, set down in quite another world from Isabel's late nineteenth-century North Atlantic leisure class, has no choice; her ideal of conduct is inseparable from her husband's literal power of life and death over her. All Isabel seems to stand to lose in 1881 is her self-esteem (and perhaps her money too).

The rational argument of James's novel has come up against its aesthetic, and both stand locked together on the brink of the novel's – and Isabel's – future. This great fiction of James's middle period feels at its ending inconclusive; it strains forward but has no language – no argument, no aesthetic – to express what can come next.[40] It cannot tell us whether Isabel goes back to her husband or not; or whether James's novel form will be able to imagine a woman who might say yes instead of no, without having to become the instant she said it a Mme Merle, cast out from sympathy, ruined.

In the transitional novels of the 1890s James explores the roots of Isabel's gesture of renunciation, and the roots of that cultural ideal of chaste, refusing femininity, by writing novels and stories centred in female childhood and adolescence. In *What Maisie Knew* and 'The Turn of the Screw' he is particularly interested in the teachers who transmit the ideal; the Mrs Wixes and Miss Overmores and the hungry deluded governesses from country vicarages. Mrs Wix sits with Maisie in their room in Boulogne and reproaches her with her absence of a 'moral sense', while all the pleasuring world of France offers itself up to the child from outside the window. By the end of the novel Maisie has learned how to renounce. At the end of 'The Turn of the Screw' the pedagogue who has too much of her own dignity and importance invested in ideals of innocence and sexlessness destroys the child who will not pretend to see the ghosts he cannot see. The adults have all their meaning and value invested in ideas and ideals which exist with terrifying independence from anything that children can see or believe in; James, through entering the innocences and ignorances of children can unlearn those adult frames, re-open a space in which to see the world cleanly and without Mrs Wix's 'straighteners'.

These fictions represent a crisis, virtually, in the *oeuvre*, a crisis of authority. There is no appeal within them against the adult, pathological version of things: Mrs Wix's dingy (and easily bought-off) proprieties, the vicarage girl's contaminated sex-obsessions. Only the fictions themselves confirm that what the children see is more real. And significantly this pathology of propriety, that James sees being imposed like distorting glasses upon the children's perception of the real, is mostly ministered by women, women whose imagination has been tainted by seclusion, narrowness, and ignorance, and who zealously perpetuate therefore the very conventions of perception through which they themselves (and this irony is particularly acute in 'The Turn of the Screw') have been excluded and diminished.

The subject of *The Awkward Age* is a transition in *moeurs* in late nineteenth-century English 'society'. Nanda is allowed to grow up not only knowing all the sexual facts but bumping up against them daily in her mother's *fin-de-siècle* idly promiscuous fast set. Her cousin Aggie is brought up according to the old custom, only her innocence, in a society that has long ago broken with all the prohibitions of its grandmothers, can only be a fragile sham sustained conveniently until the point of marriage. But the novel is not simply a celebration of a new openness, any more than it is simply a lament for the old closed perception. In a sense the novel is about the power of the past – Mr Longdon's revisiting from the past, almost from the dead, is its central motif – and about the persistence of the aesthetic of an ideal of femininity long after the fact, haunting these girls for whom ignorance or even innocence could only be a disastrous preparation, given the *fin-de-siècle* world they need to navigate.

In the complex tangle of values in the novel, it is Nanda herself, hopelessly initiated, who most acutely appreciates the aesthetic of her grandmother's kind of womanhood, Isabel's kind, that refuses and sacrifices and sets the impossible high standard. 'Ah', says Nanda, 'say what you will – it *is* the way we ought to be!'(259). And by a similar perverse twist the man Nanda loves is the very man who cannot accept her modern initiated knowingness. Her choice of Vanderbank is no accidental perversity; it is precisely because she is unencumbered with the old-fashioned superstitions of femininity that she is free to admire the old-fashioned magic of his type. His 'sacred terror', as Mitchy calls it, is the same superb male presumption of advantage which puts her out of question for him. Partly, he simply cannot imagine himself partnered by anyone who understands so much about his male mystique.

As James's fictions concentrated more and more on unpicking the complex feminine dependencies, he was also more and more interested, naturally, in men's power, a power that in *The Portrait of a Lady* only the monster Osmond was allowed to have over Isabel. And just as Nanda, liberated from superstition, loves Van, who is haunted by the superstition of the gentleman; so James, as he learned to see through the phenomenon of the glossy nineteenth-century male worldling, was all the more able to render him with especial tenderness. The men, the lovers, of the late novels – Van, Chad, Gloriani, the Prince, and, complicatedly, Merton Densher – are the truly splendid products of nineteenth-century upper-class culture: polished, privileged, callous, scrupulous; with thoroughbred fierce pride and flawless good taste; beneficiaries of the sexual double standard (no-one has ever wanted Vanderbank to be innocent or ignorant). In the late novels it is in relation to the imperturbable-seeming power of these men that James understood the real risks his women were taking when they refused refusal and innocence, and adventured for happiness and knowledge for themselves.

James, however, is never simply the chronicler of women's 'marginality and alterity' inside a late nineteenth-century leisure class. His representation of a gender differentiation in which men and women are profoundly co-dependent means that alongside his particular history of ideals of chaste and innocent womanhood, and of the privilege of men in relation to those ideals, he is bound to do justice also to the power of women.[41] Nancy Armstrong in *Desire and Domestic Fiction* has argued provocatively that while the nineteenth-century English novel might appear to explore female subjection, in fact it promotes the centrality of female subjectivity and the female experience; and that in its offer of 'social redemption through the domestication of desire', and by making sexual politics its centre, the novel marginalises other politics, of class, religion, region. She is surely right at least in her insistence on how, for all that the English novel tradition renders the realities of the female 'plight', it also enacts in its very form and content the new importance of female experience; and she may even be right that we need to be wary of how 'the rhetoric of victimisation has worked its way into the heart of literary critical theory'.[42]

Less iconoclastically, Michiel Heyns in an essay on 'The Beast in the Jungle' also wants to resist the reductiveness of the 'woman-as-victim stereotype', and suggests that '"The Beast in the Jungle" enables us to see that the alternative, "female", narrative may be the privileged one, in holding the key to the surface narrative'. Heyns offers a subtly complicating account of how 'power' is distributed between John Marcher and May Bartram in the story: 'She sees what he sees, but she also sees more than he, and what she sees is *him*: if he beguiles the world, she has access both to his mask and to his vision.' Heyns also suggests interesting (and perhaps disturbing) ways in which that female advantage of insight might work in relationship with women's cultural disadvantage; how women might take on an 'ethical privilege' in return for their underprivilege in terms of action and experience. (When Maggie Verver wants to 'openly appropriate power', she has to forfeit that 'ethical privilege'. Heyns credits the 'sheer toughness' of James's imagination in *The Golden Bowl*: 'he can see that if the meek are to inherit the earth they have to out-manoeuvre the arrogant'.)[43]

It may even be that in the writings of the 1890s, while James is, so to speak, working through the particular gendered forms of his era to their roots in training and imagination, there are 'victims' in some sense: these are certainly stories about the 'meek'. Maisie, Miles's and Flora's governess, Nanda, Mrs Brook, Fleda Vetch have only empty hands at the end of their stories to show for all they had promised themselves or dared to hope for. It is not so much that they suffer from their experiences, as that they never really embark on experiences at all: their promise is all wasted. Maisie, Nanda and Fleda have perhaps the 'ethical privilege' of understanding what has happened to them better then anyone else inside their novels: but any one of them, we suspect, would gladly exchange that privilege for compensations less abstract.

But in the last novels, while certainly Mme de Vionnet, Maria, Kate, Milly and Charlotte 'lose', they carry life away with them in armfuls; they are expelled, one way or another, from a scene disrupted, changed absolutely by their having been there. Retributive justice, if it is present at all, is opaque in these novels, nothing is necessarily fair, just as nothing necessarily lasts: but there is a surplus of experiences and fulfilments, for the women as well as the men. And these fulfilments, these 'differences made' and pleasures tasted and lives lived out, have little to do with the kinds of opportunities suggested by 'ethical privileges' of knowing better or seeing more clearly (although some of these women still, and importantly, do have the advantage in seeing and knowing). The language of ethical privileges belongs to a world of ethical adjustments; the energies of these late books seem not to cluster so much around 'right' or even 'truth', but rather where experience is thick and turbulent and passionate.[44] At the centre of that turbulence, women are powerful: Kate and Milly between them 'make' Densher, and Charlotte and Maggie 'make' the Prince, just as surely as Mme de Vionnet has 'made'

Chad; it is only through their connections with the women that the men are able to become themselves.[45]

Something in the whole movement of the development of the *oeuvre* had been bringing James up to that threshold which in *The Ambassadors* he finally crossed: no longer at the periphery but at the very heart of this novel the lovers, like lovers in the real world, take off their clothes and embrace ('We can arrange it – with two grains of courage. People in our case always arrange it' says Merton to Kate in *The Wings of the Dove*, 326). Strether learns to blush at how he has been dressing the possibility of his friends' sexual relationship 'in vagueness, as a little girl might have dressed her doll' (468); the writer who had always read Balzac and Flaubert no longer scrupled to name the simple facts that the French novelists had always told.

The development that brought James to this threshold was not the squeamish fascination of voyeurism – although that possibility had worried him as it has worried Strether. Instead it was as though some counter-impulse had been operating in his work to the one that had had him unpicking and unmaking the persuasive power of the aesthetic of renunciation and refusal. In proportion as James had understood how that aesthetic was founded in sacrifice and bondage – how it could only bring Isabel's free spirit to the *impasse* of the end of *The Portrait of a Lady* - an alternative possible value had grown in his imagination to counterbalance his loss. Isabel in her kiss with Caspar Goodwood felt herself in danger of being swept away, she beat her feet to find solid ground to stand on. In the late fictions it is as though James, doubting that Isabel's watertightness was the whole story, had wanted in his work an aesthetic abandoned to flood and risk, whose core was natural rather than moral, driven by what Walter Benjamin called in a different context the 'explosive will to happiness' (Benjamin's essay on Proust is endlessly suggestive for a reading of late James):

Nor is it hard to say why this paralyzing, explosive will to happiness which pervades Proust's writings is so seldom comprehended by its readers. In many places Proust himself made it easy for them to view this *oeuvre* too, from the time-tested, comfortable perspective of resignation, heroism, asceticism. After all, nothing makes more sense to the model pupils of life than the notion that a great achievement is the fruit of toil, misery, and disappointment. The idea that happiness could have a share in beauty would be too much of a good thing, something that their *ressentiment* would never get over.[46]

What Strether and James imagine, finally, is not the morality but the happiness of the lovers' embraces.

James has not simply substituted a French male sexual cynicism for his old English propriety. The pleasures at the novel's heart are unmistakably ephemeral and vulnerable, and James is especially interested in how defenceless his women are once they step outside the shelter of the conventional propriety which the women writers had worked so determinedly to consecrate in the English tradition. As well as being his homage to things sensual and things French, *The Ambassadors* is also James's critique of the Continental sexual system in so far as it cruelly privileges the male: Chad will move on, and Mme de Vionnet has no recourse to any rhetoric of righteousness, nor any appeal save to a stoic *vieille sagesse* passed on through the immemorial tradition of such inequities and such abandonments. But having registered all that, the essential gesture of the novel is not Mrs Newsome's, or anyone's, disapproval. It is Strether's recognition – fired, envious, perturbed; and his submission, eventually, to the flood of the realities of sensual pleasure and momentary happiness which cannot be explained or moralised or extended into an infinite future but which sit nonetheless 'like a lion in the path'.

The real pleasures of the world are not moralised in the late novels; but they are not depoliticised either. This is very much the argument Benjamin makes out for *A la Recherche du Temps Perdu*: deeply infatuated with the appearances – flawed, super-subtle, absurd, seductive – of his extraordinary Parisian élite, Proust is the writer who can most accurately and most inwardly describe the processes and the pains of class identity. The James of the late novels is not an unpolitical writer; he is more political in these novels succumbed to the deep appeal of privilege and pleasure than he ever is in *The Princess Casamassima*, his middle-period novel explicitly and conscientiously concerned with class. Class privilege in his late novels is not an iniquitous static framework sighed over by conscience from outside; it is a minutely differentiated, conflictual process imagined from inside, driven by the life energy of all those who strive with one another for their place near the golden flame. The distribution of privileges and pleasures is not just, but it is *real*: the telegraphist in 'In the Cage' understands that so painfully clearly.[47] Instead of a greasy tea-table, banquets; instead of the prison of mean employment, Florence and Venice. Instead of the safe partnership in a grocery, the letting down one's beautiful hair for a lover; instead of inconsequence, power.

The late novels do not represent any kind of polemical argument against the *fin-de-siècle* leisure class they represent. But they are explorations deep within the imagination of that class – its imagination of itself – of the dynamics of privilege, its real pleasures, its real pains. Privilege is not passive, it is a perpetual performance and contest; exhilarating, exhausting. In *The Wings of the Dove* the girls and the men alike find themselves cast in social roles – the charmer, the ironist, the dove – that pinch and chafe and suffocate; roles lightly entered upon overgrow the individuals until sustaining them becomes a matter of social life and social death. At important points the effort of privilege spills over into moments of lapsed restful contact with a world outside the brilliantly lit inner circle: Milly rests in Regents' Park among men sleeping on the grass, Merton brushes sleeves with Venetians in brown jackets, Kate and Merton walk the streets like the housemaid with the baker.

In *The Golden Bowl* four lovers circle one another, change partners, embrace, at the very pinnacle of privilege, exempt from all ordinary material considerations. They do not seem to imagine themselves answerable to any world outside, only to the exigencies of a perpetual high performance of intelligent good taste, so that even as the Prince and Maggie talk to one another across the pieces of the smashed golden bowl both are aware that 'the occasion was passing, that they were dining out, that he wasn't dressed, and that, though she herself was, she was yet, in all probability, so horribly red in the face and so awry, in many ways, with agitation, that in view of the Ambassador's company, of possible comments and constructions, she should need, before her glass, some restoration of appearances' (425). In their extraordinary lives the ordinary questions of what to do, or what to be, never arise; instead what they endlessly earnestly discuss is where to go, where next in the material paradise their wealth can purchase (the English country house, the London mansion, the historic 'collectable' Continental cities, or the open opportunities of America) to set down the golden tent of their free-floating privilege.

Why are we still interested, after almost a hundred years, in *The Golden Bowl*: in that immense expenditure of complex reflection and exquisite manner upon the tiny space of its story? Whatever this is, it is not a universal fable of love relationships. The kind of the love, the pathology of it, the pleasures and the pains in it, belong not incidentally but in their essence to an extraordinary moment in the history of a particular leisure-class civilisation, founded on an immense economic and social inequity, embodied in a vast complex system of caste distinction, of social ritual and taboo. The more James's late manner exaggerates the glamour and heightens the charm of the aesthetic of his *fin-de-siècle* leisure class, the more the fictions also find their strong purchase on its strangeness, its arbitrariness, the sacrifices built into its foundations. All these fine artificial creatures – but the women especially – walk on knives.

Neither that civilisation nor its pains and pleasures are much like ours (it is not the inequity that has vanished, it is the ritual and the taboo and the caste distinction). But just as the past in James's novels reaches both its long shadows and its long illuminations into the present of his stories, so the mysteries James explores reach forward into our own different world as if they still held secrets for us, as if even the most occult initiations of extreme privilege could speak to us across the time and change between. That tension in the *oeuvre* between on the one hand the almost elegiac rendering of a now vanished cultural aesthetic – the beauty of custom, of ritual, of appearances – and on the other hand James's revolutionary interrogation of the function of women's consciousness and women's representation within that aesthetic, seems particularly telling now, seems part of the essential history of our selves.

CHAPTER I

'Just you wait!': reflections on the last chapters of
The Portrait of a Lady

Critics (and presumably readers) have been tripping up on and debating
the ending of *The Portrait of a Lady* since the novel first appeared in 1881: in
those early days with unsophisticated perplexity and often impatience.
Even the very sympathetic review by James's friend W. D. Howells in
Century balks at James's leaving us 'to our own conjectures in regard to
the fate of the people in whom he has interested us' before submitting
to swallowing his treatment meekly: 'We must agree, then, to take what
seems a fragment instead of a whole, and to find, when we can, a name
for this new kind in fiction.'[1]

In *The Portrait* James has constructed his *impasse*: the spirited Isabel in
an impossible marriage, having made what feels like a terminal rupture
in disobeying her husband and coming to England to be with her dying
cousin, tempted momentarily by the renewed importunity of Caspar
Goodwood. But he does not seem to have left us all the instructions for
how we get out of it. Does Isabel have to return to her hated husband and
his punishments for her defection ('It will not be the scene of a moment;
it will be a scene of the rest of my life', 565)?[2] What other possible
futures does the novel allow us to envisage for her? *Is* Caspar a solution?
These speculations sound very like Isabel's own, in her railway carriage
crossing Europe on her way to Ralph (although she has not calculated
yet on Caspar's offer), and she too feels that the 'middle years', the years
ahead, the immediate question of what she will *do*, are wrapped from
her in a 'grey curtain', she only has a 'mutilated glimpse' of any future
(M 492[3]).

These days we are more sophisticatedly perplexed. The problem is not
simply one of James 'frustrating the reader's curiosity' about a handful
of 'characters'.[4] As readers – or at least as critics – we are irreversibly
committed to the idea that a serious novel will have moved beyond
'"objectively realistic representation" to a stage of reading the signi-
fications that lie behind or within reality'.[5] What James means us to

understand Isabel might do at the end of his novel *matters*, because James is elaborating a crucial moment in the development of that theme of marriage and adultery which, it has been argued, is one of the funda-mentals to the whole novel 'project', from the beginnings of the theme in *La Nouvelle Héloïse, Elective Affinities*, and so on.[6]

One of the energies driving the nineteenth-century development of the novel is that head of steam built up by the contradiction between the form's tendency on the one hand towards a resolution in adaptation to social forms and norms (its inbuilt drive, for example, towards happy endings in marriages); and on the other hand, its narratives rooted in a subjective individualism that cannot always square with resolution, that cannot but register individual reluctance, resistance, *differentness*, and raise unanswerable protests against the 'contract'. In Tony Tanner's elegant formulation, it is the 'tension between law and sympathy which holds the great bourgeois novel together'.[7] The *impasse* James has engineered at the end of *The Portrait of a Lady*, between submission to the form of marriage and commitment to the individual pursuit of happiness and freedom, is a place the English-language novel has visited numerous times already by 1881.

The 'solutions', or resolutions, for Dorothea Casaubon and Gwendolen Grandcourt (and for that matter for Jane Eyre) come from offstage, in the form of convenient demises; but we know already from something in the texture of *The Portrait of a Lady* – partly to do with just how very self-consciously it inscribes itself into that tradition of novels structured around strained marriage contracts – that James is pressing the development of the tradition to a new point where that kind of formal manipulation will not answer. An authorial rescue (Osmond falling out of a small high window at the Palazzo Roccanera?) would intrude here like an outmoded piece of theatre.

James introduces the possibility of another way out of the *impasse* – also traditional, even if traditionally (in the English-language novel) out-lawed – in the shape of Caspar Goodwood offering himself in defiance of all convention and all contract. The offer opens up under Isabel's feet – abyss, escape – but in her first panicking recognition of it she flies, away from the lover and back to the security of the lighted house. Has James proposed the third ingredient of the classic adulterous triangle – the 'other man' – only in order to eliminate him from the equation? It is difficult now to read the 1881 ending of the novel as if we did not know the New York Edition revisions, but originally it finished with Henrietta's injunction to Caspar:

"Look here, Mr Goodwood," she said; "just you wait!"
On which he looked up at her. (M 520)

Taking that by itself, it does not seem ridiculous to interpret it as a reviewer in the *Spectator* did in 1881, relishingly appalled at what he calls James's 'pure agnosticism':

never before has he closed a novel by setting up so cynical a sign-post into the abyss, as he sets up at the close of this book. He ends his *Portrait of a Lady*, if we do not wholly misinterpret the rather covert, not to say almost cowardly, hints of his last page, by calmly indicating that this ideal lady of his, whose belief in purity has done so much to alienate her from her husband, in that it had made him smart under her contempt for his estimates of the world, saw a 'straight path' to a liaison with her rejected lover.[8]

Most contemporary reviewers, after some puzzled hesitation, saw that Isabel's 'straight path' was away from and not into the arms of Caspar Goodwood, but their hesitation was understandable. Without the New York Edition underscoring, Henrietta's injunction and Caspar's look are deeply equivocal: *uninterpretable*, surely? How could we read them and *be sure* Caspar has nothing to hope for? Although when James added his final sentence in 1905 (the year he worked on the revisions for the New York Edition) he may have imagined he was making obvious what insensitive readers had only too densely missed, he was in fact tipping into definiteness a 'close' which, intriguingly, had closed nothing, had hovered on the brink of a future which it did not offer to make out any better than Isabel could herself in her 'mutilated glimpse'. In the 1881 edition Isabel is sent back to Rome, but we only have an unclear idea as to *what for*, and what could happen next: we can only piece together into a guess all the fragments of Isabel's own and her friends' speculation. In the New York Edition at least we are made sure that what could happen next cannot be Caspar:

"Look here, Mr Goodwood," she said; "just you wait!"
On which he looked up at her – but only to guess, from her face, with a revulsion, that she simply meant he was young. She stood shining at him with that cheap comfort, and it added, on the spot, thirty years to his life. She walked him away with her, however, as if she had given him now the key to patience. (592)

It makes for a neatly ironic measure of cultural shift that the language used in the *Spectator* to deplore James's 'agnosticism' – 'the tendency of life, he holds, is to result in a general failure of the moral and spiritual hopes it raises' – sounds remarkably like a strain of late twentieth-century disapproval of James's conclusion to *The Portrait*. Only where the *Spectator* reviewer upbraided James for giving Isabel to her lover we are now outraged (with some better justification perhaps) that he seems to be giving her back to her husband. It is of course no mere accident of narrative that it is *Rome* Isabel returns to. The city cannot help standing for the weight of past empire and the constraints of tradition, for 'law' against 'sympathy'; although James is too complex a writer to labour this value one-sidedly, and the novel is rich with the consolations as well as the constraints for Isabel of Rome's and Europe's pastness. (When she sits looking from St John Lateran across the Campagna, she registers the 'endurance' as well as the 'splendid sadness' of the old ruins: 'she leaned her weariness upon things that had crumbled for centuries and yet still were upright', 518.) The argument, though, that the ending of *The Portrait of a Lady* represents a willed conservatism on James's part, a sort of resistance in the spirit but submission to the letter of the law, needs to be met; and is seminal to an interpretation of James's attitude to pleasure and to the proprieties in his later novels.[9]

Before we can justly decide what order of gesture James's is at the end of *The Portrait of a Lady*, and whether he is cutting away at a stroke all the equivocation of the second half of the novel in a resort to a transcendent and absolute value – 'the traditionary decencies and sanctities of marriage'(ML 404) – we need to penetrate further back, to see how that equivocation – that *impasse* – is constructed in the first place. Significantly, most interpretations of the ending as a conservative return of Isabel to her husband (whether sympathetic or unsympathetic to James's gesture) depend upon a reading in which James has constructed Isabel as flawed; as committing, out of hubris or lack of self-knowledge, some fatal punishable error, or exhibiting – the psychoanalytic sin – some 'inner damage'. In other words, the logic of the conservative ending is perceived as being that if James feels justified in punishing her, he must have had her do something to be punished for (even if he / we perceive her punishment as tragic).

This is the retributive model of fictional structure. Interestingly, from the evidence of contemporary reviews of *The Portrait*, literary criticism of our 'agnostic' twenty-first century is more prone to the retributive model than James's contemporary and relatively unsophisticated reader. The reader in 1881 might require Isabel to be punished, certainly, if she reneged on her marriage; but he (occasionally she) does not require it because Isabel has 'an inability to extend her imagination beyond the superficial, the conventional' or because she 'refuses to let the "light" of her own sexuality shine'.[10] Here and there in 1881 (the American reviewers like her – and believe in her – more often than the English reviewers) she gets a most sympathetic reading:

The fine purpose of her freedom, the resolution with which she seeks to be the maker of her destiny, the subtle weakness into which all this betrays her, the apparent helplessness of her ultimate position, and the conjectured escape only through patient forbearance – what are these, if not attributes of womanly life expended under current conditions?[11]

The open-endedness of this reading – its absence of fictional determinism – surely approximates more closely to the experience of reading the character than any punitive closed system.[12] 'Under current conditions' – with the sharpness of contemporaneity – the woman struggling between her personal unhappiness and her ideal of loyalty in marriage evoked, not astonished psychopathology (there must be something the matter), but (at best) tact and respect.[13]

Rather than having worked from the idea of a closed, predetermined psychology, James has in fact taken the risk in *Portrait of a Lady* of inhabiting a psychology in flux, still in formation, full of the potential for surprises.[14] Searching through the treatment of Isabel's advancing disenchantment to discover what she has it in her to do in her *impasse*, what we come away with is an Isabel whose consciousness and experience are not single and unified but made up of bewilderingly contradictory elements; intuitions and ideals, fragments learned and instinctual, obstinacies and vanities and self-doubt.[15] She convinces herself, and us, both that she cannot co-exist with Osmond and that she cannot leave him. She literally voices both possibilities, gives in the words that visit her brooding reflections *both* values their weight and power: the 'traditionary decencies and sanctities of marriage' (M 404), 'the violence there would be in going when Osmond wished her to remain' (M 474), as well as 'the rapid approach of a day when she should have to take back something that she had solemnly given' (M 404) and her worry that she does not know 'what great unhappiness might bring me to' (M 428).

As well as what Isabel consciously reflects on, James gives us in tangible fact the deep instinctual resistance of her spirit to Osmond that goes on at a level below consciousness, in the comedy of how helplessly, provokingly defiant she is with him even as she believes herself most to be conforming to the letter of his law. When he tells her to sit on the sofa she chooses the chair (M 421). How fiercely, staunchly, she resists him in argument (compared, say, to Dorothea with Casaubon): 'There is a thing that would be worth my hearing – to know in the plainest words of what it is you accuse me' (M 422). And how *adequate* to him, intellectually, verbally, her defiance is (compared, say, to Gwendolen's): 'I don't think that on the whole you are disappointed. You have had another opportunity to try and bewilder me' (M 423). She cannot help (James knows uncannily the operations of married conflict) the very punctiliousness of her obedience becoming a twisted critique of what he commandeers her obedience for.

Incidentally, there is some comedy, too, in Isabel's believing she keeps the secret of her unhappiness so effectively. She proclaims it in fact at every pore, surely, for anyone attuned to her (for example when she replies to Lord Warburton's remarking her husband must be very clever that he 'has a genius for upholstery' M 337): not because she wants to be pitied, or even because she wants them to know, but simply because she does not have the faculty of pretence.

Osmond's response to his wife's galling rectitude-with-reservation is not to dissimulate the inequity of his conventional, obligating advantage over her ('he was her appointed and inscribed master', 462) but simply to invoke it. (Again, uncanny insight into that spiralling married refusal of one another's terms of reference: if she accuses him of being tyrannous, he'll answer with exaggerated tyranny.) Isabel in the subtlety of her psychological flux, in which conventional obligations have long been entangled with the filmy stuff of an intuitive and personal value-system, has come up against the brute archaic power-fact still, for all its different dressing up, inherent in nineteenth-century marriage. It is no mere incidental joke that the Countess, after Isabel tells her Osmond has forbidden her to travel to England, says, 'when I want to make a journey my husband simply tells me I can have no money!' (M 474).[16] What is someone made of subtler stuff to *do* with brute fact?

It is the nature of the irony that plays around the portrait of Isabel which is at issue in deciding how retributive or open-ended James's 'solution' is, and what his attitude is, finally, to her 'formlessness', her psychology in flux. In the later dialogically structured novels James dispenses with an omniscient narrator capable of commenting, for example, that Isabel 'was probably very liable to the sin of self-esteem' (M 41), or that she *'flattered herself'* that she had gathered a rich experience' (M 279). Here in *The Portrait of a Lady* he is still employing that conventional apparatus of

discursive commentary which it is easy to interpret as some kind of direc-
tional inscription, or 'last word', on the primary illusionistic fabric of the
novel. Yet when James informs us from his superior vantage that Isabel
has 'an unquenchable desire to think well of herself' (M 42) that trajectory of comprehension could hardly produce the illusion of life by itself:
the commentary has to be carried into conviction on the back of a wave
of other 'experiences' of Isabel – her talk, her situation, her appearance,
her adventures, and, by the second half of the novel, her *own* insistent
self-commentating narrative and analysis which almost replaces the intrusive authorial one. The illusion, finally, overspills the circumscription;
an explicit commentary can be contained within a novel which is by no
means circumscribed by that commentary.

Alfred Habegger suggests that the 'pattern' for Isabel's story comes
from James's ironic reading of contemporary American women novelists: in numerous early reviews for *The Nation, The North American Review*
and others James expressed his exasperation with so many 'middle-aged
lovers' who spent their time 'breaking the hearts and wills of demure little
schoolgirls', those same schoolgirls who had most passionately professed
desires for freedom and self-sufficiency. It seems very plausible that James
should have made this anomaly – a much-reiterated high value on personal freedom going along with a profound unacknowledged desire to
submit to a suspiciously paternal-seeming master – a hidden ingredient
in the psychological baggage of an Isabel formed, after all, in the same
America as Anne Moncure Crane and Elizabeth Stoddard (the novelists
Habegger makes reference to). No doubt it is closely tied up with Isabel's
'unquenchable desire to please' (M 28) and her 'infinite hope that she
should never do anything wrong' (M 42); and it is probably connected
too with one very characteristic movement of Isabel's thought, out of
complacency and into a painful and hurriedly repressed self-doubt. It
happens, for example, just after she has refused Lord Warburton:

Who was she, what was she, that she should hold herself superior? What view
of life, what design upon fate, what conception of happiness, had she, that
pretended to be larger than this large occasion? . . . she was wondering whether
she was not a cold, hard girl; and when at last she got up and rather quickly
went back to the house, it was because, as she had said to Lord Warburton, she
was really frightened at herself. (M 95)

That fear at herself is reiterated throughout the novel, particularly in the
last sections as she contemplates, having no idea what she will do next, the
crisis in her marriage: 'I am afraid . . . Afraid of myself! If I were afraid

of my husband, that would simply be my duty. That is what women are expected to be' (M 441); and, 'constantly present to her mind were all the traditionary decencies and sanctities of marriage. The idea of violating them filled her with shame as well as dread' (M 404). 'Marriage meant that in such a case as this, when one had to choose, one chose as a matter of course for one's husband. "I am afraid – yes, I am afraid," she said to herself' (M 474).

These are all James's representations, no doubt, of the operations of what Habegger calls Isabel's 'hidden internal bondage': they are easy for us to recognise, now, as part of an especially feminine equipment, results of a cultural patterning at the deepest and most unconscious level.[17] Habegger is plausible, too, when he suggests James might be ironising, even, qualities of Isabel's dignity in suffering at the Palazzo Roccanera: the 'noble nickel-plated mask worn by so many women's heroines of the time' is also part of the cultural equipment, and part of Isabel's 'unquenchable desire to think well of herself'.[18] James's irony, though, is simply a component in a whole movement that opens up a generous space for imagining Isabel, one that is much larger than her own ideas about herself, or, for that matter, James's 'ideas' about her. He recognises a treacherous double bind in contemporary imaging of the female, and describes how the individual fluid consciousness finds its stumbling and inevitably incomplete account in and through and around those images.

If James is at pains to register this 'pathology' of a feminine ideal, it would be misrepresenting the overall effect of *The Portrait*, however, not to stress how he also registers in Isabel a resilience, an energy, a self-confidence, all independent of the outcome of her idealistic experiments. (It is in fact the irresistible surging of that self-confidence that causes some of her moments of self-doubt in the first part of the novel: how *dare* she be so sure she does not want to marry Lord Warburton?) We know this resilience of hers is independent of her early optimistic rhetoric because we have one of the strongest expressions of it at one of her worst moments, when she is travelling across Europe back to Ralph:[19]

This impression carried her into the future, of which from time to time she had a mutilated glimpse. She saw herself, in the distant years, still in the attitude of a woman who had her life to live, and these intimations contradicted the spirit of the present hour. It might be desirable to die; but this privilege was evidently to be denied her. Deep in her soul – deeper than any appetite for renunciation – was the sense that life would be her business for a long time to come. And at moments there was something inspiring, almost exhilarating, in the conviction. It was a proof of strength – it was a proof that she should some

day be happy again. It couldn't be that she was to live only to suffer – only
to feel the injury of life repeated and enlarged – it seemed to her that she was
too valuable, too capable, for that. Then she wondered whether it were vain
and stupid to think so well of herself. When had it ever been a guarantee to
be valuable? . . . Was it not much more probable that if one were delicate one
would suffer? It involved then, perhaps, an admission that one had a certain
grossness; but Isabel recognised, as it passed before her eyes, the quick, vague
shadow of a long future. (M 492)

In Isabel's self-interrogation here, she passes in review several major
items in the Victorian female agenda. Are not delicate things supposed
to suffer? Is not renunciation a key gesture in the feminine repertoire?
Faced with the insoluble contradiction of her unhappy marriage, would
not the delicate thing to do be to pale away and die? If so, then delicacy
(that prime ingredient of Victorian femininity) is not for Isabel: *cannot be*,
because life surges in her from somewhere deeper than the Victorian
ideal, and if that convicts her of a certain 'grossness', by Victorian standards, then so be it. She is learning all the time, and knows now to let this
ideal past her with a shrug. It is James's creation of this energetic field
around her rather than her specific utterances that engages us with the
youthfully presumptuous Isabel at the opening of the novel; the presumption of youth borrows at any given cultural moment whatever rhetoric
is current to express reach and appetite and potential. And it is Isabel's
energies that Osmond had not counted on when he planned his cultural
manipulations, her mind 'attached to his own like a small garden-plot to
a deer-park', where he would 'rake the soil gently and water the flowers;
he would weed the beds and gather an occasional nosegay' (M 378).
Instead among the carefully tended hybrid blooms he calls honour and
decency thrust the rank weeds of Isabel's 'pure mind': 'We don't live
decently together!' she cries (M 472).

If we do not believe that James is interested in punishing Isabel for her
presumption or for the inadequacy of her ideas, by invoking at his ending
a sacrifice to law in returning her to Rome and to her husband, then
we are left with a novel in which the tension between law and sympathy
is unresolved at its close. We understand from her return that she still
feels herself answerable to law, to what 'seems right' (Ralph says, 'As
seems right – as seems right? . . . Yes, you think a great deal about that',
M 507). We know, too, that Isabel's return is partly for Pansy, who figures
as the sister / daughter left behind in the very mill of the conventional,
helpless to resist it because she does not have Isabel's energy; so that the

return certainly has its aspect as a gesture of female solidarity.[20] 'I don't think anything is over', Isabel says (M 507).

But the return to Rome also feels provisional.[21] She has, after all, made her first crucial gesture of disobedience to Osmond, which alters everything; they have acknowledged to one another that any such disobedience will be irrevocable.

To break with Osmond once would be to break for ever; any open acknowledgement of irreconcilable needs would be an admission that their whole attempt would prove a failure. For them there could be no condonement, no compromise, no easy forgetfulness, no formal readjustment. (M 405)

We have a novel that ends poised on the brink of something, balanced over a choice it does not – with any finality – actually *make*. In so far as a choice is made – albeit a provisional, opaque, equivocal one – it is a choice against Caspar Goodwood, and it is Isabel's. She saves herself, by flying from England: the loss of control, the wave of sudden new passionate – erotic – sensation she experienced in Caspar's arms is not what she wants, now, as a solution to her marriage. She wants to stand on her feet. ('In the movement she seemed to beat with her feet, in order to catch herself, to feel something to rest on', M 519.) The flight from drowning sends her back for that confrontation with her marriage which lingering in England only postponed. The involuntary helplessness of passion is the alibi classically offered wives exiting their unsatisfactory marriages: and Isabel wants none of it. She wants a clear head.

The function of Caspar's intervention, though, draws our attention to just how *Portrait of a Lady* is *not*, in fact, composed around the classic adulterous triangle; James's interrogation of the law as represented by the traditionary sanctities and decencies of marriage is not to consist in this novel of testing it primarily against the pressures of passion, of abandonment, of ecstasy. The conflict is all within the civilised temple, around an internal moral contradiction and opposed conceptions of honour, one outward and conventional, one personal and instinctive: between versions, in fact, of what is *right*. When Caspar does offer himself, and for a moment – in spite of the fact that the actual words of his appeal to Isabel are in the spirit of the most enlightened New World rationalism – the novel opens to a glimpse of that other, Dionysiac thing, a 'comet in the sky' (M 517), 'the hot wind of the desert', 'something potent, acrid, strange' (589), it can only come in the context of the rest of the novel as a sidelight, a surprise, something Isabel has left out of count and cannot make space for suddenly. If she is 'natural', then her nature is something straight and sunlit; it is instructive to compare her English churchyard at Ralph's funeral ('the air had the brightness of the hawthorn and the blackbird', M 509) with the lusty paganism of Charlotte's and the Prince's Matcham in *The Golden Bowl* ('sunny, gusty, lusty English April, all panting and heaving with impatience, or kicking and crying . . . like some infant Hercules who wouldn't be dressed', 250).

Readers complain of a sexual numbness in the novel, and it is true that one of the ways in which James fails to convince us of the likelihood of an Isabel choosing an Osmond is in failing to create for us his sexual attractiveness for her; although Habegger's clues about Isabel's search for the dream-father and his quotation from Constance Fenimore Woolston's astonished recognition of how James had 'divined' something in female fantasy do help.[22] (Creating convincingly the sexual attractiveness of men for women is to be one of James's distinctive achievements in the late period, from the vacillating Sir Claude through the fatal Vanderbank to Merton Densher and Chad and the Prince.) It is impossible for us to imagine reading an Isabel who says *yes* to Caspar; the whole dynamic of *The Portrait* runs against it. Yet at that late moment his offer is suddenly almost overwhelmingly tempting. It is not the open-air fresh reasonableness of his arguments that tempts Isabel, but an erotic she has never opened to before; it reaches her now perhaps just because she is broken down and in extremity.

Revising the novel in 1905, James is careful to specify that this sex which tempts her is bodily, animal, participatory ('the very taste of it, as of something potent, acrid, and strange, forced open her set teeth', 589); not the etherised swoonings Yellow Book seducees were prone to. She is afraid of Caspar – he is 'dangerous' – for the first time, as she takes in 'each thing in his hard manhood that had least pleased her, each aggressive fact of his face, his figure, his presence' (591). There is a thundering recognition in that '*had* least pleased her': in retrospect the whole callowness of her maiden reading of him appears, her treating him as her conquest to be wound in and out on her silver thread, to be exasperated with, to be pitied. Now the very hardness of him that had seemed – to her maidenliness – repellent and awkward, is revealed as dangerous and desirable. It is in fact the 'maidenliness' of Isabel that is under threat and collapsing in this scene, the persisting 'virginity' of her type even into marriage and motherhood: and as she speeds her 'straight path' to the lighted house we can both appreciate the consistency of the Diana-like flight and survival intact (she is Isabel *Archer*, after all), and regret the sexual womanliness she has not tasted: is not, perhaps, ever to taste.[23] She makes her enigmatic pause at the door to look around her: why? Is it in an unacknowledged hope that he has followed her and will prevent her going in? But even Caspar is too much of a gentleman for that.

In 1905 James no doubt had a different perspective – having written into his late novels such different, non-virginal women as Kate, Mme de Vionnet and Charlotte – on just *what* he had created in Isabel: her type, its maidenliness, its essential chastity. (Perhaps he felt more certain that from Isabel's type there *was* no hope, ever, for Caspar; and hence his addition of the determining last sentence.) His comment on the type in his later novels is more ironic, their fate less straight, more twisted. Nanda in *The Awkward Age* would have abased herself in order to get Van, and weeps bitter tears at retiring to her nunnery at Mr Longdon's. Fleda in *The Spoils of Poynton* travelling to fetch the trophy of her sacrifice of her lover to decent conduct, the Maltese cross to treasure secretly into a maiden-auntish old age, finds the whole fine thing gone up in dirty smoke. We fear that the Isabels of one generation, making their sacrifices to their ideals of honour, become the Lady Julias (in *The Awkward Age*) of another; the treasures of their refusals, their abstentions, are an equivocal legacy for their hungry and curious grand-daughters.

What James has finely understood in 1881, in Isabel's scene with Caspar, is the actual operation, in behaviour and language, of this 'virginal' cultural ideal of womanhood; 'good' girls profoundly impressed with the need to 'please' and not to do 'wrong'. What the erotic threatens here is not simply a social form. As Thomas Mann wrote about *Anna Karenina:*

Custom and morality, how far are they distinguishable, how far are they – in effect – one and the same, how far do they coincide in the heart of the socially circumscribed human being? The question hovers unanswered over the whole novel. But such a work is not compelled to answer questions. Its task is to bring them out, to enrich the emotions, to give them the highest and most painful degree of questionableness.[24]

A cultural ideal of womanhood is enmeshed tentacularly, tenaciously, at the very roots of the construction of literary femininity. We watch the rehearsal of a familiar literary pattern: man presses woman to give herself to him; woman is overcome by the desire to give in to him, but a cultural overvoice that judges against herself never remits its condemnatory commentary. 'What bliss?' says Anna Karenina with disgust and horror. For Mme de Renal in *Le Rouge et le Noir*, 'all at once that terrible word:

adulteress, came to her'. 'It's wrong', says Chekhov's lady with a lapdog, 'You'll be the first not to respect me now.'[25] And we seem to see that pattern in operation *within* the psychological flux and fluidity of a 'real' woman, within Isabel's personality and selfhood (illusion overspills circumscription again). Isabel has no language in which she can say yes; her language says no for her, rehearses in her own mouth a familiar protest, attempts to circumscribe in thin conventional words the inchoate flood of her actual experience.

'... The world's all before us -and the world's very big. I know something about that.'

Isabel gave a long murmur, like a creature in pain; it was as if he were pressing something that hurt her. 'The world's very small,' she said at random; she had an immense desire to appear to resist. She said it at random, to hear herself say something; but it was not what she meant. The world, in truth, had never seemed so large; it seemed to open out, all round her, to take the form of a mighty sea, where she floated in fathomless waters. (M 518)

'Ah, be mine as I'm yours!' she heard her companion cry. He had suddenly given up argument, and his voice seemed to come through a confusion of sound.

This however, of course, was but a subjective fact, as the metaphysicians say; the confusion, the noise of waters, and all the rest of it, were in her own head. In an instant she became aware of this. 'Do me the greatest kindness of all,' she panted. 'I beseech you to go away!'

'Ah, don't say that. Don't kill me!' he cried.

She clasped her hands; her eyes were streaming with tears.

'As you love me, as you pity me, leave me alone!' (M 519)

Isabel *cannot speak* what Caspar can, that 'the world is very big'; even though that is, for a moment, her actual experience. She is in pain 'as though he were pressing something that hurt her', she can only answer that 'the world is very small', as if the utterance came from an infinitely lesser space of possibility. She says to him, 'Are you mad?', although at that moment it is she who is experiencing sensations like madness, a confusion of sound and noise of waters in her own head. When she begs him, 'As you love me, as you pity me, leave me alone!', she offers the archetypal virtuous compromise with sexual temptation, inviting the desired profanation – the kiss – and admitting her incapacity to resist even while articulating the still predominant desire *not* to succumb, to be honourable, to be *good*. A still predominant honour is helpless none the less – because femininely weak – in the path of the onrush of desire.

It is a compromise convenient for literature, crushing for the female subjectivity that finds its account there. However ambivalent we may

feel about Isabel's Diana-like chastity, we cannot want her to succumb
to the compromise, to act *yes* while still only able clearly to articulate
no. Edith Wharton's stories, even though written out of very divorced
and extra-marital *fin-de-siècle* New York, are full of women more or less
broken in that particular double bind: distinct from, of course, though
not unrelated to, the double bind that has freedom-loving girls in search
of a master to submit to.[26] (Wharton is also very good, in connection
with Mann's remarks, on the impossibility of disentangling within the
individual subjectivity social verdict and self-condemnation.)

In *Anna Karenina*, *Le Rouge et le Noir* and *Lady with a Lapdog*, it goes
without saying that the 'consciousness' of the fiction inhabits a much
more open space than can be filled by the rehearsal of dismayed feminine
virtue by Anna Karenina, Mme de Renal or Anna Sergeyevna. In all
these cases, the enveloping 'larger' space around the female moralising
feels specifically male; the male author / narrator may value and admire
or even count on this female will-to-chastity (Chekhov's Gurov finds it
boring), but he knows it co-exists with a world of other sexual varieties.
The male consciousness has an advantage of worldliness it may even
deplore (Tolstoy, for example, who throws so much weight behind Anna's
'intuition' of her own transgressiveness) but cannot wish away.

What is distinctive in the rehearsal of the pattern at the end of
The Portrait of a Lady is how James's account of it stands within and
not outside the troubled self-contradicting female subjectivity. This has
partly to do, of course, with his writing in the English / American and
not the 'improper' European tradition: the English fictional space was
precisely *supposed* to be co-existent with a 'female' virtue (we remember
what a mess this makes of the end of *The Mill on the Floss*). But behind
James's position lies all his saturation in that European tradition, and his
scorn, sometimes, for the 'soap and water' of English fictional 'propriety':

I have been seeing something of Daudet, Goncourt, and Zola; and there is
nothing more interesting to me now than the effort and experiment of this
little group, with its truly infernal intelligence of art, form, manner – its intense
artistic life. They do the only kind of work, today, that I respect; and in spite of
their ferocious pessimism and their handling of unclean things, they are at least
serious and honest. The floods of tepid soap and water which under the name
of novels are being vomited forth in England, seem to me, by contrast, to do
little honour to our race.[27]

James treats the scene from within Isabel's subjectivity not because he
cannot imagine or approve of other perspectives, but because he wants
and needs to engage in an interrogation of 'propriety' from within.

(Possibly this makes his love scene read as somewhat 'maidenly', along-side its European counterparts.) But the danger with a male enveloping worldliness and how it fictionalises female 'virtue' is that the treatment can verge on 'connoisseurship', on relishing the 'piquancy' of a less evolved consciousness than the narrative's own. We have no reason to wish to see Mme de Renal liberated from her conventional notions of the wickedness of adultery: they are, on the contrary, intrinsic to her charm, not because *Stendhal* believes in the least that she ought to be faithful to Monsieur – after all, this is the writer who later in the same novel cre-ates relishingly, and without a trace of squeamishness, a Mathilde de la Mole! – but because the fact *she* thinks she ought to speaks an innocence the male narrative can only yearn for and never return to. And because Mme de Renal is conventionally 'moral', Julien's conquest of her is all the more piquant. Purity – 'goodness' – can still have a 'value' (in the connoisseur's sense) even for a palette that has long entertained all the other colours.

James's interrogation of the value of 'traditionary decencies and sanc-tities', though, is sited at the very point where convention focuses: in the 'goodness' of 'good' women themselves. James has committed himself enthusiastically to that tradition in English fiction of siting narratives within female consciousness; but he is also to commit himself progres-sively to broadening the scope of that female consciousness to include the big unchaste world of European fiction. An image crops up on Isabel's journey to Ralph which not only seems to suggest in embryo the imagery James uses to express in *The Golden Bowl* Maggie Verver's slow process of uncovering the real beneath the innocent-seeming surface, but also could serve as an account of the whole drive behind the renewal and development in James's writing from *What Maisie Knew* onwards:

She had plenty to think about; but it was not reflection, or conscious purpose, that filled her mind. Disconnected visions passed through it, and sudden dull gleams of memory, of expectation. The past and the future alternated at their will, but she saw them only in fitful images, which came and went by a logic of their own. It was extraordinary the things she remembered. Now that she was in the secret, now that she knew something that so much concerned her, and the eclipse of which had made life resemble an attempt to play whist with an imperfect pack of cards, the truth of things, their mutual relations, their meaning, and for the most part their horror, rose before her with a kind of architectural vastness. (M 491)

The architectural vastness could be Maggie's pagoda, the whist game looks forward to the bridge game Maggie prowls around, at once excluded and controlling. The intuition of vast secret structures of behaviours underlying surface proprieties suggests the problems of 'knowledge' for the heroines of *Maisie* and *The Awkward Age*, as well as Milly Theale's vulnerability and Woollett's obtuseness.

Meanwhile back at the end of *The Portrait of a Lady* Isabel, having been plunged dizzyingly under the surface by her discoveries about her husband and by Caspar's kiss, scrambles back out onto the dry land of her belief in herself, leaving us with the sensation of an opaque and not entirely fulfilling ending to the novel. The novel tests out 'traditionary decencies and sanctities' on their own terms and ends in an impasse: Isabel has taken the first steps out onto a bridge which as yet only reaches into the air and has no dry land the other side to come down on. The 'proprieties' are ironised in the novel – even tragically; and James has accurately recorded the inbuilt constraints, the double binds, in a 'good' woman's psychology and in her language; but he has not found another voice for his woman yet. She thinks and feels beyond the conventional, but she cannot say or act: he cannot imagine it for her. She does not have a language to override what 'seems right', nor to say yes to that erotic that opens up for her late, and frighteningly.

The challenge Isabel's unfulfilment sets for the development of this theme in James's writing – the formal / conventional stretched and tested by the subjective / affective – is to create a language for womanliness which is not anchored in goodness, or chastity, or unsexuality. James of course was not in any vanguard in English-language fiction in terms of his subject matter: heroines were flying from husbands to lovers in their throngs, long before James dreamed up Kate or Mme de Vionnet or Charlotte. Yet what so many 'daring' novels testify to is the linguistic and ideological persistence of ideals of 'goodness' long beyond the fact. (For example, again, Edith Wharton's troubled adulteress in 'Souls Belated'; and of course Sue Bridehead in *Jude the Obscure*.) What is really a radical development in late James is the convincing creation of a space and language in fiction for a womanhood liberated to kick over the traces with no more ado than a man. If Charlotte is destroyed at the end of *The Golden Bowl* it is not because of the operations of her own conscience. If Merton makes a judgement against Kate at the end of *The Wings of the Dove*, it is not because she came to his room: on the contrary, that was his sign of her good faith. If Mme de Vionnet is unhappy, it is not because she thinks she is sinful, but because she knows she cannot keep Chad.

Perhaps in the end the bridge is never built to bring Isabel safely down on another side: perhaps the sort of development James has to make out of her impasse is more like a leap, a free fall. Certainly the women of the later novels inhabit a space where it is no easy matter – where it is in fact wishful thinking – to find footholds and control as Isabel sturdily insists. And although those women may have the sexual fulfilment she eschews, there are no certainties in their universe to match that real centre of *Portrait of a Lady*, more pivotal in fact than Caspar's kiss, when Isabel and Ralph finally – on his deathbed – share the truth about her marriage in a transcendent scene of mutual enlightened intelligence:

nothing mattered now but the only knowledge that was not pure anguish – the knowledge that they were looking at the truth together . . .

' . . . You said just now that pain is not the deepest thing, No – no. But it is very deep. If I could stay – '
'For me you will always be here,' she softly interrupted. It was easy to interrupt him.
But he went on, after a moment –
'It passes, after all; it's passing now. But love remains . . . '

'And remember this,' he continued, 'that if you have been hated, you have also been loved.'
'Ah, my brother!' she cried, with a movement of still deeper prostration. (M 507)

There is plenty of mutual enlightened intelligence in the late novels, but transcendent it is not; it is contingent, vulnerable, temporary. (What becomes, for example, of the exceptional mutuality of Kate and Merton at the opening of *The Wings of the Dove*, described as if they found themselves face to face at the top of a pair of ladders looking over their respective garden walls?) With new freedoms for James's heroines comes a loss of certainty; a free fall intimately related, of course, to the developments in James's form, where whatever was left of the controlling intrusive narrator and his containing ironies is sunk in the opaque subjective dialogic medium of the late fiction.

CHAPTER 2

'As charming as a charming story': governesses in What Maisie Knew and 'The Turn of the Screw'

In a review of a children's novel in 1875 Henry James complained:

It is evidently written in good faith, but it strikes us as a very ill-chosen sort of entertainment to set before children. It is unfortunate not only in its details, but in its general tone, in the constant ring of the style. The smart satirical tone is the last one in the world to be used in describing to children their elders and betters and the social mysteries that surround them . . . Miss Alcott . . . goes too far, in our opinion, for childish simplicity or paternal equanimity. All this is both poor entertainment and poor instruction. What children want is the objective, as the philosophers say; it is good for them to feel that the people and things around them that appeal to their respect are beautiful and powerful specimens of what they seem to be. Miss Alcott's heroine is evidently a very subjective little girl, and certainly her history will deepen the subjective tendency in the little girls who read it.[1]

It would be stretching a point to pretend that this description of Louisa May Alcott's *Eight Cousins* exactly fits *What Maisie Knew*, the novel that James himself wrote twenty-two years later. *Maisie* is at great pains never to be 'smartly satirical', and of course although its subject is a child it was not written for a child to read. But it represents none the less a revolution in James's thinking, to have come round from the review's position of satirical disapproval to the point of making a whole novel out of the history of a highly subjective little girl discovering that 'the people and things around [her] that appeal to [her] respect' are very far from 'beautiful and powerful specimens of what they seem to be'. This discovery in *Maisie* is a part of her growing up, and not 'pert', 'vulgar', or 'depraved'.[2]

It is generally agreed that James's writing in the late 1890s, after the crisis of his failure in the theatre and his disappointment in not achieving the kind of mass readership for his novels he had perhaps hoped for, underwent just such a revolution in thinking. The 'late style' begins to be recognisable from *What Maisie Knew* onwards, with its new 'difficulty' and its retreat from a commentating, hierarchising narrative voice. At the same time James produced a series of fictions centred on studies of childhood or adolescence: almost as though he was making, out of his disappointments and doubts, a re-entry in his writing into the vulnerability and openness of childhood and adolescence, and through it a new interrogation of the very sources of adult authority, of the authority of the 'objective' referred to so confidently in the 1875 review. Under particular scrutiny are not only the children of those turn-of-the-century novels and stories themselves, but also the adults in those fictions who are directly responsible for the children's initiations: the educators, the transmitters of adult knowledge, particularly the governesses.[3]

In his 1906 and 1907 *Harper's Bazar* essays on the manners and speech of American women, James wrote nostalgically about the governess or schoolmistress of the past who had served as 'the closed vessel of authority, closed against sloppy leakage'; her strict primness was 'one of the ways in which authority can be conveyed'. The essays protest at the so different femininity of contemporary girls:

'Don't let us have women like that,' I couldn't help quite piteously and all sincerely breaking out; 'in the name of our homes, of our children, of our future, of our national honour.'[4]

But even in the context of this extravagant camped-up conservatism, James cannot help choosing words which suggest his ambivalence towards 'closed vessels of authority'; and that ambivalence is the very subject matter of *What Maisie Knew* and 'The Turn of the Screw' (1898). In these fictions the whole point of all the governesses – Mrs Wix, Miss Overmore and the girl from the Hampshire vicarage – is that they are extremely 'leaky vessels', and the 'precious ripe tradition' they embody comes under the most sceptical scrutiny.

To establish how fundamental this interrogation of authority and tradition is to the whole development of James's work and style through the transitional period of the 1890s, it is worth re-examining Tony Tanner's suggestion that it is 'the tension between law and sympathy which holds the great bourgeois novel together'.[5] In early novels such as *Washington Square* and *The Europeans*, the operation of that tension as structural principle is self-evident. Without Dr Sloper's 'law' (and he has to be *right* about Morris) there is no space, no narrative, for Catherine's 'sympathy': a Catherine who could marry whichever dreadful man she liked would not be interesting. In *The Portrait of a Lady* the law–sympathy tension is, as we have seen, within Isabel herself. Her struggle is to sustain the two polarities in relation: to do what 'seems right' relative to both the 'law' *and* her own freedom. And she experiences – problematically – their interdependence: that any transgression of hers against the 'law' will also be against her idea of her free self.

What feels different as soon as we turn to *What Maisie Knew* is how the structuring around law and sympathy has altered its equilibrium. There is plenty of 'law' in the novel, invoked at one point or another by most of the adults (except for Sir Claude) and especially by Maisie's teachers, but it is not constructed there as authority: the narrative meticulously unlearns for us any objective and authoritative over-reading, begins instead with Maisie's blank page and develops through her interpretative gropings. The pronouncements of 'law', of what is 'right' and 'wrong', when they come, are looming phenomena which Maisie has painfully to reckon with, and which are unmistakably going to have to take up a great deal of room in her imaginative space; but they remain objects of puzzled and troubled perception, they are not justified inside the experiencing subjective intelligence of the novel.

In Boulogne, while Mrs Wix and Maisie are waiting for Sir Claude to return, Maisie falls under the spell of her first foreign country: everything it invites her to is in a different language, both literally and metaphorically, from her life in London; a language Maisie is not able properly to interpret yet, but which seems to represent a possibility of exciting liberations. The liberations she dreams of in Boulogne need not be literal: what matters is her openness, her sense of scale, of far-off horizons and beckoning experiences. But all the while, Mrs Wix's 'dingy decencies' and 'frumpy old-fashioned conscience' are urging in her ear in familiar and reproachful English:[6]

'Haven't you really and truly any moral sense?' . . . after this the idea of a moral sense mainly coloured their intercourse. She began, the poor child, with scarcely knowing what it was; but it proved something that, with scarce an outward sign save her surrender to the swing of the carriage, she could, before they came back from the drive, strike up a sort of acquaintance with. The beauty of the day only deepened, and the splendour of the afternoon sea, and the haze of the far headlands, and the taste of the sweet air. It was the coachman indeed who, smiling and cracking his whip, turning in his place, pointing to invisible objects and uttering unintelligible sounds . . . made their excursion fall so much short that their return left them still a stretch of the long daylight . . . The bathers, so late, were absent and the tide was low; the sea pools twinkled in the sunset and there were dry places as well, where they could sit again and admire and expiate: a circumstance that, while they listened to the lap of the waves, gave Mrs Wix a fresh support for her challenge. 'Have you absolutely none at all?' (193)

Responsible, aghast at Maisie's depravity, conscientiously fulfilling her duty as guardian and pedagogue, as 'closed vessel of authority', Mrs Wix intrudes her 'dingy' apparatus of sin and shame upon the sensual movement and beauty of the day, as if she would like to prevent Maisie having any but blinkered glimpses of it through her own 'straighteners'. Laying the groundwork for the familiar female double binds, she bemoans in Maisie the lack of consciousness of a system of social taboos and regulations she will not even explicate: Maisie has to piece together for herself out of muddied fumbled hints what exactly it is that is 'wrong' about Sir Claude's liaison with her stepmother. She is supposed to intuit the indecency of sex without – God forbid – knowing anything about sex. Mrs Wix insists with almost Alice-in-Wonderland tenacity that the thing – the 'moral sense' – is *out there*, real, where Maisie only sees sea and sky. By the end of their ride, with a little vulnerable gesture of willingness and compliance, 'surrendering to the swing of the carriage', Maisie signs her readiness to try to believe.

Later the same evening, Mrs Wix continues her challenge to Maisie's 'moral sense' inside the hotel room, and we are given again the conflict within the child – paradigmatically expressed by her situation *inside* the room but looking *out* of the window – between all the multiple live promptings of experience and the monologic insistent voice of authority.

'What I did lose patience at this morning was at how it was without your seeming to condemn – for you didn't, you remember! – you yet did seem to *know*. Thank God, in his mercy, at last, if you do!'

The night, this time, was warm and one of the windows stood open to the small balcony over the rail of which, on coming up from dinner, Maisie had hung a long time in the enjoyment of the chatter, the lights, the life of the quay made brilliant by the season and the hour. Mrs Wix's requirements had drawn her in from this posture and Mrs Wix's embrace had detained her even though midway in the outpouring her confusion and sympathy had permitted, or rather had positively helped, her to disengage herself. But the casement was still wide, the spectacle, the pleasure were still there, and from her place in the room, which, with its polished floor and its panels of elegance, was lighted from without more than from within, the child could still take account of them. She appeared to watch and listen: after which she answered Mrs Wix with a question. 'If I do know – ?'

'If you do condemn.' The correction was made with some asperity. (196)

The distinction made here between knowing and condemning is surely a crucial one, that expresses something radically new in the structures of representation and judgement in *What Maisie Knew*. James is opening

a space between seeing the world and moralising it – a space with room
for all the pleasuring life outside the window. It is the space Mrs Wix
with all the force of her adult authority is trying to close for Maisie, even
if as yet Maisie in the shadowed inner room can still see the lights re-
flected from outside. In the language and gestures of these paragraphs
James is explicitly separating out the premises of perception from the
presuppositions of a given social code: separating out knowing and condemning and even, finally, opposing them. Mrs Wix really believes that
Maisie's freedom to see and know without condemning is sinful. Even
as, with Calvinistic solemnity, she searches in vain for the 'moral sense'
in Maisie that she believes should be 'innate' and not 'taught', we watch
her in fact try to transmit and impose a learned system of interpretation
and condemnation. For Maisie to be 'saved' will require shutting out the
possibilities of seeing and knowing beyond the window, possibilities the
sympathy of the novel is unequivocally committed to.

Something has changed here in James's attitudes; an independence is
being made out deep inside the text from a whole received system of
social propriety, something prepared for in the interrogations of earlier
works, but only fully realised in these works of the late 1890s onwards.
That independence could only be won with the lapsing of the authoritative kind of hierarchising narrative voice and through the unlearning,
the unmaking, of certain kinds of authority within the texts. We saw in
The Portrait of a Lady how for all his power to create protest, and to test
and stretch law to its very edge, for so long as his authority as writer was
interpenetrated with the authority of a certain social order, all that testing
and stretching could not finally break out of a circularity in which there
was no narrative, no knowledge, outside interpretation and judgement.
The problem may have felt for James in its writing out as much a problem
of narrative as of his own personal 'morality'; if the structure of 'the great
bourgeois novel' *had* been dependent on the tension between law and
sympathy, then into what form could narratives grow if the conviction
of law was allowed to lapse?

Seminal to James's making out his independence from the social law
is this period in the late 1890s when he absorbs himself in the child
perspectives, entering their ignorances and innocences, effortfully un-
writing all the signs of knowing worldliness, or rather, separating those
signs from the authority, the voice, of the novel. Law (convention, propriety, the whole apparatus of social regulation) becomes external to the
narrative, becomes the circumstance within which the narrative takes

form. Instead of one of the poles of narrative being located, as it were, outside the individual, in the external world (law), all the tensions and irreconcilables, and all the dynamic of narrative development, are displaced onto the subjective, and the subjective interpretation of law. The fictions uncover the sources of social convention within the individual consciousness, and the processes by which objective law is grafted upon subjectivity. The polarity is not between law and sympathy, but between innocence and experience.

In the novels of this transitional period James significantly uses narrative devices that make impossible the kind of omniscient narrator who in the very process of telling interprets, hierarchises, judges: in *Maisie* (1897) the narrative through child 'eyes'; in 'The Turn of the Screw' (1898) a Conrad-like Chinese box of narratives within narratives, uncharacteristic of James; in *The Awkward Age* (1899) that drama-like principle of composition described explicitly in the preface as making 'the presented occasion', like a play, 'tell all its story itself' in a succession of scenes consisting mainly of dialogue.⁷ In the later novels, there is no longer any need for devices. The scruple that relinquishes monologic authority has been internalised; that middle-ground proneness of English novel-narrative to judgemental omniscience has been purged from the style itself.

In his studies of governesses, Mrs Wix with her straighteners, the carnivorous Miss Overmore / Mrs Beale, the leaky and fantasising girl from the Hampshire vicarage, James gives us virtually a pathology of propriety, of the processes of transmission of the law. All the certainties these adults construct as they transmit to the children their version of what is happening, are problematised within the text by James's representation of the children's resisting 'innocence'. Innocence reads around and through and beyond an adult discourse charged and distorted and closed in infinitely regressive short circuitings by its imagination of and fear of sin; scarred by its own processes of self-censorship and self-suppression; and muddied and equivocal with self-protection and self-interest.

This recoil from the adult, from the discourse of experience, characterises both *What Maisie Knew* and 'The Turn of the Screw'. It makes these two fictions read, in fact, as a *crisis* of authority in the *oeuvre*. There is no appeal that can be made in the world of these novels against the governesses' versions, nowhere the children can turn to find out whether Mrs Wix's 'moral sense' or the sin-burdened ghosts are *real*. Only the fiction itself represents and vindicates that appeal. We hold out hopes of a common-sense humaneness from Mrs Grose in 'The Turn of the Screw',

but although she does eventually take Flora away, her caste-submission
to the educated governess's superior propriety does not seem seriously
to falter (it is significant that she herself cannot read); she docilely takes
it from her that stealing letters and 'saying things' are enough to put the
children outside the protection of the civilised pale.

In *What Maisie Knew*, Sir Claude can clearly see the pleasuring world
that Maisie sees and hear its call: and without straighteners. But his
sight of it is a wistful glimpse backwards from an adulthood essentially
compromised: he cannot help her. When he watches 'the fine stride
and shining limbs of a young fishwife who had just waded out of the
sea with her basketful of shrimps'(184), we know things about how his
gaze follows her up the beach that Maisie does not: in fact the essential
boundary marker between child innocence and adult unreliability in
these transitional fictions is the initiation into sexual awareness. The girl
from the vicarage, trespassing beyond the marker, projects her shame
at her trespass onto Miles and Flora; Maisie at the end of her novel
is finally forced beyond the marker and into awareness, thanks to Mrs
Wix's and Mrs Beale's ministering initiations. Sir Claude, lost on the
far side of adult complications, is not merely unreliable, he is positively
drowning: his pleasure in the company of Maisie, whom he calls his
'boy', is surely partly to do with the relief from sexual complications;
and his glance at the fishwife coming out of the sea is at an Eden-like
dream of sex uncompromised by markers and consequences. (Not only
are the fishwife's naked limbs and emergence out of the sea mythic,
outside history: more prosaically, the fact that as a fishwife she is out of
Sir Claude's class holds out, for a man of the world, the promise of sexual
irresponsibility.)

These two transitional fictions locate crucially around the issue of sexual initiations; and in both of them the 'far', adult side of initiation is
represented as treacherous country. It is interesting that these two stories,
whose very subject is the legacy for the English imagination of Victorian
guilty propriety, should themselves manifest vestiges of troubled
Victorianism, in that they are only able to represent innocence as
possible for an unsexual child, unstained by the dirty water of adult
passions. If we read *Maisie* and 'The Turn of the Screw' as James finally
writing himself out of the conviction that 'it is good for [children] to
feel that the people and things around them that appeal to their respect
are beautiful and powerful specimens of what they seem to be', this first
straight look at the reality is as yet more appalled than forgiving. It is
not until *The Awkward Age* that James will find it in him to write his

sordid adult sinners not as grotesques but only as flawed, disappointed, damaged human beings.

The pathology of propriety in both these transitional fictions is represented as essentially something manipulated by women; the product of a female imagination tainted by its long seclusion, its narrowness, its ignorance. The men may seem to be the first causes, the prime movers: it is for the love of Sir Claude, or in the service of the 'master', that all the stories' development comes about. Yet while the women are actively promoting and manipulating that development, the men uneasily or indifferently absent themselves, wash their hands of responsibility. Even the men's ultimate authority and the women's dependence on them is to some extent actually stage-managed and orchestrated by the women: in the case of 'Turn of the Screw' the master does not actually exist at all within the primary narrative (the governess's one meeting with him happens outside her 'manuscript'); he is only operative as the girl's fevered imagination of him. Nancy Armstrong in 1987 offered sceptical Foucauldian insights into the 'enchantments' of 'narratives in which a woman's virtue alone overcomes sexual aggression and transforms male desire into middle-class love'; it seems as if James in the 1890s was himself sceptically probing a similar gendered complex of power, action and narrative.[8]

Is he not probing, in his treatment of governesses in *Maisie* and 'Turn of the Screw', at that old story which had been told and retold countless times by and to and about women in English fiction in the nineteenth century: the governess–master story of which *Jane Eyre* is both source and supreme manifestation? Is he not exploring how that story had penetrated to the very roots of perception of the female and of the imagining of women's fulfilment, how it had entangled itself with 'law', and how latent in its apparent innocence and cleanness were dangerous contradictions – its passionateness with its decency, its hunger with its control? The story had a dangerous power to delude, to hold out as the rewards for righteousness promises of what it could not deliver: the promise, ultimately, of the master.[9]

In Mrs Wix, James's *Jane Eyre* pastiche works through comic realism. A parodistic fragment of the old story is dropped down into another world altogether, a world where there is no-one to fall in love with Mrs Wix's sobriety or her grey dresses. Her very dinginess, her straighteners, her ill-at-easeness amidst gallic pleasurings, all derive by some crooked mocking line from Jane's sober grey wool and cool disapproval of Adèle's French fineries. Even the dead child seems a detail out of the Victorian store: but realism reads its way round the pathetic tale of Clara-Matilda and picks up its sordid hint of a differently unhappy story, of illegitimacy perhaps (where is Mr Wix and why is he never mentioned?). Mrs Wix's nursery stories are not, as in *Jane Eyre*, robust North English folklore, but tell of 'distressed beauties' and 'perfect gentlemen, strikingly handsome' (72): the governess–master story reduced to absurd and fatal paradigm.

In her moment of greatness Mrs Wix breaks out and makes a passionate appeal to Sir Claude; makes the classic *Jane Eyre* step across gender and caste divide, charged with all those years of schoolroom imaginings, emboldened by the new finery Sir Claude has paid for (she should have listened to Jane who *knew* new clothes would turn her head). In accents she has never tried out before – and to Sir Claude, to her employer, to a gentleman! – she reveals herself at last peremptory, vociferous, accusatory, equal, and *female*:[10]

Maisie could scarcely believe her eyes as she saw the good lady, with whom she had associated no faintest shade of any art of provocation, actually, after an upward grimace, give Sir Claude a great giggling insinuating naughty slap. 'You wretch – you *know* why!' And she turned away. The face that with this movement she left him to present to Maisie was to abide with his stepdaughter as the very image of stupefaction; but the pair lacked time to communicate either amusement or alarm before their admonisher was upon them again. She had begun in fact to show infinite variety and she flashed about with a still quicker change of tone, 'Have you brought me that thing as a pretext for your going over?' (197)

It has never occurred to Sir Claude, of course, that he need give any account of what he is doing whatsoever, let alone a pretext, to Mrs Wix. His hold on his gentlemanliness may be ever so shaky, but his 'stupefaction' registers none the less the deserts of difference between himself and Mrs Wix's fusty sad insignificance. He has brought her over to Boulogne precisely for her decency, and now it turns out even she harbours complications; the 'precious, ripe tradition' he had counted on for safety cries out, in its extremity, in the unsound cadences of sacrifice and self-abandonment, in the rhetoric of wish fulfilment.

'You're dreadful, you're terrible, for you know but too well that it's not a small thing to me that you should address me in terms that are princely! . . . Take me, take me,' she went on and on -the tide of her eloquence was high. 'Here I am; I know what I am and what I ain't; but I say boldly to the face of you both that I'll do better for you, far, than ever she'll even try to. I say it to yours, Sir Claude, even though I owe you the very dress on my back and the very shoes on my feet. Owe you everything – that's just the reason; and to pay it back, in profusion, what can that be but what I want? Here I am, here I am!' – she spread herself into an exhibition that, combined with her intensity and her decorations, appeared to suggest her for strange offices and devotions, for ridiculous replacements and substitutions. She manipulated her gown as she talked, she insisted on the items of her debt. (201)

In this *Maisie* world of manipulating women and vacillating men (Beale is not weak exactly, but the Countess does *pay* him) it is Sir Claude's fatality to be desired. No wonder that after Mrs Wix's outbreak he abandons his moment's dream of escape (with Maisie his 'boy', and to France and the fishwife) and resigns himself to Mrs Beale, a Blanche Ingram among governesses.

It is possible that among the things Maisie is *refusing*, in that first gesture of her independence at the end of the novel, is just this Victorian female love-pathology, the melting and the sacrificing, the cult of the man (Mrs Wix discussing her 'secret feelings . . . by the hour' with Maisie in the schoolroom); the high tone and the sordid accommodations. It is 'realism' that Maisie awakes to, at the end, a recognition beyond delusions that however nicely she and Sir Claude get on, there is no place for her innocent play-romance in the adult economy of emotions: competitive, possessive, conflictual, sexual. He does not even wait to wave to their steamer from the balcony: she knows he has gone to Mrs Beale. Sir Claude does not think much about Maisie when she is not there: it is very important for Maisie to know that. It is on the way to healing a certain debilitating habit of the female imagination.

This is a habit which the leaky governess of 'The Turn of the Screw' is very prone to. One of the features of her volatile and inconsistent narrative is how it perpetually imagines itself exposed to a male gaze, to her master's attention; and how it gains its significance and importance from that, its rewards.[11]

I liked it best of all when, as the light faded – or rather, I should say, the day lingered and the last calls of the last birds sounded, in a flushed sky, from the old trees – I could take a turn into the grounds and enjoy, almost with a sense of property that amused and flattered me, the beauty and dignity of the place. It was a pleasure at these moments to feel myself tranquil and justified; doubtless, perhaps, also to reflect that by my discretion, my quiet good sense and general high propriety, I was giving pleasure – if he ever thought of it! – to the person to whose pressure I had responded. What I was doing was what he had earnestly hoped and directly asked of me, and that I *could*, after all, do it, proved an even greater joy than I had expected. I dare say I fancied myself, in short, a remarkable young woman and took comfort in the faith that this would more publicly appear . . . One of the thoughts that, as I don't in the least shrink now from noting, used to be with me in these wanderings was that it would be as charming as a charming story suddenly to meet someone. Someone would appear there at the turn of a path and would stand before me and smile and approve. I didn't ask more than that – I only asked that he should *know*; and the only way to be sure he knew would be to see it, and the kind light of it, in his handsome face. (35)[12]

We readers know, as Maisie learns, that really there is no such gaze, no such 'knowing'. The narrative directs us around its ostensible statement to realist readings of probability: it is obvious that the master is indifferent to his employee and oblivious of her fantasising perpetual consciousness of him. But the governess never attains to that objective purchase on her experience from outside her own narrative that Maisie does: never recognises that she has constructed her master herself. Too much, fatally too much, depends upon the verification that gaze and its imagined approval bestow upon her project of authority. Her sense of her own authority is entangled at too deep a level with the sense of it as an authority by proxy: a dangerous responsibility without answerability, the need to act without the requirement to examine the premises of action. (She does what she is told, after all; what she should; what she must.)

Of course the male watcher for whom the governess's narrative performs is not only the master (and not only Peter Quint on the tower): it is for Douglas that she writes her story down, and in his susceptible youth her narrative finds at last its male underwriter, its guarantee of her justification, and (too late and too attenuated, smelling too much of the 'sweet dim faded lavender' of genteel unfulfilment[13]) its reward, in his lifelong devotion to the memory of her truth. The pathos and quiet dignity of Douglas's country-house ghost-story frame to 'The Turn of the Screw' are just the qualities the governess has intended him, and us, to read into her narrative. But in his meticulous mimetic reproduction of the language and cadences of the 'old story', James is uncovering something else, something less dignified as well as less quiet, a veritable pathology of perception, in which for instance the master's very indifference and neglect are contorted into privilege and consolation:[14]

It was striking of the children . . . never to fail – one or the other – of the precious question that has helped us through many a peril. 'When do you think he *will* come? Don't you think we *ought* to write?' . . . 'He,' of course, was their uncle in Harley Street; and we lived in much profusion of theory that he might at any moment arrive to mingle in our circle. It was impossible to have given less encouragement than he had done to such a doctrine, but if we had not had the doctrine to fall back upon we should have deprived each other of some of our finest exhibitions. He never wrote to them – that may have been selfish, but it was a part of the flattery of his trust of me; for the way in which a man pays his highest tribute to a woman is apt to be but by the more festal celebration of one of the sacred laws of his comfort; and I held that I carried out the spirit of the pledge not to appeal to him when I let our young friends understand that their own letters were but charming literary exercises. They were too beautiful to be posted; I kept them myself; I have them all to this hour. (89)

This daughter of a clergyman finds the language and apparatus of religion to hand – 'doctrine', and 'festal celebration of . . . sacred laws' – to reconcile herself to the arrangements of patriarchy and class system which consign her to narrowness and unfulfilment, and to insist upon the significant presence of the in fact absent watcher.

With consummate doubleness, she both encourages the children to count upon the imminent appearance of the master, and pockets their letters to him in a gesture that not only presumes but effects their futility. It is in this that the pedagogy of the governess consists: she teaches the children to believe in a fulfilment that cannot happen, and to address themselves to an authority who will never hear them. She perpetuates her own pathology: not out of innocence (the mere perpetuation of the watertight tradition) but in a narrative fractured around its own bad faith. The very cadences of longing and sweet, funny hopefulness – 'we lived in much profusion of theory that he might at any moment arrive' – are the flowery surfaces concealing the violences sprung at their roots, in their very vocabulary. The 'young friends', the 'charming' and 'beautiful' letters, the 'adorable children': these are the emphases which invariably produce within the narrative tension of 'The Turn of the Screw' a violently dissenting anti-reading, against sweetness and against innocence. 'Their more than earthly beauty, their absolutely unnatural goodness. It's a game . . . a policy and a fraud' (82). Beauty and charm and adoration are intoxicating poisons the vigilant narrative has perpetually to articulate against:

There appears to me, moreover, as I look back, no note in all this more extraordinary than the mere fact that, in spite of my tension and of their triumph, I never lost patience with them. Adorable they must in truth have been, I now reflect, that I didn't in those days hate them! (89)

The little wretches denied it with all the added volume of their sociability and their tenderness, in just the crystal depths of which – like the flash of a fish in a stream – the mockery of their advantage peeped up. (87)

with their voices ['our small friends' voices', New York Edition] in the air, their pressure on one's heart and their fragrant faces against one's cheek, everything fell to the ground but their incapacity and their beauty . . . It was a pity that I needed once more to describe the portentous little activity by which she sought to divert my attention – the perceptible increase of movement, the greater intensity of play, the singing, the gabbling of nonsense and the invitation to romp. (62)

The changed reiteration of the diminutive in that last passage is significant. The 'small' that is tender, protective, coy in the account of the children's charms becomes the 'little' that is lashing, sceptical, hostile in the governess's conviction of Flora's contamination. Both energies seem to come from the *same source*.

The excessive protestations of abasement and service to the master, and the very commitment of the narrative itself to the presumption of his gaze, also have their violent underside of resentment and refusal in such a narrative divided against itself. As the narrative progresses, or the governess finds herself farther and farther committed into the fragile and fantastic narrative web she has spun, we watch the process of the transmutation of the master out of the underwriting authority for her invention into the enemy of it. He becomes the one to whom it had better not be reported, the one from whom it must be kept secret, the one who the governess-missionary wincingly recognises will conspire with Flora to misunderstand, to make her out 'the lowest creature'.

' . . . Flora has now her grievance, and she'll work it to the end.'
    'Yes, Miss; but to *what* end?'
    'Why, that of dealing with me to her uncle. She'll make me out to him the lowest creature-!'
    I winced at the fair show of the scene in Mrs Grose's face; she looked for a minute as if she sharply saw them together. 'And him who thinks so well of you!'
    'He has an odd way – it comes over me now,' I laughed, '– of proving it! But that doesn't matter. What Flora wants, of course, is to get rid of me . . . It's *you* who must go. You must take Flora.'
    My visitor, at this, did speculate. 'But where in the world – ?'
    'Away from here. Away from *them*. Away, even most of all, now, from me. Straight to her uncle.'
    'Only to tell on you – ?'
    'No, not "only"! To leave me, in addition, with my remedy.' (119)

Miles is to be feared for, left alone, the 'remedy' for his governess who girds herself for her final test of strength, Macbeth-like, amidst the falling away hourly of the reassurances and the old superstitions that have sustained her; excepting the one or two superstitions to which she is committed too far to retreat:

within a minute there had come to me out of my very pity the appalling alarm of his being perhaps innocent. It was for the instant confounding and bottomless, for if he *were* innocent what then on earth was *I?* (136)

In spite of her moments of 'perverse horror' at what she is doing – 'To do it in *any* way was an act of violence, for what did it consist of but the obtrusion of the idea of grossness and guilt on a small helpless creature who had been for me a revelation of the possibilities of beautiful intercourse?' (132) – an act of violence it is to be, and the Macbeth analogy does not seem disproportionate to the violence of the language of the last pages of the story: 'fighting with a demon for a human soul', the 'ravage of uneasiness', 'the hideous author of our woe', 'the drop of my victory and all the return of my battle' and the 'wide overwhelming presence' that 'filled the room like the taste of poison' (137).

It is the language of violent conflict; it is also more specifically the language of the gothic, of violence interiorised, domesticated; of the suffering underside of reasonableness and respectability; and of the vision of the madwoman in *Jane Eyre.* Almost until the last moments of the struggle in the dining room, the governess is *knitting:* and we remember that one of the worst condemnations she and Mrs Grose have ever actually articulated of that 'horror of horrors' Miss Jessel is that she goes outside *without a hat* (108). She encounters Peter Quint for the second time when she goes in search of a pair of gloves 'that had required three stitches and that had received them – with a publicity perhaps not edifying – while I sat with the children at their tea' (41): almost as if the tiny shame links itself subliminally with the terrible apparition. James is locating that specific and predominantly feminine terrain in the nineteenth-century imagination where the very minutiae of refinement give rise to the worst dreams; where the vast disposition of thundering life-forces is around the tea table and the sewing basket.

The governess's crucial act of assertion of authority in the newly masterless house that last evening is to dine downstairs: 'to mark, for the house, the high state I cultivated' (126). In all seriousness, now, she acts out the possession and authority which she had entertained in playful language at the opening of her narrative ('I could take a turn into the grounds and enjoy, almost with a sense of property that amused and flattered me, the beauty and dignity of the place'). In place of fantasies of obedience and reward, she now paces the house in an assertion of dominance, 'clutching the helm', 'very grand and dry', causing it to be known that 'left thus to myself, I was quite remarkably firm' (125). At first reading her language here is in complete contrast to her conventional gushing, grateful and self-doubting girlishness at the beginning of the story:

> In spite of this timidity – which the child herself, in the oddest way in the world, had been perfectly frank and brave about, allowing it, without a sign of uncomfortable consciousness, with the deep, sweet serenity indeed of one of Raphael's holy infants, to be discussed, to be imputed to her and to determine us – I felt sure she would presently like me. It was part of what I already liked Mrs Grose herself for, the pleasure I could see her feel in my admiration and wonder as I sat at supper with four tall candles and with my pupil, in a high chair and a bib, brightly facing me, between them, over bread and milk. There were naturally things that in Flora's presence could pass between us only as prodigious and gratified looks, obscure and roundabout allusions.
>
> 'And the little boy – does he look like her? Is he, too, so very remarkable?'
>
> One wouldn't flatter a child. 'Oh miss, *most* remarkable. If you think well of this one!' – and she stood there with a plate in her hand, beaming at our companion, who looked from one of us to the other with placid heavenly eyes that contained nothing to check us.
>
> 'Yes; if I do – ?'
>
> "You *will* be carried away by the little gentleman!'
>
> 'Well, that, I think, is what I came for -to be carried away. I'm afraid, however,' I remember feeling the impulse to add, 'I'm rather easily carried away. I was carried away in London!'
>
> I can still see Mrs Grose's broad face as she took this in. 'In Harley Street?'
>
> 'In Harley Street.' (25)

How does the governess's narrative transform like this from its beginnings in a language of subordination to its climactic disastrous assertions of dominance? What is the development between her perception of Flora's Raphael-like 'holy innocence' this first tea-time and the vituperative fury of the scene by the lake, where she sees Flora's face as a 'small mask of reprobation': her 'incomparable childish beauty . . . suddenly failed', and like a 'vulgarly pert little girl in the street, she hugged Mrs Grose more closely and buried in her skirts the dreadful little face' (116)?[15] What James seems to be exploring is how these apparently mutually contradictory values – the sweetness and the foulness, the adoration and the loathing, the submissiveness and the domination – are intimate co-presences in a language essentially *dyadic*, constructed around a Manichean vocabulary of positives and negatives. The one excess entails the other: all the potential for the governess's visions of horror is there in her vision of an impossibly radiantly innocent childhood. And the bad faith of the narrative hovers from before she has ever even seen Peter Quint, as a miasma of overstatement ('one of Raphael's holy infants'), of mendacity ('There were naturally things that in Flora's presence could pass between us only as . . . obscure and round-about allusions'), of false logic (why do they proceed to flatter Flora, having said they shouldn't?), and of helplessness to control (the 'placid, heavenly eyes . . . contained nothing to *check* us' recalls the omnipresent possibility of being 'carried away').

Most important of all, the bad faith is in the monologic solipsism of a narrative that fails consistently to make its move into dialogue, on to the separateness of others. The governess talks *about* Flora but not *to* her. It pretends to be a story of service and sacrifice in Miles's and Flora's name; they and their childishness certainly become the fetish objects of her missionary project ('I . . . covered her with kisses in which there was a sob of atonement', 30). But there is a sense in which all her obsessive attentiveness to them misses their actuality in the text; smothers all their speech in interpretation; expends much energy on coercing them to 'tell the truth' but can within its own logic only ever hear their offer of it as postponement and ploy:

I was of course thoroughly kind and merciful; never, never yet had I placed on his little shoulders hands of such tenderness as those with which, while I rested against the bed, I held him there well under fire . . .
  'You must tell me now – and all the truth. What did you go out for? What were you doing there?'
  I can still see his wonderful smile, the whites of his beautiful eyes and the uncovering of his clear teeth, shine to me in the dusk. 'If I tell you why, will you understand?' My heart, at this, leaped into my mouth. *Would* he tell me why? I found no sound on my lips to press it, and I was aware of replying only with a vague, repeated, grimacing nod. He was gentleness itself, and while I wagged my head at him he stood there more than ever a little fairy prince. It was his bright-ness indeed that gave me a respite. Would it be so great if he were really going to tell me? 'Well,' he said at last, 'just exactly in order that you should do this.'
  'Do what?'
  'Think me – for a change – *bad*!' I shall never forget the sweetness and gaiety with which he brought out the word . . . He had given exactly the account of himself that permitted least of my going behind it. (79)

As soon as she asks the question she sets up the impossibility of believing any answer but her pre-selected (impossible) one: that he has been with Quint. There is a circularity to their thus betraying themselves to her suspicions: unless they tell her her suspicions are correct, she is bound to hear their 'lies' as confirming those suspicions. But a realist reading *around* the governess's narrative directs us to attend to Miles's offered explanation with all the seriousness his governess cannot afford. He seems to have been alerted precisely to that entrapment within their governess's interpretation of things which insists too much on their innocence and goodness; he wants to break into her dyad of perfect innocence and devilish foulness by offering his own ordinary imperfection: he wants her to 'think me – for a change – *bad*!'.[16]

We can seek out a reading through and behind the governess's fantasising presentation of the children's strangeness: James affords us plenty of occasions when we hear them, through the entanglements of her interpretative web, doing their utmost to speak plainly, to make sense. These are indeed likely to be peculiar children: orphaned, with an indifferent father-substitute, attaching themselves to a succession of paid minders all more or less driven and preoccupied, if not simply subservient like Mrs Grose. They are surrounded with all the material care belonging to the power-to-command of a privileged caste; but in fact, because they are not adult and not able to command, they are vulnerable to whatever more or less sublimated resentments may be felt by those of lower caste or those whose caste status (like the governesses') is ambivalent, insecure. They are haunted by sudden deaths and disappearances *which no-one ever speaks of.*

If we give them a reading uncontaminated by the governess's dyadic values, these are indeed not 'innocent' children. They inhabit a real un-innocent world which naturally they are groping to understand. They are acutely sensitive to their new governess's moods (which she imposes more and more peremptorily) and even as she promotes that sensitivity she reads it with characteristic doubleness as a sign of their corruption. Theirs is the sensitivity of children who are quite used, for instance, to weeping governesses with secrets ('She had looked at me in sweet speculation and then had accused me to my face of having 'cried'. I had supposed the ugly signs of it brushed away', 62). They are used to adult motivations obscure but dangerous; and behind the innocent-seeming codes of adult surfaces, to hidden realities which children are not allowed to name. (Miles is presumably expelled from school for transgressing – too innocently, ironically enough – this interdict.) They are indeed haunted, they have presumably been through all this with Miss Jessel before: they know about demented governesses and indifferent men.

Their new governess never speaks to them about the deaths, or her fears, she never asks them about the *real* Peter Quint and Miss Jessel; her narrative never opens onto genuine dialogue, it is only the space in which she acts out her role:

The large, impressive room ... the great state bed as I almost felt it, the full, figured draperies, the long glasses in which, for the first time, I could see myself from head to foot. (24)

"How do you know what I think? [the governess asks].

"Ah well, of course I don't [Miles replies]; for it strikes me you never tell me."(93)

She addresses the children either in baby-talk or, later, with a coy know-ingness that both invites and fears their complicity: but she presumes always that they can in fact read the hidden realities behind her surface code (and that very presumption becomes further proof of their contam-ination). *We* presume, in fact, that they do indeed *try very hard* to read her, to fathom and to please her, like Maisie struggling to discover the 'moral sense' that Mrs Wix insists is there; they are indeed more initiated than is compatible with their governess's ideal of Raphael-like holy innocence. 'We must do nothing but what she likes', Miles anxiously suggests to Flora and Mrs Grose after he has first broached the subject of his re-turning to school, and made his first gesture of appeal to his uncle, to an outside and objective authority, against his governess's threatening quivering refusal to let him go.

At the end of the story, abandoning baby-talk, the girl addresses them in screams and vituperation, in the whole unleashed arsenal of feminine 'sensibility', in the gothic of prostration, of fainting fits and embraces and falling against things for support. ' "No more, no more, no more!" I shrieked, as I tried to press him against me, to my visitant' (137). (This is uncharacteristic: James's women on the whole eschew the Victorian hysteric body-vocabulary. At most they cry. If anything, it is his men whom he puts through the 'gothic' range: in 'The Jolly Corner' and 'The Beast in the Jungle', for example.) And it is at those moments of fracture, as the code founders and the suppressed breaks through, that the frightened children struggle to make themselves heard. Flora shouts aloud, 'I don't know what you mean. I see nobody, I see nothing.'

Flora refuses to see; Miles (and we remember the weak men and ma-nipulating voracious women of *What Maisie Knew*) tries, little gentleman that he is, desperately to save himself by obliging, looking first for Miss Jessel – is *that* not who she wants? that was who she wanted, by the lake – and then, when that does not please, for the other one he guesses that she means. (They have intuited enough about her obsessions, to guess. And anyway, it would seem natural that her obsessions coincided with the children's own, that they too would be preoccupied, haunted, by the secrets and the deaths.)

his head made the movement of a baffled dog's on a scent and then gave a frantic little shake for air and light, he was at me in a white rage, bewildered, glaring vainly over the place and missing wholly, though it now, to my sense, filled the room like the taste of poison, the wide, overwhelming presence. (138)

But although Miles tries to oblige, he cannot say he sees what he does not see, what is not there. Only the children, within the text, refuse to see what is not there; candidly they articulate their scepticism, they accuse, they name names, oppose their personal realism to the trajectory of adult fantasy. All the adults, including and especially the comfortable listeners to Douglas's old story, are complicit in accepting the governess's version of what happens, accepting in obedience to the conventions of the old story that she sees what is not possible, the dead returned to life.[17]

It is this complicity which makes 'The Turn of the Screw' a story about much more than one individual pathology.[18] The very survival of the story in Douglas's manuscript, the very hush which the blasé sophisticated listeners of a different generation still accord to the old-fashioned tale, suggest the persuasiveness and persistence of the governess's version of things. Worldly ladies and gentlemen seem to need to believe in her slightly comical fusty respectable *rightness*: the ritual circumstances of the re-telling and Douglas's piety signal that we are in the presence of a foundation myth, some fundamental underpinning of caste and gender tradition, a childhood-learned core of magic and belief. The narrative experiment of 'The Turn of the Screw' does not consist simply in the analysis of a disturbed individual: it is launched rather into the exploration of the wider field suggested by Millicent Bell, 'social classes and their relation to one another and ... gender in this context'.[19]

Bell analyses at length in her essay 'Class, Sex and the Victorian Governess: James's 'The Turn of the Screw'' the especially anomalous position of the governess within nineteenth-century class structure:

a woman burdened with the task of upholding and transmitting the increasingly 'Victorian' domestic ideal, though she herself was single and unable to count on the prospect of a marriage; she was a 'lady' in the nineteenth-century sense of the term, yet anomalously earning her own living.[20]

It is required of her that she both embody in her own existence and perpetuate in her teaching systems of thought of which she is not in fact the beneficiary. James makes her story therefore the focus for his explorations of those systems of thought. Her own anomalous 'false' position refracts as violences and hiatuses into her narrative just those inconsistencies and suppressions which are tangled in the very premises of ideals of propriety, of ladylikeness, of feminine innocence and ignorance. What is forced out of the narrative in efforts of innocence, and in the effort to identify 'nature' with innocence, will return as sub-text, as shadow reading, as the revelation of the hidden contents of the 'respectable' surface. The governess *cannot afford* to hear the children; to believe the children would be to undo that dyad of innocence and guilt which is holding together all the contradictions, all the false logic, of her own role. She can only be ladylike and modest and contented and important by imagining the children are foully contaminated with guessed-at desires. If she admitted the mere ordinary reality of the children, she might have to discover that she herself is inferior, thwarted, raging, desiring, and doomed to unfulfilment.

Despite all the surface appearance of accusation of 'them', a great deal of the governess's language actually obliquely suggests her *own* guilt. She wonders, ' "What will they think of that? Doesn't it betray too much?" It would have been easy to get into a sad, wild, tangle about how much I might betray' (67). 'I tried to laugh, and I seemed to see in the beautiful face with which he [Miles] watched me how ugly and queer I looked' (91). 'I was like a jailer with an eye to possible surprises and mistakes' (90). In her sightings of Miss Jessel, her very readiness to condemnation hints that what she sees and fears in the broken woman weeping on the stairs is a vision or a premonition of herself, her own capacity to be broken and betrayed: 'she vanished without looking round at me. I knew, for all that, exactly what dreadful face she had to show' (74). Knows, because it and its dreadfulness are familiar from that long treacherous mirror in her room? Her unpityingness has just the flatness of self-chastisement.

When the governess comes upon her predecessor in the schoolroom, 'she . . . looked at me long enough to appear to say that her right to sit at my table was as good as mine to sit at hers' (97). Miss Jessel exacts a recognition of identity: the screams – 'You terrible, miserable woman' – might be the governess's protest at herself.[21] When she berates against Flora to Mrs Grose we seem again to hear incontinent fury at herself, a transfer onto the child of shame and disgust that is in origin self-shame: 'Oh, I see her perfectly from here. She resents, for all the world like some little high personage, the imputation on her truthfulness and, as it were, her respectability . . . Ah, she's "respectable", the chit!' (119). The vision of her broken predecessor is of that propriety and intactness and control which it is her life's struggle to sustain, invaded and brought down; by the foulness of Quint, the foulness of sex and of sin.

As Miss Jessel 'appears' in relation to the governess's anxieties about herself, so Peter Quint 'appears' on the tower at the very moment she imagines walking into the fulfilment and completion of the master's gaze ('Someone would appear there at the turn of the path and would stand before me and smile and approve . . . I only asked that he should *know*', 35). Quint is the master's surrogate, who wears his cast-off clothes, and, actor-like, exercises in the master's absence (Mrs Grose thinks) too much of the master's authority. Like the master he is 'remarkably handsome', and the sexual frisson this draws from the governess in the text is a shudder at something devilish, the dyadic counterpart of the benign swoon of uncontrol produced in her by the master's equivalent good looks ('I was carried away in London', 25).

There is a telling moment early on where the governess suddenly extends the taint she has been attributing to Quint into her thoughts of the master; she speculates that he too, like Peter Quint, was 'not so very particular perhaps about some of the company he himself kept' (51). The almost proprietorial chaffing knowingness, over this man she has only met twice, is a first sign of what is to come in the gradual translation of her idealised master into the resented enemy of her project as the story progresses. How could she possibly know what company he kept: from what under-depths of female imaginings of male freedoms does such knowingness come? (We remember Charlotte Brontë's gauche man-of-the-world manner in *Jane Eyre*, over Rochester's wild oats.) Is this part, in fact, of the unexamined content of the myth of the adored master? Is Peter Quint the embodiment even of what the governess *requires* the master to also be?

Almost as soon as Quint is glimpsed she unloads onto his figure a dread and foulness that has been waiting for him to appear, waiting in her very language as the dyadic 'dark' that shadows too exclusive an insistence on innocence and beauty; he becomes the repository for and the embodiment of the whole hoard of her sexual and social taboos and fears. Mrs Grose complains that Quint was 'much too free': his character as the governess constructs it with the help of Mrs Grose threatens the whole system of propriety and 'place' that binds these two women to the safety of submission and dependence. He stole (waistcoats), he drank, he had 'secret disorders' and 'vices more than suspected', he moved in and out of the constraints of the house and grounds, he had other (of course 'lower') social contacts.

He talked to Miles (too freely, no doubt), and 'spoiled' the boy, whatever we understand by that: possibly (it is one of the realist 'counter-readings' to the governess's narrative that James hints at for us) offered the boy a relatively uncomplicated cross-caste companionship. Being too free with Miles and 'spoiling' him sound distinctly preferable to the governess's obfuscations and her preoccupation with Miles's being 'spoiled' in the way she chooses to understand the word. In his moment of extremity at the end of the story Miles casts around for an escape (he has already spent the day outdoors) and says he has to see Luke. Who is Luke? One of the servants the governess shares her isolation with and yet never names? (She reflects when discussing Quint with Mrs Grose that some of them, too, are 'too free' (50).) Might we guess that Miles is grasping for the safety of the stables or the kitchen, invoking the different (and masculine) authority of tackle and traps against this female spirit-conjuring?

Peter Quint is like the governess's dream of her master and yet dangerously unlike him: the essential dividing marker between them is that Quint is not a 'gentleman'. On the wrong side of the caste marker that makes the master a gentleman and herself a lady lies the undoing of the governess's whole identity and *raison d'être*. The caste marker holds apart those dyadic possibilities of love fulfilment around which her imagination circles: her fantasised reward in the master's approving gaze, and Miss Jessel's degradation, ending in exposure and death, when she succumbs to the attention of Peter Quint. The vision of Quint signals for the governess the dangerous real content of the apparent innocence of her fantasy of the master, and her whole project of realisation through the master's recognition. Or, to express it differently, Peter Quint and Miss Jessel provide the ugly realism that haunts the governess's idealising fantasy of her master; they are the parodistic enactment of the impossible romance. They provide the counter-narrative to the governess's dreams, her high-mindedness and inexplicit, swooning fulfilments of recognition from an unseen watcher; instead, they act out class degradation, pregnancy (we presume), exposure, shame, and death.[22] (The close presence of that brute other realistic possibility behind the fairy tale is present, also, in *Jane Eyre*: in the look, for example, that Mrs Fairfax gives Jane the night she comes upon them kissing after Rochester's proposal in the garden.)

In the governess's narrative, it is only 'gentlemanliness and ladylike-ness', or propriety, that hold back the possibility of her own 'love story' becoming the story of Peter Quint and Miss Jessel: and the children get caught up in the deployment of energies around this. The boy and girl, in their presumed but doubted sex-innocence, must be protected, for the sake of the lady and the master, from the sex-knowledge of Peter Quint and Miss Jessel. Invested in the children, in other words, is the fetish of the governess's own innocence.

But that is not all the story. As well as the governess's dread of the ghosts, there is also her jealousy of them, and her curiosity. Miss Jessel has had what the governess herself longs for: the crude sexual maleness of Quint is after all something projected not only by the governess's fear but by her desire. The boundary of propriety is something that both saves her *and prevents her.* The walking into the gaze wants more than mere absent approval, the body in its gesture of surrender to the imagined presence asks for more than it dares to acknowledge:

Someone would appear there at the turn of a path and would stand before me and smile and approve. I didn't ask more than that – I only asked that he should *know*; and the only way to be sure he knew would be to see it, and the kind light of it, in his handsome face. That was exactly present to me – by which I mean the face was – when, on the first of these occasions, at the end of a long June day, I stopped short on emerging from one of the plantations and coming into view of the house. What arrested me on the spot – and with a shock much greater than any vision had allowed for – was the sense that my imagination had, in a flash, turned real. He did stand there! (35)

Once these ghost-emanations from an underworld of her imagination have shown themselves to the governess, *she wants to know*, she prefers 'the fullness of [her] own exposure'. The alternative seems more dreadful, would condemn her to a perpetual exclusion: 'What I had then had an ugly glimpse of was that my eyes might be sealed just while theirs were most opened' (87). What the governess offers as missionary sacrifice in her determination to go on seeing ghosts reads in fact as more like hungry need: the quiet of Bly without her ghosts is the emptiness of a theatre without a play. *They are her story*, the story that transforms the 'grey prose' of her office and 'the stupid shrubs I knew and the dull things of November' (40, 129) into experience, into a life; into, what's more, romance:

The place, with its grey sky and withered garlands, its bared spaces and scat-tered dead leaves, was like a theatre after the performance – all strewn with crumpled playbills. There were exactly states of the air, conditions of sound and of stillness, unspeakable impressions of the *kind* of ministering moment, that brought back to me, long enough to catch it, the feeling of the medium in which, that June evening out of doors, I had had my first sight of Quint, and in which, too, at those other instants, I had, after seeing him through the window, looked for him in vain in the circle of shrubbery. I recognised the signs, the portents – I recognised the moment, the spot. But they remained unaccompanied and empty, and I continued unmolested; if unmolested one could call a young woman whose sensibility had, in the most extraordinary fashion, not declined but deepened . . . I had then expressed [to Mrs Grose] what was vividly in my mind: the truth that, whether the children really saw or not – since, that is, it was not yet definitely proved – I greatly preferred, as a safeguard, the fullness of my own exposure. I was ready to know the very worst that was to be known. (86)

This fear of being left 'unmolested' by her ghosts connects significantly with that rhetoric of resignation in the governess's bright talk in the opening chapters about her fulfilment in looking after the children. Close by her reassurances in the prose there always nestle the signs of her resentment, of her dread that there will be nothing *more* than this:

The attraction of my small charges was a constant joy, leading me to wonder afresh at the vanity of my original fears, the distaste I had begun by entertaining for the probable grey prose of my office. There was to be no grey prose, it appeared, and no long grind; so how could work not be charming that presented itself as daily beauty? (40)

The question insists that it is already answered; yet, once asked, it remains operative against all her ecstatic reassurances. It is the same question, of course, that Charlotte Brontë / Jane Eyre asks eloquently at Thornfield: this material sufficiency and respectability and employment – why is it not *enough?*

The nexus of gender and power conflicts that concentrates itself in the governess's sightings of Peter Quint is even more complex, too, than simply issues of sexual fear and sexual desire.[23] There are frequent moments when she seems not so much in sexual relation with Quint as in a rivalry of authorities. She outgazes him, in their penultimate encounter on the stairs, turns the tables on the power he had over her when he watched her from the tower, when he was the watcher she had and had not been longing for. This time, in a complex manoeuvre of authorities, she asserts caste against his sexual advantage: 'I definitely saw it turn, as I might have seen the low wretch to which it had once belonged turn on receipt of an order' (71). The neutral pronoun triumphantly unsexes Quint.

There are also moments where, just as happens with Miss Jessel the broken governess, Peter Quint appears as a parodistic distorting reflection of the governess herself; he the employee-usurper of authority, he the actor, 'much too free', he in the final scene with the 'prowl of a baffled beast'. Surely these are displacements onto the ghost of aspects the governess cannot afford to recognise in herself? As the story winds up to its climax, as she asserts her dominance in the emptying house, and as she forces her terrible un-innocent knowledge onto Miles ('strange passages and perils, secret disorders', 52), does she not more and more resemble the Peter Quint that she has conjured up?

The interrogations of adult objectivity in 'The Turn of the Screw' and *What Maisie Knew* are crucial markers in the development of James's late work. Both stories seek out under the surface of social decencies and norms a totemic core of belief tightly entangled in fetishes of sexual innocence, child innocence, femininity and female powerlessness: it is at the rehearsal of this core of belief that Douglas's audience sits enthralled and complicit. The adult objective law becomes simply the version of the story that the adults tell: in a recoil of mistrust and distaste at how that version manipulates and betrays, James falls back for his 'truth' upon the vulnerable uninitiated children.

Both fictions render his perception of the bad faith and damaged perceptions of the women in whose ministering and mothering voices the broken story is to be retold, the totem is to be perpetuated. At the same time both fictions represent with sympathy the causes of the damage, the entrapping mechanisms of innocence and sacrifice, the beguiling stories of reward and fulfilment, and, in 'The Turn of the Screw', the inevitability with which disempowerment and unfulfilment will return to haunt the story in neurosis and dissimulated revenges.[24] The sleep of the innocence of these women produces monsters. The world of the little girl at the Hampshire vicarage was supposed to be made up of the happinesses that cat and pony bring; she was supposed to be 'slavish idolater' to her brothers while they showed no corresponding 'fine consideration' for her 'inferior age, sex, and intelligence' (68). She cannot afford to let this little boy whose voice is a 'high casual pipe with which ... he threw off intonations as if he were tossing roses' escape from her to grow up into the deep-voiced world of men, of absent and indifferent masters.[25]

CHAPTER 3

'The sacred terror': The Awkward Age
and James's men of the world

From the vantage point of *What Maisie Knew* and 'The Turn of the Screw', both fictions centred in childhood, the adulthood lying beyond the marker of initiation into sexual knowledge looks like treacherous country. In *The Awkward Age* (1899), centred in adolescence, James makes some tentative explorations into that country on the far side of the marker, and finds out that after all it has firm ground and breathable air. It is a more forgiving fiction than its two predecessors: at least, it is not tensed around that same recoil from the sexual and mistrust of the adult which animates *Maisie* and 'The Turn of the Screw'. Even from inside the sordid tangle of impropriety and treachery of *The Awkward Age*, James finds it may be possible, after all, to *talk*; there may be language, and even candour, beyond the breakdown of the old law, and the old story; there may be ways of talking *about* taboo rather than simply inhabiting a language (as in *Maisie* and 'The Turn of the Screw') broken *over* it. It may be possible to imagine adults who can hold apart 'knowing' and 'condemning'.[1]

If we are reading these fictions of the late 1890s as transitional within James's *oeuvre*, he was at the same time excitedly reading the specific cultural detail of those years as transitional for English leisure-class society: in *The Awkward Age* transition is his explicit subject, located as it is between the secure proprieties of Lady Julia's generation and the incalculable consequences of the openness of Nanda's. In his notebooks, just before and after the sketch which is the seed for *The Awkward Age*, James made notes from Brada's *Notes sur Londres*, a journalistic analysis from the French perspective of change in contemporary English society:

What Brada speaks of in particular, as the two most striking notes to him are *Primo*, the masculinization of the women; and *Secondo*, the demoralization of the aristocracy – the cessation, on their part, to take themselves seriously...

The idea of this little book is the Revolution in English society by the *avènement* of the women, which he sees everywhere and in everything. I saw it a long time ago – and I saw in it a big subject for the Novelist . . . [Quoting from Brada] *'car c'était une belle chose après tout, que de voir une puissante aristocratie, une société si riche et si forte, tant d'êtres divers tenu en respect par quelques fictions qui suffisaient à défendre l'edifice sociale; c'était une salutaire illusion que de supposer toutes les femmes chastes, tous les hommes fidèles, et d'ignorer, de chasser resolument ceux qui portaient quelque atteinte visible à cette fiction.'* [because it's a wonderful thing after all, to see a powerful aristocracy, a society so rich and strong, so many different individuals, kept in check by a few fictions which are enough to sustain the social edifice; it is a happy illusion to suppose that all women are chaste and all men faithful, and to chase off resolutely anyone who visibly gives the lie to such a fiction.]

I seem to see the great, broad, rich theme of a large satirical novel in the picture, gathering a big armful of elements together, of the *train dont va* English society [the rate it's going] before one's eyes – the great modern collapse of all the forms and superstitions and respects, good and bad.[2]

In Brada's perception of a turning tide in English society, the apparatus of sexual prohibition and regulation and the defence of the social edifice (that is, the system of class and the protection of leisure-class privilege) are inextricably entangled. The 'salutary illusion' that women are chaste and men are faithful is an important part of what has safeguarded that social edifice. And that safeguarding system of sexual prohibition depends in turn, Brada suggests, on sustaining the 'femininity' of women; if they become 'masculinized' (that is, if they have access to traditionally masculine forms of knowledge, masculine freedoms to know), then the whole edifice is jeopardised.

In Brada's integration of the sexual with the political, James recognises his subject: not only the subject-to-be of *The Awkward Age*, but the whole nexus of the preoccupations he has been writing around since he began, the preoccupations that are first tried in the 'international theme'. What do *moeurs* mean, what are the ultimate sanctions for behaviours, if they are prescribed differently in different cultures? What does it mean to be a 'good' girl (as Daisy Miller is good), if it means something different in different places? What can Isabel's 'goodness' go on meaning to her in the new world of her marriage, whose surfaces offer no purchase for that 'goodness'? In the novels of the late 1890s these probings of mores and propriety have twisted themselves further and further out of neutrality and into a crisis of belief. Those core values of female innocence and goodness which have been central to a feminised English-language novel tradition seem to require from James, in *Maisie* and 'The Turn of the Screw', fundamental re-examinations, rewritings. Is it possible that the 'old story' of sacrifices and rewards, restraints and fulfilments, had an aspect that was corrupted and corrupting? In the 'great modern collapse' of all the 'forms and superstitions and respects', the ghosts of which broken promises will return to haunt the ruins? In order properly to understand the implications of that collapse, James like Brada will find his focus in the phases of transformation of sexual mores; in the proprieties the most intimate points of contact between individuals become the key with which to unlock an understanding of an age and its significant historical transformations.[3]

James refers to Brada as 'he' and 'him'; in fact, she was a woman, but the mistake is understandable. The unapologetic cynicism of her comments depends upon that French tradition of the disaffiliation of the writer from the bourgeois project, a disaffiliation whose roots lie in *Lucien Leuwen* and *Le Rouge et le Noir*, and in Rousseau. The French novel tradition, unlike the English one, had been mostly in the hands of men, and its freedom to speak from outside propriety was inseparable from male freedoms in a given cultural system to think and know from outside that propriety. (Once a tradition is located in that 'outside', of course, it is possible for some, few, women to write there too: James in his writings on George Sand makes much of how she took her freedoms 'exactly like a man'.) From the perspective of a French anti-bourgeois intellectualism which had never been affiliated to the idealising project of decency and chastity and duty, the 'modern collapse' of the old 'superstitions' in English society will simply mean the removal of a hypocritical gloss from an unaltered reality; will afford some natural satisfaction at the deflation, finally, of the famous English hypocrisy. A properly chic cynicism will even lament the end of such a useful fiction, that had served so effectively to hold together a society 'so rich and so strong'.

Even in James's first notes, however, Brada's seamless cynicism at the collapse of the convenient fiction of propriety that holds together the social edifice is translated into something more complex. Reading the transformation from a centre, a *feminine* centre, in which ideals of 'innocence' and 'goodness' had a potency not wholly ironised by their juxtaposition with a different 'reality', the change that comes with the collapse is not so slight, not superficial. James's phrase 'the great modern collapse of all the forms and superstitions and respects, good and bad' is open-ended. It does not suggest that the subject of *The Awkward Age* is simply to be elegy, that 'long argument for the old lavender' it has sometimes been taken for.[4] But equally, a 'great collapse' of 'forms' suggests more than a cheerful change of labels; it suggests upheavals in the very structures of imagination, in the very stories a society has told itself and lived by.

The problem of getting the balance right in a reading of *The Awkward Age* between lament for a world passing and excitement at new energies liberated seems to centre on Mr Longdon.[5] He is fifty-five (James was the same age at the time of writing the novel) and his country retreat makes us think of James's Lamb House at Rye; readings have sometimes tended to identify Mr Longdon with the novelist, and therefore to hear his voice as privileged, as James's own. At its most extreme, this reading has given us an interpreter of a corrupt *fin de siècle* whose old-fashioned and shockable innocence is underwritten in a critical vocabulary positively sacral, belonging to the world of the governess of *Turn of the Screw*, with its dyadic language of cleanness and innocence (Mr Longdon) and corruption and guilt (Mrs Brook). But the apparatus for the enforcement of those kind of judgements, for the separating out of the clean from the polluted, is determinedly eschewed in *The Awkward Age*; explicitly so in James's explanation of his method in the preface, where the 'presented occasion', like a play, is to 'tell all the story itself'. What is the reliance on dialogue in the novel for, if not to suspend the 'version' of a Mr Longdon in flexible and evolving relationship with, say, the 'version' of a Duchess?

If there is a self-portrait of sorts in the novel it is scrupulously ironised. We might even say that Mr Longdon's wisdom, his values, his moral universe, do sound something like the more confident, secure narrator-voice of *The Bostonians*, say, or *Washington Square*; only here that narrator voice is relegated from (to use the Bakhtinian vocabulary) monologic centrality to being only one of the voices, the values, of the heteroglossia of the novel. In conversation with the Duchess, Mr Longdon does not always have the last word. They are talking here about Mrs Brook's relationship with Van:

His silence, for a little, seemed the sign of a plan. 'What is it he hasn't done with Mrs Brook?'

'Well, the thing that *would* be the complication. He hasn't gone beyond a certain point. You may ask how one knows such matters, but I'm afraid I've not quite a receipt for it. A woman knows, but she can't tell. They haven't done, as it's called, anything wrong.'

Mr Longdon frowned. 'It would be extremely horrid if they had.'

'Ah, but, for you and me who know life, it isn't *that* that – if other things had made for it – would have prevented!' (288)

The 'wrong' that is no more than part of a system of euphemism for the Duchess ('they haven't done, as it's called, anything wrong') – just as the 'innocence' she has arranged for Aggie is part of a system of

marriageability – strikes Mr Longdon with all its *old* weight, of judgement, of sin. But then the only vocabulary his old-fashionedness has to
meet 'wrong' in, the language of good manners and gentility, seems as
inadequate here (as comical) as her cynicism: 'It would be extremely
horrid if they had.'

'Ah, but for you and me who know life . . .' the Duchess goes on, appealing round the closure of judgement to other qualities she chooses
(teasingly, but accurately, as it turns out and she perhaps intuits) to suppose in him: an openness, finally, to the facts, to a changeable reality; an
interest in knowing that reaches beyond the closure of condemning. 'It
isn't *that* that – if other things had made for it – would have prevented!'
Whether the 'old forms and superstitions and respects' were 'good' or
'bad', a whole world of reality lies beyond the boundaries where those
forms had seemed to hold back possibilities; and *The Awkward Age* leans,
like Mr Longdon, across those boundaries and into that world.

Not only is Mr Longdon not the privileged interpreter of *The Awkward
Age*; he is by no means an inflexible, static value. A case might even be
made that he undergoes a Strether-like 'conversion', not quite to im-
moralities, but at least to talk. In his final scene with Nanda he is almost
garrulous; so eager to articulate his exasperation at Van, his interpretation of Van's reasons and Van's conduct, as to almost qualify him for
inclusion in Mrs Brook's insatiably articulating and interpreting 'set'. It
is Mr Longdon who has made his adjustments to 'the great modern collapse of all the forms', who has learned to imagine Nanda's informed and
initiated condition outside the old language of taint and pollution; in the
process, of course, of informing and initiating himself.[6] It is Vanderbank
whose imagination has failed. Mr Longdon's new-found garrulousness
represents an openness to the new forms, or to whatever it is that succeeds the end of the old; Vanderbank's irreproachable good taste and
unfailing charm remain disastrously (disastrously for Nanda, that is) part
of a closed system.[7]

In Nanda's and Van's love story, at the centre of *The Awkward Age*, we can
examine the crux of the transition in English *mores* from an era when an
essential value was invested in an ideal of innocent femininity to an era
when all the apparatus of totem and taboo protecting that essential value
was breaking down under the weight of its own sheer improbability. Van
asks Nanda at the end of their last interview to 'Look after my good name'
(360) with Mr Longdon, and there in the very forms of his language is
expressed his incapacity to change. His 'good name' is a fetish from inside

a system of honour, that system whose end Brada pretends to deplore, a system dependent ultimately upon the appearances of a male initiated protectiveness standing guard over a female innocence and ignorance, a female 'chastity'. The essence of good name is appearance – your 'name' takes its value in the mouths of others: Nanda's actual virginity is not to the point, when it comes to the problem of whether Van can marry her. It is her appearance of contamination that makes her impossible, her failure to dissimulate the ordinary unprotected experience that any intelligent girl in this *fin-de-siècle* London was bound to pick up.

Van's unacknowledged relationships with other women are not to the point either, relationships we know about from the Duchess (that useful informant): 'Vanderbank's a man whom any woman, don't you think? might be – whom more than one woman *is* – glad of for herself: *beau comme le jour*, awfully conceited and awfully patronising, but clever and successful and yet liked' (187). In fact Van's sexual experience outside legitimate courtship is, albeit unacknowledged, positively a component of his conventional male honour, his 'good name'. After all, sexual innocence cannot stand guard over innocence: it would not know what to guard against. That Van's experience is part of his attractiveness for Nanda is apparent in their exchange in the park at Mitchy's 'weekend' over Van's silver cigarette case, the case that is undoubtedly a present ('such things always are – people don't buy them for themselves', 161), and from someone he cannot name to her. Nanda turns the case over and rubs it against her cheek, she interrogates him about it. The male mystique is supposed to be potent for her. But she is not supposed to make conscious and articulate its potency; or to recognise, as she so plainly does, its representations (the case), or to interrogate them ('by whom was it given you? . . . you must have forgotten').

Nanda asks him for a cigarette, and she says she would like a cigarette case of her own. 'Why, it holds twenty', he demurs: oughtn't her feminine capacity to be less (or oughtn't she to know the rule that would have her represent it so)? 'Well, I want one that holds twenty.' Her relationship to his otherness – to his male history, his freedoms – is supposed to be in defining herself against them, not in naming them, nor trying them for herself. Van's charm thickens around him almost in direct proportion to his unease. All his sophistication seems bent upon making harmless – making innocent – these damages Nanda does herself, these betrayals of knowledges and understandings she should not have, within his system: '"I want so to give you something," he said at last, "that in my relief at lighting on an object that will do, I will, if you don't look out, give you either that or a pipe"' (161). 'We're such jolly old friends that we really needn't so much as speak at all', he enthusiastically suggests (159).

Almost everything Nanda says to Van has this effect of making her more impossible as his wife: it is the very gestures with which she offers herself to him ('Oh, Mr Van, I'm "true"!', 161) that inhibit him, at the moments he seems to come closest to making *his* gesture, his offer of marriage and a permanent protection. Van's dilemma represents the paradox of the old forms and superstitions of gender: posited upon a femaleness so prone to awakening male desires that it has to be safe-guarded by a complex apparatus of modesty and segregation, male de-sire finally becomes focused not so much on the protected females but on the protecting apparatus of femininity itself. Nanda's availability, her offer of her own vulnerability, her virtual confessions of her own passion, are not desirable, for Van, even though generations of girls have been constrained on the grounds that their availability would be impossibly enflaming.

Nanda's knowingness, her articulated knowledge of the world and of herself and of Van, break the closed circle of a feminine mystique upon which male desire has come to depend; break a whole system of gender relations in which male initiated knowledge (contaminated) and female ignorance (innocent) renew one another and make one another whole. For all his sophistication, Van's imagination of himself is so closely structured around that male–female polarity that he cannot transcend his conservative instincts, in spite of his good will. He is 'superstitiously haunted', to use James's own words from another context, 'by the con-ception of the gentleman'.[8] Almost to the very end he holds Nanda off, deflects the straightness with which she addresses him, by talking to her tenderly *de haut en bas* as if she were still the little girl whose innocence could redeem the painful adult story he is all too uncomfortably aware of: 'And your writing touched me – oh, but really. There were all sorts of old things in it . . . I see you go in for sets – and, my dear child, upon my word, I see, *big* sets. What's this – "Vol. 23: The British Poets". Vol. 23 is delightful – do tell me about Vol. 23. Are you doing much in the British Poets?' (351). It is not that Van is old-maidish or virginal in his scruples; it is quite the opposite. Nanda's knowingness curdles the very piquancy of that separateness-in-contamination upon which his male conquering potency depends.

The Awkward Age, then, takes its step across the restraining walls of the old system, and is a critique, finally, of a system of gender from a point of purchase outside. In all its *talk* it is searching out a language not simply subject to one culture's imaginings of gender and sexuality but able to transcend those imaginings and talk *about* them. In a complex manoeuvre of double consciousness, however, the novel also works to recreate inside its talk the power in imagination of the very system it deconstructs. The measure of narrative complexity does not consist in how securely an ultimate narrative authority locates itself in an ironic position outside the false position of the mere material: the complexity – the irony – is a matter of inhabiting the transition, rather than looking back from the safety of the far side. *The Awkward Age* is not an elegy, Pound's lament for the 'old lavender'; but it is not a revolutionary project, either.

Van's masculinity is not simply ironised, or analysed. In the very act of imagination in which he sees through Van, James wants to render him with all his power to move, all his commanding presence, his aesthetic; he wants to imagine the bottomlessness of the very phenomenon he is at the same time embarked upon seeing all round. He reproduces in his text the flutter of Van's passage through his world; his power to move is talked *about*, from the Duchess who calls him the man that 'any woman . . . might be . . . glad of . . . *beau comme le jour*' (187), to Mitchy in his last interview with Nanda: 'He *has* turned up at last then? How *tremendously* exciting!' (361). And Van's actual presence has to strike the reader with the same conviction as Chad strikes Strether in the café on the Avenue de l'Opéra in *The Ambassadors*: 'He saw him in a flash as the young man marked out by women' (98). In Van's talk, his manner, James records the 'type': the soothing reticence; the self-deprecating charm; the unfailing kindness (except perhaps with Mrs Brook) that somehow wards off intimacy; the quickness of his wit; and those refusals, that thoroughbred fine pride that shies at obediently taking jumps (after all, he refuses a fortune with Nanda). For all the exhibition of confessional ease with Mr Longdon in the bachelor flat, his intelligence and his charm are a finished surface that deflects as much as it absorbs; his irony is essentially self-protective:

'It will be tremendously interesting to hear how the sort of thing we've fallen into – oh we *have* fallen in! – strikes your fresh ear. Do have another cigarette. Sunk as I must appear to you, it sometimes strikes mine. But I'm not sure, as regards Mrs Brookenham, whom I've known a long time –'

Mr Longdon again took him up. 'What do you people call a long time?'

Vanderbank considered. 'Ah, there you are –! And now we're "we people"! That's right; give it to us. I'm sure that in one way or another it's all earned. Well, I've known her ten years. But awfully well.'

'What do you call awfully well?'

'We people?' Vanderbank's inquirer, with his continued restless observation, moving nearer, the young man had laid on his shoulder the most considerate of hands. 'Don't you perhaps ask too much? But no,' he added, quickly and gaily, 'of course you don't: if I don't look out I shall have, on you, exactly the effect I don't want. I dare say I don't know *how* well I know Mrs Brookenham.' (34)

In James's writing from the late 1890s onwards, it is in this double movement of creation, this seeing all around and at the same moment this consent to the sheer power of the phenomenon in itself, that the novels' dialogic essence consists. The dialogism is not simply a matter of the characters *speaking* for themselves (so that we have Mr Longdon's version suspended in flexible relation with the Duchess's, say): it is in that gesture of submission the late novels are so preoccupied with making, to the power of the characters *being* what they are. In the opening chapters of *The Ambassadors*, Strether's wondering enchantment with Appearances (the exceptional capital A is in the first chapter), which of course is to be darkened and complicated as the story unfolds, is emblematic of all the late novels' concentration on the sheer power – the imaginative persuasiveness – of forms. The possibilities of dining *tête-à-tête* by the light of a pink shaded candle before the theatre, or walking the old walls of Chester, are enchanting not because they signify something beyond themselves, but because they *exist*: and so elaborately, in such complexity, evolved over such long histories. Their very arbitrariness (he might not be there, he could be at Woollett, where forms are other) is their authority and their mystery. The authority and the mystery are nothing the novel can contain, it can only surround them.

Through the novels of the middle period James worked to explore and eventually disestablish forms – 'law' – both in writing himself through and beyond a whole received perception of gender and sexual propriety (in *Portrait of a Lady*, for instance) and in writing himself into a habit of narrative scepticism, a scrupulous eschewing of certain kinds of narrative authority. Then, in the transitional novels of the late 1890s and in the late novels, it becomes apparent how that same hard-worked-for independence from the law and the old forms becomes the means by which the law and the old forms are rendered and appreciated. It is precisely in creating an intellectual space in which, say, a certain convention of gender is understood and seen through, that James is able to wholly render the power, the poetry, the imaginative persuasiveness, of that convention.

The Awkward Age offers a critique of Vanderbank's 'masculinity', seeing round it, rendering how incompletely it answers to new, changed possibilities. But alongside that the novel also creates the perception of the power, the persuasiveness, of his 'type' as he lives it out. And this double consciousness of possibilities is not only sustained for us as readers; characters within the novel are quite capable of it too, they discuss themselves the paradox that it is Van's very limitations, his very belonging to an inflexible typology, that make him ultimately *more* desirable than, say, the open-minded and flexible Mitchy. It is Mitchy who first gives a name to the 'power-to-move' of Van's type:

'What I mean is that I don't give out the great thing... The great thing's the sacred terror. It's *you* who give that out.'
    'Oh!' ...
    'Ain't I right, Mrs Brook? – doesn't he, tremendously, and isn't that, more than anything else, what does it?'
    The two again, as if they understood each other, gazed in a unity of interest at their companion, who sustained it with an air clearly intended as the happy mean between embarrassment and triumph. Then Mrs Brook showed that she liked the phrase. 'The sacred terror! Yes, one feels it. It *is* that.' (227)

And later, to Mr Longdon:

'There are people like that – great cases of privilege.'
    'He *is* one,' Mr Longdon mused.
    'There it is. They go through life, somehow, guaranteed. They can't help pleasing.'
    'Ah,' Mr Longdon murmured. 'If it hadn't been for that...!'
    'They hold, they keep, every one,' Mitchy went on. 'It's the sacred terror.' (343)

It is Mitchy and Nanda (not Vanderbank) who name that very scruple in Van which makes it impossible for him to marry Nanda, it is in *their* vocabulary that the phenomenon is surrounded:

'You're so good that nothing shocks you,' she lucidly persisted. 'There's a kind of delicacy you haven't got.'
    He [Mitchy] was more and more struck. 'I've only that – as it were – of the skin and the fingers?' he appealed.
    'Oh, and that of the mind. And that of the soul. And some other kinds, certainly. But not *the* kind.'

'Yes' – he wondered – 'I suppose that's the only way one can name it.' It appeared to rise there before him. '*The* kind!' ... 'The man with "*the* kind", as you call it, happens to be just the type you *can* love? But what's the use,' he persisted as she answered nothing, 'in loving a person with the prejudice – hereditary or other – to which you're precisely obnoxious? Do you positively *like* to love in vain?' (260)

In the same way, although the treatment of the dead Lady Julia is complex, and her example as icon of unpolluted femininity in one sense burdens the living women in the novel, the power – the persuasiveness – of the icon is testified to by the very characters who are least capable of imitating its perished brittle narrowness. 'Ah, say what you will,' says Nanda, 'it *is* the way we ought to be!' (259).

It is by definition only those who do not have '*the* delicacy' who can discuss and name it; yet because the likelihood of a secret contamination had always been a part of the male mystique, it is possible at least for Van to *listen*. He can be part of Mrs Brook's set *and* find himself incapable of marrying Nanda because Mrs Brook's set has contaminated her. The new-feminine, on the other hand, born out of the collapse of the old forms, is almost necessarily committed to scepticism: for the women to know anything at all is to exclude themselves in the same moment from the innocence upon which the old form depended. The women in these late novels are more likely to be committed, then, to 'seeing around', to the struggle with and the manipulation of representations; the men are more likely to continue afloat upon that tradition of male worldliness, so richly developed in its aesthetic appeal, and *preventing* them so little. How different the 'consciousness' of Charlotte's 'performance' as society beauty is to the Prince's 'performance' of himself, in *The Golden Bowl*. In the antiquarian's shop in Bloomsbury, it is Charlotte who, sceptical of the accidents of form – the arbitrary divides of class and race – is uncomfortably aware of the shopkeeper as conscious agent. For the Prince those forms are so final, so conclusive, as to simply put the man outside the sphere of his perception: 'He took, always, the meaner sort for granted – the night of their meanness or whatever name one might give it for him made all his cats grey' (99). The old forms – the old 'law' – *serve* the Prince. For Charlotte the very traditions of romance, of the privileges of intelligent feminine beauty, work equivocally, so that she fears even as she fulfils; they contain (and traditionally, of course) the seeds of her undoing, just as the shopkeeper's consciousness she is so reciprocally conscious of will precipitate eventually her suffering and her punishment. We remember that the Prince waits for 'the doing by the woman of the thing that gave her away . . . the man could always expect it without lifting a finger' (61). Charlotte's only advantage is at least to be aware that she is doing it: 'Giving myself, in other words, away – and perfectly willing to do it for nothing. That's all.' (94)

The gloss, the worldliness, the liberty, of these men, these most per-fected and privileged products of nineteenth-century upper-class culture, with their mixture of callousness and scruple, brutality and delicacy (Mitchy's 'sacred terror' conveys both the deep, the magical appeal, and the scent of blood) had always, by James's own account, stirred his imag-ination; in *Notes of a Son and Brother* he recalls a schoolboy encounter in the Rue de Rivoli:

There swung into view the most splendid, as I at least esteemed him, of my elders and betters in the Rue Balzac, who . . . with his high hat a trifle askew and his cigar actively alight, revealed to me at a glance what it was to be in full possession of Paris. There was speed in his step, assurance in his air, he was visibly, impatiently on the way . . . I but went forth through the Paris night in the hand of my mamma; while he had greeted us with a grace that was as a beat of the very wings of freedom!9

All the irony of an old man's perspective on the dazzled child he was, all the long retrospect in which the dandyisms of an era have had time to decay to dusty pathos, serve to see around the phenomenon for what it was, yes: but only in order that, in the same moment, the writing will recover the live gloss, the power-to-move, the one-time authority of a 'type', the completeness of the thing-in-itself. It is the live gloss, of course, that no amount of biographical industry can restore now to the name of a Jocelyn Persse or a Morton Fullerton, those friends James paid homages to that seem out of all proportion to the meagreness of what they left 'for the record'. He wrote to Persse 'I rejoice greatly in your breezy, heathery, grousy . . . adventures, and envy you, as always, your exquisite possession of the Art of Life which beats any Art of mine hollow.'10 Only the novels can initiate us now into a male mystique whose magic consisted in all the lost ephemera of dress, manner and form.11

James's interest in these men is something like Walter Benjamin's account of Proust's fascination with aristocracy, with its 'language estab-lished along lines of caste and class and unintelligible to outsiders' and those 'lives planted so firmly in their social habitat . . . inextricably inter-twined in the thicket of their fate'.12 And like Proust's, James's interest in recreating all the power of fashion, of form, is inseparable from his in-terest in the passage of time: James sees that form as historically created, historically contingent, he sees *all round it* and in the same movement vibrates to it with an intense sympathy – and not only in the *Autobiography* but even in those novels supposed to be contemporary with the phenomena they describe – as if for something vanished, irreplaceable, precious *because it existed*.

The past in *The Awkward Age* – that 'lost simplicity' and all those lost ways of being – are imagined and hinted toward in numerous oblique, tentative, impressionistic touches; between the lines, almost, of the explicit memories. 'I belong to a different period of history', says Mr Longdon. 'There have been things this evening that have made me feel as if I had been disinterred – literally dug up from a long sleep' (30). Mrs Brook with an unfathomable degree of irony says to her husband: 'Mamma *was* wonderful. There have been times when I've felt she was still with us, but Mr Longdon makes it vivid' (75). Nanda tells Vanderbank that she has discussed the changes in 'young girls' with Mr Longdon at Beccles:

'He can't shut his eyes to the facts. He sees we're quite a different thing.'
  'I dare say' – her friend was fully appreciative. 'Yet the old thing – what do *you* know of it?'
  'I personally? Well, I've seen some change even in *my* short life. And aren't the old books full of us?' (249)

Van's rather conventional young-fogey's lament for 'values' is often read as James's own attitude within the novel: 'London doesn't love the latent or the lurking, has neither time, nor taste, nor sense for anything less discernible than the red flag in front of the steam-roller. It wants cash over the counter and letters ten feet high' (43). But this is unsubtle, too *comfortable* – has something of Van's characteristic imperviousness – beside how the past affects Mr Longdon, Nanda, Mrs Brook, Vanderbank. They are all chilled in the long shadow it casts. The past's very unalterability, its consistency and completeness unto itself, haunts their present, presides over it; its potency threatens to drain the present of significance. 'Ah', says Nanda, 'say what you will – it *is* the way we ought to be!'
  In a phase of cultural transition, while it is impossible to imagine oneself back inside the old forms which have broken open, to imagine oneself outside those forms is to imagine oneself nowhere. Mrs Brook's whole set is defined by being in transition. The past, the previous generation, is a matter of constant reference. Some of this reference is set up by the return – almost *from* the past – of Mr Longdon; but the contrast he

seems to bring out for all of them is not simply their reassuringly making connections for him. Implicit in their talk and manner all the time even without Mr Longdon is a defiance, sometimes exhilarated, sometimes jaded, of 'the old system'; a modernity which defines itself not really in new forms, but in a sort of scandalising game of dares with the old ones. The breaches they make in the containing walls of the old system are not to get out by. Mrs Brook, for instance, always gives as the reason for her involvements with the Lady Fannys and Carrie Donners that she is devoting herself to *keeping* them from running away:

'Surely I've not to remind you at this time of day how Captain Dent-Douglas is always round the corner with his post-chaise, and how tight, on our side, we're all clutching her.'
    'But why not let her go?'
    Mrs Brook, at this, showed a sentiment more sharp. '"Go"? Then what would become of us?' She recalled his wandering fancy. 'She's the delight of our life.'
    'Oh!' Vanderbank sceptically murmured. (141)

In this *fin-de-siècle* drawing-room world where irony is a way of life, her role is as mock guardian of the proprieties. The French novels that litter the rooms of this generation are occasion for extravagant rehearsals of scruples, offences, delicacies which everybody knows that nobody believes in any more (the *women*, always, have to be shocked at the books which the *men* bring):[13]

'Mitchy dear, those two French books you were so good as to send me and which – really, this time, you extraordinary man!' She fell back, intimately reproachful, from the effect produced on her, renouncing all expression except that of the rolled eye. (77)

Nanda is incapable of her mother's performance of travestying respectability, of mock innocence. Hers is the next inevitable stage of the cultural evolution: after irony, flatness, open-endedness and acceptance. She has no sense of humour; it is *funnier* to be perpetually parodying than to be unsurprised and candid. Out of the very thoroughness of her knowing Nanda remakes an 'innocence' that is almost diametrically opposite to Lady Julia's kind, and yet bears a family resemblance to it; her incapacity for the game of irony and parody stands in for Lady Julia's 'ignorance'.

Nanda's liberation is not anything she ever wanted. It is an effect historically produced; she has grown up during a period of cultural transition, and her freedom is a manifestation of it. Mitchy celebrates for her, at the end of the novel, all her new freedoms to know and to name (among them to know and to name herself), the freedoms Lady Julia never had: 'This luxury, you see, now, of our freedom to look facts in the face is one of which, I promise you, I mean fully to avail myself . . . We've worked through the long tunnel of artificial reserves and superstitious mysteries . . . You go down to the roots? Good. It's all I ask!' (366). But Nanda is silent while he speaks; both she and Mitchy know he offers this 'liberation' as compensation, in fact, for what – and as a consequence, precisely, *of* her liberation – she *cannot* have.

In the second half of *Portrait of a Lady* we are privy to Isabel's baffled struggling between opposed and equally potent imagined possibilities – to be 'good' (to please), and to be 'free'. In that novel James cannot imagine for Isabel the kind of purchase on her own bafflement he gives Nanda. But Nanda's intellectual liberation, that is, her 'seeing round' the fatal bondage in her own imagination, does not show her a straight path *out* of it. Wherever we think Isabel's 'straight path' is taking her when she flees from Caspar's kiss, it is interesting that it is she, who is still subject to the old self-contradictory ideals of womanhood (free, and yet good), who *acts*, who imagines there *is* a straight path to follow; while Nanda is held in an impasse special to a certain kind of reflective consciousness, a certain kind of self-knowingness.

But Nanda cannot wish herself back into bafflement; consciousness cannot unwish itself. The very metaphors in which she imagines consciousness have a forward trajectory:

'Aggie's only trying to find out –'
  'Yes – what?' He asked, waiting.
  'Why, what sort of person she is. How can she ever have known? It was carefully, elaborately hidden from her – kept so obscure that she could make out nothing. She isn't now like *me*.'
  He wonderingly attended. 'Like you?'
  'Why, I get the benefit of the fact that there was never a time when I didn't know *something* or other and that I became more and more aware, as I grew older, of a hundred little chinks of daylight.' (371)

The hidden thing once uncovered cannot be re-concealed; the daylight of Nanda's vision cannot be snuffed out, she cannot put herself back inside whatever dark place broke open around her burgeoning consciousness. Aggie in the novel is the very exemplar of the impossibility of wishing a way back into ignorance: the sham of her innocence and its consequences bear no relationship (or only a parodistic one) to the authentic problem of the innocence of an Isabel or a Lady Julia. Knowledge is not a choice; once the 'old story' has been seen through, or seen around, it can only henceforward be play-acted.

Readings of the novel have tended to concentrate on Nanda, and have tended to write Mrs Brook away in the other – the dark, the polluted – part of that dyadic, moralising critical language which finds Mr Longdon the embodiment of 'absolute moral values'.

Her *history* has been mostly ignored. But Mrs Brook comes furnished with a past as vivid and specific and crucial to understanding as if she was a character from an Ibsen play: it is an interesting quirk of literary history that while criticism has mostly lent its sympathy to Hedda Gabler and Nora Helmer it has mostly come down very hard upon poor Mrs Brook. Nora Helmer's flow of chatter on the edge of hysteria is not, for all its comparative unconsciousness, absolutely unlike Mrs Brook's creative extravagance, her wails, her deprecations, her wide-eyed appeals; both are performances, both sustain the fiction of happiness (or perhaps in *The Awkward Age* the fiction of brilliance), the 'brave face'. Van's discrimination against Nanda, incidentally, bears a family resemblance to Thorvald Helmer's 'A songbird must have a clear voice to sing with – no false notes'. Nora's anxieties about a time when 'I'm no longer as pretty as I am now', 'when Thorvald's . . . lost interest in watching me dance, or get dressed up, or recite' are the essence, surely, of Mrs Brook's crisis in the novel.

The crisis of Mrs Brook is the other significant story of the novel: at least as important as, and inseparable from, Nanda's. The question of Nanda's 'coming downstairs' is not only a problem for the *moeurs* of a society in transition, it is also the moment at which her mother faces the beginning of the end of her youth, her life as a focus of sexual attraction; the moment at which she understands her *replacement* by her daughter. Nanda and her mother communicate in guarded, scrupulous politenesses: 'they had for each other, in manner and tone, such a fund of consideration as might almost have given it the stamp of diplomacy' (232). But the 'smash' Mrs Brook brings about at Tishy Grendon's can only have come out of a motivation extreme and violent that lies beneath the surface of that mutual accommodation. She *cannot bear* Nanda to have Van. She loves him for herself: but there is more to it even than the desperation between rivals, Van is her youth, to give him up to her daughter is to accept the end of her own life as a lover of men (and would illustrate neatly in passing the inequity that the man who is after all her own age can have if he wants it his 'second chance' at the new generation at the very point the mother is passed over).

In Nanda's last interview with Van, when she finally succeeds in making him talk sensibly to her, adult to adult, it is she who has understood this inequity and her mother's situation best:

'I just ask you – I even press you. It's because as she said, you've practically ceased coming. Of course I know everything changes. It's the law – what is it? – "the great law" of something or other. All sorts of things happen – things come to an end. She has more or less – by his marriage – lost Mitchy. I don't want her to lose everything. Do stick to her. What I really wanted to say to you – to bring it straight out – is that I don't believe you know how awfully she likes you. I hope my saying such a thing doesn't affect you as "immodest." One never knows – but I don't much care if it does. I suppose it *would* be immodest if I were to say that I veritably believe she's in love with you. Not, for that matter, that my father would mind – he wouldn't mind, as he says, a twopenny rap. So' – she extraordinarily kept it up – 'you're welcome to any good the information may have for you: though that, I dare say, does sound hideous. No matter – if I produce any effect on you. That's the only thing I want. When I think of her downstairs there so often nowadays practically alone, I feel as if I could scarcely bear it. She's so fearfully young.' (356)

There is a nuance of precocity in that clairvoyance; just a touch – unconscious in Nanda – of the cruel privilege of youth, to pity what it replaces (Nanda's straightness might remind us of the unsettling leverage young Hilde Wengel exerts in *The Master Builder* on the lives of her enmeshed and compromised elders). But Mrs Brook's own sense of her history with Van is saturated with time-consciousness, with her awareness of ageing and loss:

There was a time, in fact, wasn't there, when we rather enjoyed each other's dim depths. If I wanted to fawn upon you . . . I might say that, with such a comrade in obliquity to wind and double about with, I'd risk losing myself in the mine. But why retort or recriminate? Let us not, for God's sake, be vulgar – we haven't yet, bad as it is, come to that. I *can* be, no doubt – I some day *must* be: I feel it looming at me out of the awful future as an inevitable fate. But let it be for when I'm old and horrible; not an hour before. I do want to live a little even yet. So you ought to let me off more easily – even as I let you. (317)

The whole history of Mrs Brook furnishes us with so many reasons why, instead of accepting gracefully her transition to middle age, she rages against it, and in her rage pulls down her world self-destructively on her own head (the 'smash' at Tishy's loses her Mitchy as well as Van – surely his *marriage* alone would never have stopped him coming). In Ibsen it is always the fathers we need to know about to understand the women (Nora's, Hedda's). For Mrs Brook, the crucial figure is her mother. Counterbalancing the sacral rosiness that tends to accumulate around the memory of Lady Julia in the talk of Mr Longdon and Nanda and

Vanderbank are some brute facts. Who married Fernanda to Edward Brookenham? What kind of 'innocence' in the mother could have promoted and sanctified this monstrous coupling; what notion of 'good' and uncontaminated girlhood consigned this intelligent passionate woman to that waste?

The quality of Lady Julia and Vanderbank's mother that seems to be most commemorated is their power of *refusal*: all the things they did not do and did not know; the men they did not marry; the changes they could not have lived with. Van says that his mother was 'taken in time', saved from suffering when her daughter Blanche Bertha Vanderbank metamorphosed into modern Nancy Toovey (41). What grandeurs of high-minded femininity are conjured by 'Blanche Bertha', its portentous chastity, its moody poetry.[14] No wonder the daughter of the mother who chose that name needed to wriggle, with whatever loss of dignity, out from under it. And Mr Longdon himself suggests some of the more twisted convolutions of that feminine power-in-abstention:

'I think she rather liked the state to which she had reduced me, though she didn't, you know, in the least presume upon it. The better a woman is – it has often struck me – the more she enjoys, in a quiet way, some fellow's having been rather bad, rather dark and desperate, about her – *for* her. I dare say, I mean, that, though Lady Julia insisted I ought to marry, she wouldn't really have liked it much if I *had*.' (47)

This is another twist of the 'old story': the abstentions and reticences the woman imposed upon herself turn out to have their price, for others: the 'better' the woman, the more sternly – and righteously – she exacts it.

Whenever the conversation waxes lyrical over Lady Julia's graces Mrs Brook's eyes widen even further than usual and she sounds at her most limpidly judicious.

'Of course I revere mamma just as much as he does, and there was everything in her to revere.' (144)

'Mamma was so sincere. The fortune was nothing to her. That shows it was immense.' (142)

'... compared with her, I'm a poor creeping thing. I mean ... that of course I ache in every limb with the certainty of my dreadful difference. It isn't as if I *didn't* know it, don't you see? There it is, as a matter of course: I've helplessly, but finally and completely, accepted it.' (150)

How does she mean these things? Mrs Brook's sincerity is at any given point a difficult thing to define, not because there is so little of it but because in fact, in spite of her mannered drawl, her gushes, there is so *much*. Everything she says has its aspect as performance (even those comic married silences in which she hands Edward his tea) but she is an actress whose eyes convince us that for all she is wedged into her part she is also at every moment intensely, feelingly alive. She 'means' and 'ironises' in the same breath, she is not capable of her mother's or Nanda's transparency, she represents that opaque transitional moment at which discourse becomes sceptically aware of its own premises and yet cannot articulate itself outside a parodistic relationship to the old habits, the old cadences, the old gestures.

Alone with Nanda, when Nanda says, 'I could have done much better if I hadn't had the drawback of not really remembering Granny', Mrs Brook moans, 'Oh, well, I remember her!' with 'an accent that evidently struck her the next moment as so much out of place that she slightly deflected' (234). This moment of exasperation is not because she knows something – something factual and awful about Lady Julia – that the others do not. It is just that all the graces look differently depending on just from which angle they strike their beneficiaries. It is not difficult to imagine how a Lady Julia's old-fashioned ideals of femininity might have acted upon a daughter of different temperament and in a different era, to produce some of the tensions, the suppressions, the resentments which we feel pent up in Mrs Brook, as she paces the petty cage of her miserable marriage, steps out along the high wire of her public performances.

James wrote about *Hedda Gabler* that it was 'the portrait of a nature, the story of what Paul Bourget would call an *état d'âme*, and of a certain state of nerves as well as soul, a state of temper, of health, of chagrin, of despair'.[15] And if one of Ibsen's contributions has been to our understanding of certain qualities of 'femininity' produced by deforming social and cultural pressures (Hedda, Nora), then surely Mrs Brook is the product in James's art of the same kind of analysis? Her circumstances – her mother, her marriage, her long, presumably unconsummated flirtation with Van – and what they have made of her are at least as much James's subject as her *effect*. In her long-suffering, plaintive diatribe to Nanda it is impossible to mistake at least some of the truth about her life: 'money, money, money at every turn, running away like water', and, 'your father's settled gloom is terrible, and I bear all the brunt of it' (259). The plaintive and the long-suffering are notes as habitual as the drawl of innuendo Nanda winces from elsewhere ('So tremendously made up to, you mean – even by a little fussy, ancient man? But *doesn't* he, my dear . . . make up to you?', 237). But Mrs Brook's complaint is bigger even than the sum of its fairly grinding parts: it flashes out for an instant at a remark of Nanda's:

'He goes himself on Saturday, and if I want I can go a few days later.'
  'And what day can you go if *I* want?' Mrs Brook spoke as with a small sharpness – just softened in time – produced by the sight of a freedom on her daughter's part that suddenly loomed larger than any freedom of her own. (240)

It is unfair of her here to be irritated at just that 'modern' independence she has encouraged – for her own purposes, mostly – in Nanda. But the very freedom that has been her convenience and has cost Nanda so much is also suddenly enviable, unattainable: it is, for that moment, everything Nanda's mother has not had.

Critics have often speculated that the advent of Ibsen on the London stage was fortuitous at a stage in James's development when he was working to loosen the surface of his realism and liberate the freehand of his late designs; and they have suggested a relationship between the towers and the pagodas, the wild ducks and the doves, the tarantellas and the bridge tables.[16] Even the late James 'manner' might conceivably owe something to Ibsen's dialogue, the stiffish communications of his characters, their talk undressed of the muffling familiarity of its everyday clothes. Certainly Ibsen continues to provoke James's sometimes exasperated, sometimes ecstatic criticisms throughout the 1890s. Ibsen weaves his 'more or less irritating spell' in the preface to *The Awkward Age*; 'from the moment he's clear, from the moment he's "amusing", it's on the footing of a thesis as simple and superficial as that of *A Doll's House*' (20). But in *London Notes* (January 1897), writing about *John Gabriel Borkman*, James finds that in spite of Ibsen's vision 'so indifferent to the comedy of things', 'the whole thing throbs with an actability that fairly shakes us as we read', 'the sturdy old symbolist comes this time with a supreme example of his method', and Ibsen has a 'rare mastery of form'.[17]

The likeness may be no more, of course, than a matter of cultural synchronicity; and the unlikeness at first sight seems so much *more* striking (James's fascination with urbanity and social sophistication, for instance, which Ibsen is not interested in). Yet if we are thinking of James's writing in the late 1890s as mediating in some sense Continental ('masculine') cynicisms and English-language ('feminine') innocences within the novel tradition, it seems relevant to consider that in the Scandinavian drama a similar conflict of systems was being enacted. Ibsen's plays are *about* the cracking and straining of gender conventions of male contamination and female innocence; and the plays themselves also *represent* the confrontation, or rather the dialogue, of a new anti-hypocritical sexual realism with a tradition of moralising Protestantism.

For James, as for Ibsen, 'the great modern collapse of all the forms and superstitions and respects, good and bad' was most surely approached through what Brada called the 'masculinisation of the women'; that is, through the opening up, within the women characters in their fictions, of a *knowledge* of themselves: a conscious awareness of their femininity, of the function of femininity within a gender system, and of the sacrificial ideal buried in the foundations of that system. In his exploration of Mrs Brook as well as of Nanda, James works to break down that separation of 'masculine' and 'feminine' knowledges upon which the perpetuation of the system depended: the masculine-cynical 'unclean honesty' represented by the novels of a Maupassant, say, or a Balzac; and the feminine-optimistic idealism perpetuated by the propriety of the English-language novel tradition. In his fictions he represents an intermediate, transitional possibility; women whose relationship to 'innocence' is all problematised, whose knowledge from outside innocence liberates them, but endangers them too, puts them at the mercy of a cultural machinery still predicated upon dyads of innocence and guilt, cleanness and pollution.[18]

CHAPTER 4

Blushing in the dark: language and sex in
The Ambassadors

Tone is everything in *The Ambassadors* (1903): it is the very subject of the novel. Strether has to mediate, like James in his letters from Paris to his family at home in the 1870s, Old World sophisticated *moeurs* for New World decencies. Is there a tone he can find – playful? ironic? appealing? – in which he can reconcile a Sarah Pocock or a Mrs Newsome with a Mme de Vionnet? Will he be able to make out a language in which the one can imagine the other? All those thick missives he dispatches across the Atlantic represent his sincere effort to translate the one tone-world into another; to bring about, by his own sheer efforts of imagination-in-language, their mutual transparency.

It is in the very nuances of his language, too, that he stands most accused by Sarah of defection (like the younger Henry accused by William James of 'French tricks' in his letters): the crimson spots burn brighter in her cheeks and she is – significantly – lost for words when he tries on her his little *galanterie*, his sample of 'how Parisians could talk':

'And yet, dear Sarah,' he freely broke in, 'I feel when I hear you say that, that you don't quite do justice to the important truth of the extent to which – as you're also mine – I'm *your* natural due. I should like much better,' he laughed, 'to see you fight for me.'

She met him, Mrs Pocock, on this, with an arrest of speech. (342)

The challenge, then, for a reading of *The Ambassadors*, is to find a tone in keeping with the spirit of the novel itself. And the danger that always hovers is that the critical mode will not be able to sustain the novel's lightness, its poise between New World earnestness and Old World elegance where *both* – however the balance finally tips – have their weight. Of its nature criticism tends towards earnestness. Although readings of the novel cannot but take its essential point, its essential tenderness towards the transgressive love affair, it is surprising how often there lurks submerged in the critical prose a Puritanical schoolmaster who sounds more like

Woollett than Paris, discussing the novel in terms of Strether's mistakes, his culpable blindness, his self-deceptions, his misplaced idealism.[1]

There is some support in the text for this inbuilt critical inclination to read the novel as a *lesson* (the retributive model of fictional structure again, as in Isabel's having to have done or been something wrong, in order for her to be punished: Strether has to be guilty of some mistake, in order for him to be corrected). Strether himself often finds the idiom of the lesson, the moral exemplar, close to hand when he is interpreting his own experience. Good Woollett product that he is, his introspections tend to sort his experience in terms of a language of 'duties', 'responsibilities', 'scruples', and the need to 'justify himself'.[2] Most of all (very New World) he feels the need to 'make of it all what he could' (466), that is, to read the whole painful process of his changing his mind as a learning curve from which it would be unworthy of him not to profit.

However, even as Strether is prone to the explications of a Woollett pedagogy, so he is also prone to a perpetual self-irony in which his own earnestness and dutifulness – what Ian Watt calls his 'enormous sense of responsibility about personal relationships' – are as much fair game as all his other qualities. Watt diagnoses this 'ironic ambivalence' of Strether's in his masterly close analysis of the first paragraph of the novel; in the very detail of the vocabulary and grammar we 'are getting into Strether's mind, and we have been prepared to relish the irony of its ambivalences'; Strether is 'comically loyal to what he would like to feel'.[3] Some of the irony at Strether's earnestness is the narrator's; but (and Watt is right to insist that this is not a novel which insists upon its 'intellectual distance' from its protagonists) some of the irony is Strether's own.

What Strether ruefully contemplates, as in the course of the novel his moral frameworks for interpretation endlessly complicate themselves, is that after all there may be no lesson in this story. There may be imperatives of character and upbringing which belong to a world of lessons and dutifulness, so that, for instance, he *has* to say to Maria Gostrey at the end of it all that he must not, 'out of the whole affair', have 'got anything for' himself (512). (We may alternatively choose to read that as the most courteous possible expression of a refusal which is really on other grounds; 'dear old Maria' may be Strether's great friend but it is not *she* whose womanliness has come to embody all the 'life' he enjoins upon little Bilham, the 'life' he envies Chad, and is himself too late for.[4]) But the story itself overspills, finally, the successive patternings Strether's New World conscientiousness cannot help trying to urge upon it. There is no moral system within which Strether can explain to a Mrs Newsome that a Mme de Vionnet is 'good' for Chad. When Maria or little Bilham are persuaded to agree that she is 'good', they mean of course – and Strether allows them to get away with meaning – that different 'good' they might apply to painting, or wine, or air. This is, finally – even criticism has to face it – a novel not about goodness but about pleasure.

Benjamin's essay on Proust furnished some hints, in the last chapter, for James's complex attitude towards his young men of the world. In finding the right tone for a reading of *The Ambassadors*, it helps again.

Nor is it hard to say why this paralyzing, explosive will to happiness which pervades Proust's writings is so seldom comprehended by its readers. In many places Proust himself made it easy for them to view this *oeuvre* too, from the time-tested, comfortable perspective of resignation, heroism, asceticism. After all, nothing makes more sense to the model pupils of life than the notion that a great achievement is the fruit of toil, misery, and disappointment. The idea that happiness could have a share in beauty would be too much of a good thing, something that their *ressentiment* would never get over.[5]

The place where James's fiction can finally unlearn that 'time-tested, comfortable perspective of resignation, heroism, asceticism' has to be France. The novel is a homage, really, to all those possibilities France has stood for in the cultural 'map' James has been making out in his fictions; all those possibilities – of happiness's 'share in beauty'? – which from his very earliest writings he has perceived as existing in dynamic and essential contradistinction to the Protestant values of an Anglo-Saxon cultural tradition.

In his essay on Maupassant of 1888, for instance, the decent American in James cannot help recoiling in distaste from the explicit sexual content of the stories:

whatever depths may be discovered by those who dig for them, the impression of the human spectacle for him who takes it as it comes has less analogy with that of the monkey's cage than this admirable writer's account of it.[6]

However, the whole piece is addressed as if to an Anglo-Saxon propriety, and insists upon how, no matter how a reader's sense of the proper – a literary ideal of 'noble and exquisite things' – may be offended by so much from the monkey's cage, that same reader will be – problematically – stirred and persuaded by the powerful realism of the writing. Out of the *same sensuality*, it seems, come both the offending sexual content *and* the power of the writing to move and convince. That sensuality, when it is not monkeys, persuades the hesitating reader as unanswerably, royally, as a 'lion in the path' (James's own phrase from the same essay):

We are accustomed to think, we of the English faith, that a cynic is a living advertisement of his errors ... It is easy to exclaim that if he judges life only from the point of view of the senses, many are the noble and exquisite things that he must leave out. What he leaves out has no claim to get itself considered till after we have done justice to what he takes in.[7]

France is invoked in James's *oeuvre*, in his cultural mapping, to stand for the sensual and the beautiful, for pleasure, with whatever complications that brings for Anglo-Saxon propriety and its preference for 'resignation, heroism, asceticism'. In *What Maisie Knew* it is the sounds and smells of Boulogne life which float up to Maisie's hotel room in counterpoint to Mrs Wix urging her lessons in conscience and condemnation upon Maisie inside. When James wants to express his outrage at the desecration of France in the late essays on the Great War, it is an imagery of earth and growth and fruitfulness that comes to hand:

But I verily think there has never been anything in the world – since the most golden aspect of antiquity at least – like the way in which France has been trusted to gather the rarest and fairest and sweetest fruits of our so tremendously and so mercilessly turned-up garden of life. She has been gardened where the soil of humanity has been most grateful and the aspect, so to call it, most toward the sun, and there, at the high and yet mild and fortunate centre, she has grown the precious, intimate, the nourishing, finishing things that she has inexhaustibly scattered abroad.[8]

Italy too, of course, has its special function in the novels.[9] But an Italian culture is never sharply focused as an alternative *system*, an alternative way of seeing, to the moralising and conscientious Anglo-Saxon one; issues of history and national identity apart, this is really a question of *literature*. What we feel from the very beginnings of James's writing is that his relationship to the French nineteenth-century literary tradition is fundamental, not auxiliary; the polarity in his imagination between a George Eliot and a Balzac, say, or a Hawthorne and a Flaubert, is at the very basis of his perception and his curiosity.[10]

In a sense *The Ambassadors* enacts precisely the evolution of that relationship throughout James's own fictions. Strether's origins, his deep dutiful sense of a responsibility to 'home', his instincts of respectful tenderness towards the products and the qualities of 'home': these are like the deep roots James's early and middle-period fictions put down in the English fictional tradition and its 'piety, in the civil and domestic sense'.[11] Strether's middle-aged adventure, his sheer incapacity to resist another way of seeing as it persuades itself upon him; this is like James grappling with Maupassant. He *ought* to be able to feel, as W. D. Howells did in re-action to some of James's anecdotes from Paris-Babylon, that he 'thanks God he's not a Frenchman'.[12] Instead he (Strether, James) finds himself prevented from keeping to that straight and narrow: the persuasiveness, the authority, the unanswerability of pleasure as a system unto itself, sit like a lion in his path. Ultimately, like Strether, James finds himself, his poise, somewhere outside both systems, seeing into and appreciating both and not quite at home in either. In the last novels James opens his fictions onto a dialogue of *both* ways of seeing.

Ruth Bernard Yeazell sets out in her *Fictions of Modesty* just what was perceived as the essential difference between the nineteenth-century English-language and Continental novel traditions.[13] The English novel according to Yeazell, committed to centring its narratives more often than not on the evolving consciousness of its young women, had taken shape inside the 'space of courtship' between love and marriage. This was the only space left available to its young women for manoeuvre, for quest, for *choice*, once English fictional parameters were understood as more or less identical with ideals of feminine propriety. In other words, nothing could 'happen' to the young women *after* marriage. As Thackeray boasted (or complained?) in the sentences from his *Autobiography* which Yeazell uses as epigraph:

Can anyone by search through the works of the six great English novelists I have named, find a scene, a passage, or a word that would teach a girl to be immodest, or a man to be dishonest? When men in their pages have been described as dishonest and women as immodest, have they not ever been punished?

On the contrary, 'without adultery, it would not be too much to say, the Continental novel would scarcely be possible'.[14] Yeazell finds notes for one of James's own stories from 1902 which set out precisely that interdependence: '*L'honnête femme – n'a pas un roman*'; 'if she's *honnête*, it's not a *roman* – if it's a *roman* she's not *honnête*'.[15] She suggests in fact that Tony Tanner's argument for an 'intimate connection between adultery and the novel' is actually an account of Continental rather than English-language fiction.[16]

When the stuff of the Continental novel impinged on *The Portrait of a Lady* it was as a substance lurid, gothic, deadly. Osmond's and Mme Merle's adultery can only be associated negatively, threateningly, with the novel's centre of consciousness in Isabel. In her long flight across Europe to Ralph she turns over and over its alien, exotic reality, but cannot assimilate it, cannot adapt to it her sympathetic imagination formed in such a different moral air. The adulterers are punished, too, as Thackeray describes; as is conventional, the man loses a little (a little of his power over Isabel) and the woman loses everything, lover, friend, child, happiness. Osmond is a continuing factor at the end of the novel: Mme Merle, in the proper tradition of English fictional adulteresses, falls, upon her discovery, beyond the pale of the narrative.

In *What Maisie Knew* and *The Awkward Age* the exotic, lurid stuff of the Continental novel is handled more familiarly. The novels pitch themselves inside a world in which the dingy news of adultery is everyday; mixed up with, even, and contaminating, the 'innocence' of the young girls. And the ideal of that innocence itself is becoming shadowed, problematic; it seems it can only be sustained at the cost of such exclusions, such sacrifices, such distortions of language (the dyadic vocabulary of innocence and contamination in *Turn of the Screw*, the 'innocence' of a little Aggie). All this development in the writings of the late 1890s is like Strether's squeamishness, alongside the irresistible advance of his reluctant recognition. How can the innocent core of English fiction be kept immune, once it finds itself in relationship with a world of such other realities?

When in Book 11, chapter 4 Strether is finally confronted with the incontrovertible carnal fact of Chad and Mme de Vionnet's affair, and he can no longer pretend to himself that he does not know what it means when a man like Chad is 'formed to please' (511) and 'marked out by women' (167), a whole fiction of innocence collapses in a single, final gesture. It is like growing up, all at once (except that it has been prepared for by a long development); like some fictional rite of passage. The system of proprieties and concealments and euphemisms is suddenly something for children, or virgins. Strether blushes, the same night, for 'the way he had dressed the possibility in vagueness, as a little girl might have dressed her doll' (468). The innocence of that 'little girl' has depended on too much ignorance: 'It must never be forgotten that the optimism of [English] literature is partly the optimism of women and spinsters; in other words the optimism of ignorance as well as delicacy.'[17]

We can extend the words in which Strether reflects on his 'discovery' to imply issues of fictional as well as social propriety.

He moved . . . back to the other feature of the show, the deep, deep truth of the intimacy revealed. That was what, in his vain vigil, he oftenest reverted to: intimacy, at such a point, was *like* that – and what in the world else would one have wished it to be like? It was all very well for him to feel the pity of its being so much like lying; he almost blushed, in the dark, for the way he had dressed the possibility in vagueness, as a little girl might have dressed her doll. He had made them – and by no fault of their own – momentarily pull it for him, the possibility, out of this vagueness; and must he not therefore take it now as they had had simply, with whatever thin attenuations, to give it to him? (468)

Strether and James confront together the whole question of *imagining* intimacy, imagining those 'deep deep truths'. Strether up to this point has not actually been 'deceived' about Chad and Mme de Vionnet's relationship. But the language of his reflections here only confirms what James has been careful to be precise about earlier in the progress of Strether's attitude to the affair. 'He had been trying all along to suppose nothing' (468): not that he had supposed *something* (i.e. that the affair was unconsummated) which turned out to be incorrect. Of course he has tried out, over and over, the possibility that their attachment is 'virtuous', in the Woollett sense: he tries it on Maria, on little Bilham. Only we recognise the over-insistence, the too calm certitude, of someone who is trying to convince himself. He is so alert, too, to when those others, however they want to spare him, cannot help their shades of hesitation, of demurral:

Poor Strether's face lengthened. She's impossible?'
[Maria] 'She's even more charming than I remembered her.'
'Then what's the matter?'
She had to think how to put it. 'Well, *I'm* impossible. It's impossible. Every-thing's impossible.'
He looked at her an instant. 'I see where you're coming out. Everything's possible.' Their eyes had on it in fact an exchange of some duration, after which he pursued: 'Isn't it that beautiful child?' Then as she still said nothing: 'Why don't you mean to receive her?' (221)

The essence of what Strether has imagined is that he has tried, pre-cisely, to imagine nothing. He has failed to anchor his conviction in the 'virtuous attachment'; his intellectual habit, whatever he 'wants' to think, is too doubting and questing for that. (He is especially sceptical, in fact, of anything he *wants* to believe.) So instead of conviction he has left a space (an impossible-to-sustain space) in which he simply refuses to imagine anything.[18] It is a postponement: it has felt like the only way he can sustain in one consciousness the morals of Woollett and the pleasures of Paris. For what is concealed – deferred – inside that space there is in Woollett's vocabulary no name which does not condemn; there is no name in the vocabulary of Paris that is not euphemism – 'make-believe', Strether calls it. The third possibility – that he find a truthful language for it of his own – he is holding off out of habits of reticence and delicacy deeply entangled at the root of his perceptions. He has believed there are things which must not, cannot, be named. He has known there is a monkey's cage, but he has believed that no sympathy, no interest, no art, could justify the voyeurism of looking in.

In a letter to Paul Bourget written in 1888, James rehearses much the same scruples about the erotic content of Bourget's latest novel.

What can one know of these matters as far as they concern others and how can one speak about all this on behalf of anyone other than oneself? For this reason it is preferable to talk of them as little as possible, for if one speaks of them as they concern oneself, the result is fatuous, tasteless and immodest. For me, the conduct of love seems to constitute a very special part of our existence, essentially characterised by *action* and not by thought. This element of action is the affair of each one of us, but as soon as thought is brought to bear upon it – as soon as one drabbles intellectually in the matter, as a novelist or as a painter, it becomes unhealthy and distasteful. And that is why infinite tact and taste are required lest one should founder in the mud: it is a question of treatment, an entirely practical problem ... I should never wish to know what happens between a man and a woman in their bedroom and in their bed.[19]

There is a reasoned argument here which calls the issue a 'practical problem', a 'question of treatment'. A distinction is made between 'what happens between a man and a woman in their bedroom' and all the other 'parts of our existence': what happens in the bedroom has a special status as 'action' which has – to protect it, to protect ourselves? or both? – to be kept absolutely separate from our reflective selves, our 'thought'. It is impossible, James argues, to write about this 'action' because it should exist unmediated by thought. The moment thought – language, writing, painting – is allowed to imagine the 'action', then that action is spoiled, it becomes dirtied, 'unhealthy and distasteful': we 'founder in the mud'. The shame is not in the thing itself, but in the voyeur's stare. Because the thing itself and the reflective consciousness are by definition mutually destructive, there is no imagination of the action, no language for it, no way of re-creating it, which is *not* the voyeur's.

As well as the reasoned argument, there is a powerful charge in the language of the passage which goes beyond what the reasoning quite justifies. The appeal, elsewhere in the letter, to an Anglo-Saxon consensus ('almost our only reaction to him [the sensitive and eminent young man beginning his first adulterous affair] is a desire to give him a good kick in the behind') and the invocation, in support of his protests, of a collective

middle-ground common sense ('we do not want it and we do not believe in it') are not characteristic of James, and signal a defensiveness,
a felt need to raise more than just his own reasoning against the threat
perceived. Fiercely James purges himself of the shame of voyeurism, a
contamination which the act of reading the Bourget novel seems to have
brought too close. And he invokes a final inaccessibility of the sexual facts
which reads (to be infinitely tactless and tasteless) almost as a moment's
biographical insight; we glimpse at once an intensely guarded privacy
and an intensely felt exclusion. 'What can one know of these matters
as far as they concern others and how can one speak about all this on
behalf of anyone other than oneself?'

If we decide that the distinction James makes between sexual behaviour and all the other 'parts of our existence' is spurious, then his
argument breaks down. It would seem unfair, if that were the case, for
him to protest at Bourget's realist detail. 'How can these things then
possibly concern us', he writes, ' – the details of Desforges' flirtations or
of the love-making of René and his mistress and the state of disarray of
the shirts or corsets worn?'. But in James's own novels, with regard to
every other part of existence, it is precisely these details which function
as the very material of the illusion and the guarantees of its truth. The
essence of the realist curiosity is that art 'needs to know' everything else;
is it not simply anomalous to assert that it needs for its own health *not* to
know this one thing?

However, this whole issue of sex in fiction *is*, notoriously, and even
today, something like a special case: the vexed question that seemed in
some sense answered with the end of the nineteenth-century system of
fictional propriety, has re-asserted itself in the debate over pornography.
There may well be an ultimate untellability special to sexual behaviour
which has to do with precisely the problem James locates; the contradiction between the intrinsic voyeurism of fiction and the intrinsic privacy of sex ('less capable of open delineation than anything else in the
world', as James puts it in the letter to Bourget). This special problem
needs responding to with special tacts; and the failure of those tacts risks
more than just literary flatness, it jeopardises perhaps (certainly anti-
pornographers would recognise this argument) some core of individual
privacy, has a power to intrude and damage beyond the ordinary power
of fictional illusion. The sexual details in Bourget's novel certainly seem to
have offended James in the way pornography offends: they have intruded
behind his merely literary judgement and he feels attacked, personally
(to judge from his defensiveness and his tone, which rather overspills,

interestingly enough, *another* kind of tact; the letter must have annoyed Bourget, surely?).

James in this letter proposes as solution to the problem simply a literary decorum which holds off even from curiosity about the locked room in this Bluebeard's castle of realism. There is, after all, so much *else* to write about: 'despite the infinite variety of life, you devote to her and to her *underclothing* [James's italics] a quite particular and unwholesome attention'. Like Strether he chooses to make his enjoyment (his material) out of all the charms and effects and urgencies of love – after all, they are *love* stories that James writes – but simply to hold off from imagining the sexual act whose implications if not facts lie hidden somewhere at the stories' centres.

James changed his mind. In a letter to Hugh Walpole in 1910 about one of Walpole's novels, he complained that what was missing from the fiction was 'the marital, sexual, bedroom relations of M and his wife . . . which have to be tackled to mean anything'. And this is consistent, of course, with the material of James's own last three completed novels. Instead of inserting themselves into that 'space of courtship' between love and marriage which Yeazell defines as the essential place of the English-language novel tradition, and where most of James's own novels before *The Ambassadors* certainly fit, the three late novels belong instead (although with some essential qualifications which will need to be made) inside the Continental tradition of novels centred on illicit sexual relationships. (The illicit relationship is adulterous in *The Ambassadors* and *The Golden Bowl*; what makes *The Wings of the Dove* inconceivable within the tradition of James's earlier fictions is partly the fact of Kate's visit to Merton's room, but much more the sympathetic interiority of much of the treatment of Kate, who is duplicitous and – put crudely – uses her sexual favours in Balzacian fashion to achieve her financial ends.) The locked room has been opened, and what is inside does have, after all, to be 'tackled', turns out in fact to be essential to an understanding of the whole.

When Strether is confronted, finally, with evidence he cannot sidestep, when he can defer no longer the 'imagining' of what is between Chad and Mme de Vionnet he has so uncomfortably eschewed, it is almost as if he enacted James's conversion on this point. And as with Strether, this conversion for James is not really in the least a matter of a sudden all-transforming switch from no to yes; we have traced already through the novels of the middle years and of the transitional period of the late 1890s the trajectory of ever-widening inclusiveness, the history of an imagination always rebounding upon and re-interrogating its own premises and fundamentals, which finally brought James's fictions to the door of the locked room and the felt necessity of finding some way of 'tackling' what lay unexpressed and unexplored within.

That trajectory, that history, could be described in James's own words, writing about R. L. Stevenson in a review of 1900:

There is world enough everywhere . . . for the individual, the right one, to be what we call a man of it. He has, like everyone not convenienced with the backdoor of stupidity, to make his account with seeing and facing more things, seeing and facing everything, with the unrest of new impressions and ideas, the loss of the fond complacencies of youth.[20]

James quotes appreciatively just after this from one of Stevenson's letters, which contrasts 'the prim obliterated polite face of life, and the broad, bawdy and orgiastic – or maenadic – foundations'. The pagan suggestions in the Stevenson remind us interestingly, first, of Strether's reiterated imagining of Chad as pagan in *The Ambassadors*, and, second, of the transformation of the significance of a particular image in James's vocabulary between the Bourget letter of 1888 and the first of the late three novels. In the letter he complains that 'an intellect like your own should have thought it necessary to make so great a sacrifice to false gods!'. In *The Ambassadors* Strether wants to be 'expiatory' towards little Bilham because he 'has been sacrificing to strange gods': 'I feel as if my hands were imbrued with the blood of monstrous alien altars – of another faith altogether' (393). James's own use of the language of rite and creed in connection with the propriety issue seems to justify our talking about Strether's, and James's, change of mind in terms of a 'conversion'; and it certainly suggests James making connections between Anglo-Saxon systems of sexual propriety and a Protestant idealism. But most significantly, in the Bourget letter they are false gods. By the time of *The Ambassadors* the gods are only *strange* ones; Strether's sacrifice to them is uneasy and half-hearted, perhaps, but none the less propitiatory. The strange gods are real, and must be answered.

When the anonymous lady and gentleman in the boat in the ideal picture Strether has been composing reveal themselves in fact as his friends Chad and Mme de Vionnet, Strether of course experiences shock, discomfiture, distaste. Their meal at the Cheval Blanc is the least happy one they have ever shared. But, returned to Paris and alone in his room, his strong reactions are not only of shock and distaste. Along with the astringency of those there is a relief, an exhilaration at finally 'seeing and facing' (to use James's terms from the passage on Stevenson). While Strether was hovering outside the locked door of the secret, the door opened wide and the secret thrust itself upon him. And although he had held off from the secret out of a delicacy that eschewed the voyeurism of imagining it, in the new light of certainty new decorums disclose themselves, and that very delicacy, that hovering, sting him in dissatisfied retrospect.

That was what, in his vain vigil, he oftenest reverted to: intimacy, at such a point, was *like* that – and what in the world else would one have wished it to be like? It was all very well for him to feel the pity of its being so much like lying. (468)

There are all kinds of prurience, and perhaps hovering too busily around a secret while deferring actually naming it is one of them: there may be more ways of muddying and soiling secrets in imagination than simply (as in the Bourget letter) too crudely telling them. The exhilaration – or perhaps just the relief – at that eventual seeing and facing seems to be more than merely Strether's; it reverberates in James's whole *oeuvre*.

Into the world of sayable things intrudes the presence of the other realities that have only been guessed at and hinted at so far, have only been circumlocuted. And the language, the vocabulary, they finally exact in their text is the simplest, the most stating; it is neither the Woollett language of moralising high-mindedness nor Parisian sophisticated euphemism. Neither Chad nor Mme de Vionnet 'speak', there are no conceivable explanations: facts speak, bodies speak, and so unequivocally that in Strether's separate interviews afterwards with both of the lovers they simply presume he now 'knows', though no word has been said. Literally, it is the bodies that speak: Mme de Vionnet has no shawl, Chad no overcoat, these things are taken off and left at the room both of them shared the night before. A veil is torn away and what is revealed beneath is after all only ordinary human nakedness. It seems a particular felicity that after such long prevarication the sign that is finally found to stand for the secret in the locked room is something as simple, as ordinary, as the taking off of clothes.

But then it is an evening of other ordinarinesses too: it is not for nothing that the scene is staged as pastoral. Strether's pastoral is ironised, of course, when into his exquisite framed picture row not, after all, the anonymous lovers required for colour contrast and the suggestion of an erotic Arcadia where love can be both innocent and fulfilled at once, but instead his real known pair who drag with them all the world's complications and take off real clothes. But the vitality with which the pastoral is evoked in this chapter is too strong for *mere* irony. The day, the place, are too beautiful, too full of pleasures, *only* to be spoiled ('the lap of the water, the ripple of the surface, the rustle of the reeds on the opposite bank, the faint diffused coolness and the slight rock of a couple of small boats', 459). Pastoral has its other usual functions here too: as a corrective to urban over-refinement, as a means of re-acquaintance with hidden, 'natural' sources of strength. Strether and Chad and Mme de Vionnet share their rustic supper: even the most exquisitely sophisticated ladies and gentlemen need to break bread and pour wine when they are hungry; by implication, even the most rarefied of virtuous attachments will be bound to stoop to bodies sooner or later. And even ladies and gentlemen with the most tasteful possible manners will sometimes be reduced to covering their nakedness in ordinary fibs, however these may disagree with delicate stomachs. These are the chastening lessons that sophistication has conventionally taken from pastoral along with its solaces: that refinement confers no immunity to ordinary ills and frailties, and that we are all made of the same earth. This function of pastoral coincides interestingly with a realism whose concern is often with the actual lived implications of ideals of conduct.

The crucial problem for the James of the Bourget letter was the absolute inadmissibility of any reconciliation of the 'action' of sexuality and the imagination of it. To imagine it was to dirty it; thought became muddied, voyeuristic, as soon as it approached the privacies that could only exist sealed off, uncontaminated by imagining them. The impossibility of sustaining that watertight separation made James in the letter defensive, uncomfortable: was not the unthinkable guiltily thought even in repudiating the possibility of cleanly thinking it? In *The Ambassadors*, the solution to the problem is as simple as acknowledging the truth that the thing *exists already* in thought. Fiction can render it by rendering its effects in imagination; it need not pretend to enter the room behind whose locked doors imagination takes on flesh.[21] So, James has us 'imagine' Kate's visit in Venice through how it haunts Merton afterwards; or we 'imagine' all the pleasures of Charlotte's and the Prince's visit to Gloucester through their anticipations of it that spring morning at Matcham. What Strether feels as he reflects in his room alone is not only shock, and not only relief, at 'seeing and facing' what he had postponed; there is also voluptuousness, as he gives himself up at last to imagining what he had not allowed himself to think:

He foresaw that Miss Gostrey would come again into requisition on the morrow; though it wasn't to be denied that he was already a little afraid of her 'What on earth – that's what I want to know now – had you then supposed?' He recognised at last that he had really been trying all along to suppose nothing. Verily, verily, his labour had been lost. He found himself supposing innumerable and wonderful things. (468)

His imagination, finally, of the relationship between Chad and Mme de Vionnet is not of its 'goodness', or its justification: it is of its pleasures.

The moment is his loneliest one:

The very question, it may be added, made him feel lonely and cold. There was the element of the awkward all round, but Chad and Mme de Vionnet at least had the comfort that they could talk it over together. With whom could *he* talk of such things? (468)

With the imagination of their pleasures comes his acknowledgement of his exclusion from them.[22] Part of the enjoyment of his day in the countryside had been in his striking himself as 'engaged with others and in midstream of his drama' (457): in the light of his encounter with the lovers that sense of engagement seems suddenly foolish. The essential of the business that preoccupies them all is carried out in pairs, and he is not needed for it. And his exclusion is not just something for a day, it is of a whole lifetime. In *The Ambassadors*, which is essentially a novel about middle age and ageing, the imagination of the erotic is painfully entangled with the idea of youth, an inaccessible lost youth:[23]

It's too late. And it's as if the train had fairly waited at the station for me without my having had the gumption to know it was there. Now I hear its faint receding whistle miles and miles down the line. What one loses one loses; make no mistake about that. (215)

What Strether refuses when he gently-determinedly puts aside Maria's offer of herself is the let-down of mere compensation. It is part of his character (perhaps it is Woollett in him) to believe that the real, recognised loss cannot be fudged, should not be 'made up for'. There would finally be something demeaning (Woollett has its pride) in seeming to console himself for the absence of the real, the authentic thing (youth, passion, pain), with the mock-erotics of a middle-aged pastiche-passion.

Even as James's fiction finds its way of writing sex into the story, it also ruefully writes its own ultimate exclusion from an erotic that is only real outside fiction: this is the acknowledgement of that special problematic status of sex-in-writing discussed earlier. The art gestures outside art to the places it can imagine but cannot enter. Strether with his lost opportunities is the embodiment of a rueful comic apology for the sixty-year-old writer come late to make his homage to pleasure, to 'the idea that happiness could have a share in beauty', having painstakingly unlearned the 'time-tested, comfortable perspective of resignation, heroism, asceticism'.[24]

If we read *The Ambassadors* as centring on a significant moment of 'seeing and facing' in James's *oeuvre*, then in that moment the issue of the erotic and the issue of language and tone are inseparable. What Strether finally allows himself to imagine ('he found himself supposing innumerable and wonderful things'), is only possible because of the changes in the tone, the texture and the vocabulary of his thinking which have already scandalised Sarah Pocock. He has learned a different language in Paris, a language which 'gave Strether such a sense of depths below it and behind it as he hadn't yet had' (347). He has picked up archness, extravagance, indirection, perpetual irony, he has developed, in a word, *manner*: and only *manner* bestows the elasticity that finally allows him – ironically enough – to call a spade a spade, to accuse himself and his old unmannered straightness of a culpable ignorance, the innocent ignorance of 'little girls dressing dolls'. 'Straightness', the common sense of middle ground, had become a straight-jacket, it had become impossible to communicate the truth in it because the truth had turned out to be curved and nuanced and ambivalent in ways straightness could not express:

'I mean,' he explained [to Sarah], 'that she [Mme de Vionnet] might have affected you by her exquisite amiability – a real revelation, it has seemed to myself; her high rarity, her distinction of every sort.'
    He had been, with these words, consciously a little 'precious'; but he had had to be – he couldn't give her the truth of the case without them. (419)

Those great efforts of conscientiousness represented by Strether's voluminous correspondence with Woollett almost seem to represent James's own desire, in his own writing, to keep faith with the origins of his *oeuvre* in the moralising conscientious Anglo-Saxon novel tradition. As he moves into the larger open space from where there are other, less 'straight' ways of seeing, he continues to try to explain the one way to the other, to mediate different tones, to make transparent all the premises of his perception, just like Strether:

'Well, what can I do more than that – what can I do more than tell her everything?' To persuade himself that he did tell her, had told her, everything, he used to try and think of particular things he hadn't told her. When at rare moments and in the watches of the night he pounced on one it generally showed itself to be – to a deeper scrutiny – not quite truly of the essence. When anything new struck him as coming up, or anything already noted as reappearing, he always immediately wrote, as if for fear that if he didn't he would miss something; and also that he might be able to say to himself from time to time 'She knows it *now* – even while I worry'. (246)

This, the very image of a vigilant Protestant conscientiousness, also seems to describe the characteristic Jamesian exhaustiveness. The trouble is that the very exhaustiveness in itself sounds suspect – 'precious' – to Sarah and Mrs Newsome and Woollett. The more minutely Strether (and James) explains himself, the less straight he seems.

Finally when it seems as though his very efforts of conscientiousness bring down Woollett's disapproval, Woollett's silence, Woollett's ultimatum on his head, Strether takes 'the numerous loose sheets of his unfinished composition [his latest letter], and then, without reading them over', tears them into small pieces. Afterwards he sleeps '– as if it had been in some measure thanks to that sacrifice – the sleep of the just' (287). At some point in James's *oeuvre* justice – truth – exacts a break with the old forms, the abandonment of an old world of tone, and a whole commitment to an ever more nuanced, opaque, convoluted manner and language. The late manner is one to which the innocence and ignorance of Sarah and Mrs Newsome and Woollett will never find – will never want to find – access; even though in some measure it has evolved under the pressure of their expectation. The breakdown of the Paris–Woollett correspondence in *The Ambassadors* rehearses the evolution within the *oeuvre* of the late style, gives an account of the *necessity*, finally, of its quixotic, mannered, lofty inaccessibility, its aristocratic irony 'asserting a bond among the élite who can decode its inverted operation'.[25] The story (Chad's and Mme de Vionnet's, Kate's and Merton's, the Prince's and Charlotte's) exacts the style; the old straightness was not adequate, particularly, to explaining the power in the story of pleasure. In order to find out his robust plain signs for sex – Mme de Vionnet and Chad without their outdoor things, the powerful presence-in-absence of that room in which their clothes are abandoned illicitly together – James has had to free himself from that frame of plain middle-ground decency within which the Anglo-Saxon novel tradition had grown up. Plainness, in some contexts, can even come to depend upon opacity and complication.

However, if the evolution of James's late style was a matter of liberating himself from the proprieties of the Anglo-Saxon tradition, it need not follow that it represents James's English version of the Continental tradition. Strether, if he 'loses' Woollett, does not 'gain' Paris; he cannot naturalise himself there. His reiterated insistence that 'the strength of his position . . . was precisely that there was nothing in it for himself' (313) has often been taken as a manifestation of Jamesian asceticism, in that reading of the *oeuvre* which has James as the high priest of renunciation if not incapacity (Benjamin's 'time-tested, comfortable perspective of resignation, heroism, asceticism'). But in a reading of the late novels which finds them instead deeply responsive to passion, appetite, energy, Strether's insistence that he is somehow justified by not 'getting anything out of it' may stand for something rather different. The novel may indeed be heavy with an almost Yeatsian burden of ageing; the regret for lost opportunity, the yearning admiration for an inaccessible youthful completeness-unto-itself, the futility of too middle-aged a desire:

The prime effect of her [Mme de Vionnet's] tone, however, – and it was a truth which his eyes gave back to her in sad ironic play – could only be to make him feel that, to say such things to a man in public, a woman must practically think of him as ninety years old. (344)

But the compensatory lightness – as for Yeats? – comes in the fictional purchase on all that, in the being able to express it precisely so well because so finally outside of it. The compensation itself, of course, is – for added lightness – accessible in turn to further ironies, for who would not rather have the real (foolish, transient) thing than the power to tell it? (That further irony is a *locus classicus* of love poetry, in Shakespeare's sonnets, for example, in Jonson's 'On My Picture Left in Scotland', or in that letter of James's to Jocelyn Persse: 'I . . . envy you, as always, your exquisite possession of the Art of Life which beats any Art of mine hollow'.[26])

Strether's loss in life, and strength in art, is that he is 'out of it': he has made for himself eventually a tone, a poise, that is both outside Woollett's closed attitude of disapproval, and outside (if a little wistfully) the heady enchantments of sex in France. His 'genius for missing things' is the key to his grasp on things (407); his disabling 'obsession of the other thing' ('I'm always considering something else; something else, I mean, than the thing of the moment', 66) is what qualifies him for us (if not for Mrs Newsome) as ambassador, as mediator of the different worlds. Having embodied this detachment from both ways of seeing in Strether (whose spectacles – 'eternal nippers' – both separate him from the world and make him see it more clearly), James feels no need to focus it explicitly again; nobody is in the least renunciatory or detached in *The Wings of the*

Dove or *The Golden Bowl.* The detachment is established as a perspective, and the characters are free to be as embedded and embroiled *in* things as they possibly can.

Strether's wry self-deprecating comedy at the expense of his successive inglorious positions (ambassador for Woollett's offended prudery, spokesman for Paris's licentiousness) raises issues of gender entangled with issues of ways of seeing. His 'foolishness' is a confusion of his manliness, almost: his very sensitivity, his very scrupulousness, his 'enormous sense of responsibility about personal relationships' (Watt's phrase), and in the end his very *imaginativeness*, make it impossible, once he has broken with the controlling women of Woollett, that he should smoothly identify himself with the controlling *men* of Paris. Scrupulousness, sensitivity, imaginative identification with the opposite sex: these are not the qualities Strether guesses in Gloriani, admires in Chad. But they are Strether's qualities: and they commit him to a kind of limbo, beneficiary of neither gender system, berated for his weak male susceptibility by Woollett and excluded from the pleasures of Paris by a conscientiousness and a tenderness that are too feminine.

Paris holds out its promise to the body through its refinements of food and dress and comfort-in-living, tantalising with its half-revealed, half-concealed cult of sexual pleasure unburdened with shame, the mystery at the centre of all its initiations. But its promise is essentially to a male appetite; and it depends upon certain male freedoms. Chad wears them as casually and strikingly as his black crush hat, that night of his first conversation with Strether in the café:

Chad turned this over . . . 'Well, such questions have always a rather exaggerated side. One doesn't know quite what you mean by being in women's "hands". It's all so vague. One is when one isn't. One isn't when one is. And then one can't quite give people away.' He seemed very kindly to explain. 'I've *never* got stuck – so very hard; and, as against anything at any time really better, I don't think I've ever been afraid.' . . .

'. . . But our suspicions don't matter,' [Strether] added, 'if you're actually not entangled.'

Chad's pride seemed none the less a little touched. 'I never *was* that – let me insist. I always had my own way.' With which he pursued: 'And I have it at present.'

'Then what are you here for? What has kept you,' Strether asked, 'if you *have* been able to leave?'

It made Chad, after a stare, throw himself back. 'Do you think one's kept only by women?' His surprise and his verbal emphasis rang out so clear in the still street that Strether winced till he remembered the safety of their English speech. 'Is that,' the young man demanded, 'what they think at Woollett?' (171, 172)

Of course Chad's exhibition of male indifferences here ('I've never got stuck, so very hard', and 'Do you think one's kept only by women?') is partly precisely because he is being a *gentleman*; that is, he is making light of his attachments to women in general in order to conceal, as it goes without saying a gentleman must, the reality of his liaison with one woman. He is protecting Mme de Vionnet's honour by denying her power. The lie is excusable within this code because it is not to protect the gentleman himself; the affairs are no shame to him, but frankly referred to. Chad's every *aperçu* ('One is when one isn't. One isn't when one is') breathes modest, taken-for-granted *know-how*: it belongs to a male discourse where such know-how, such implications of wide sexual experience, such lightly worn trophies of the erotic pursuit are even more indispensable to male style and éclat, to male dignity and self-respect, than the walking stick and the knowing how to enter an opera box at ten o'clock at night. And in the end, the form and the habit and the manner of such male privilege convince all by themselves; we cannot help finding that Chad's assertions of his ultimate indifference ring 'true', even when we know about Mme de Vionnet. Any system which defends its attachments by denying them (so any system where male sexual adventure is defined as primarily adulterous and therefore of its nature clandestine) is too anomalous to support mutuality or reciprocity for long.

If Strether is only half understanding Chad's blasé Parisianisms that evening in the café, equally Chad has forgotten how to talk to Strether, how they talk in Woollett. For perhaps the only time we catch unadulterated in Chad's easy frankness the whiff of that male 'jungle', that 'great world covertly tigerish' which Strether identifies for himself at Gloriani's party, seeing at once that Gloriani, that 'glossy male tiger, magnificently marked' (216) has in this Paris world (so unlike Woollett) the advantage over any merely female Duchess. But by the time Strether is onto the whiff of the jungle Chad is covering his tracks: part of his being formed to please is that he is quick to intuit what does not please Strether, and he speaks henceforward about women in softer tones. In their last interview, when Strether tries to persuade Chad not to leave Mme de Vionnet, his tones are even too soft for Strether's liking; the more he says nice things about her, the more Strether hears that if the nice things need saying then they are not enough. Through Chad's protestations of her claims to his benevolence show the brute underpinnings of this gender system; 'I'm not tired of her', Chad says; and, 'she's never bored me . . . she's never been anything I could call a burden' (502).

Mme de Vionnet works very hard not to be that burden. Chad's pleasure depends upon her not boring him; her happiness depends upon his not being bored. When Strether is surprised she knows nothing about Jim Pocock he asks, 'Doesn't he [Chad] tell you things?'

She hesitated. 'No' – and their eyes once more gave and took. 'Not as you do. You somehow make me see them – or at least feel them. And I haven't asked too much,' she added; 'I've of late wanted so not to worry him.' (356)

Unlike Sarah Pocock, she is 'obliged' to have 'charm' (354). And that 'charm' Strether defines elsewhere as a performance, in which her skill is all reflective and responsive, finding out the 'tones' to fit others:

One of the things that most lingered with him on his hillside was this delightful facility, with such a woman, of arriving at a new tone; he thought, as he lay on his back, of all the tones she might make possible if one were to try her, and at any rate of the probability that one could trust her to fit them to occasions. (456)

It does not seem too crass to extend Strether's expression here as he imagines Mme de Vionnet's social versatility and skill at pleasing to implicitly suggest other more sensual skills; because of Strether's Woollett-tutored reticence, it remains of course an unfocused suggestion, only a part of the sensuousness of the day and his situation, lying on his back in the sunshine in the grass, 'luxuriously quiet'.

When Miss Barrace points out to Strether how Mme de Vionnet can make herself for Jim's entertainment and 'for Chad, in a manner, naturally, always', 'easily and charmingly, as young as a little girl', or, 'about twenty years old' (pp. 403–4) we have a glimpse of the huge female effort, the female desperateness, of this particular gender arrangement. It is poignantly important in the story that Mme de Vionnet is older than Chad, and that she has (like Mrs Brookenham) a young daughter, whose turn it is for youthful loveliness, waiting in the social wings to replace her as the object of male desire. The idea of Jeanne and her youth seems fatally entangled, somehow, in other people's speculations about Chad's future and his affections. It is not that Mme de Vionnet is *only* vulnerable because Chad is younger than her; but the disparity in their ages that so disadvantages her expresses a fundamental inequity, a fatality for femininity, built into their arrangement (*it cannot last*).

In his letter to Bourget James objected to 'this character who so often appears in French novels: the sensitive and eminent young man beginning his first adulterous affair ... Almost our only reaction to him – as

Anglo-Saxons – is a desire to give him a good kick in the behind.' The objection is part of James's irritated reaction in that letter to the whole impropriety, as he sees it, of 'drabbling intellectually' in 'the conduct of love'; but it may also be an objection to an element of the French novel tradition which sometimes appeared conventional and unexamined to James, an ideal of sexual freedom and adventure structured upon a fundamental gender inequity. He writes in his 1878 essay on Balzac:

He takes the old-fashioned view – he recognises none but the old-fashioned categories. Woman is the female of man and in all respects his subordinate; she is pretty and ugly, virtuous and vicious, stupid and cunning. There is the great *métier de femme* – the most difficult perhaps in the world, so that to see it thoroughly mastered is peculiarly exhilarating. The *métier de femme* includes a great many branches, but they may be all summed up in the art of titillating in one way or another the senses of man ... The great sign of Balzac's women is that in all things the sexual quality is inordinately emphasised and the conscience on the whole inordinately sacrificed to it ... It is their personal, physical quality that he relishes – their attitudes, their picturesqueness, the sense that they give him of playing always, sooner or later, into the hands of man.[27]

In so many nineteenth-century French *Bildungsromane* centred on the consciousnesses of young men, crucial passages in their development – the rite of initiation into sexual manhood, the social climb, the middle-aged disillusionment – are presided over by a whole cast of female types: the ingénue, the demi-mondaine (Coralie in *Illusions Perdues*, Rosannette in *L'Education Sentimentale*), the aristocratic patroness (la Sanseverina in *La Chartreuse de Parme*, Mme de Bargeton in *Illusions Perdues*), or the decent wife whose husband is unworthy, self-tormented by her own infidelity (Mme de Renal in *Le Rouge et le Noir*, Mme Arnoux in *L'Education Sentimentale*). Sometimes, if they have social status and influence, or for as long as they are desired, the women wield considerable power. (No-one would want to underestimate the command of a Sanseverina or a Mathilde de la Mole over her own destiny; and his interest in them is one of the ways in which Stendhal is distinctively different to Balzac.) But there is nothing like the same drive as in the English novel tradition towards resolution in marriage: and there is nothing like the same exploration of and search for values of mutuality and reciprocity in love. There is no convention of a novel-framework through which female characters can exact commitment, desert, equity (as, say, Elizabeth Bennet can, or Jane Eyre). Here we feel the significance of Ruth Bernard Yeazell's point about the 'space of courtship' in the English novel tradition; that narrow but crucial space where the female subjects of novels still had the (limited) power of decision over their destiny. The dynamic of the Continental tradition is located within a very different space for choice and action: within the possibility of that transgressive and post-marital relationship which Tony Tanner makes central to his analysis in *Adultery in the Novel* ('without adultery, or the persistent possibility of adultery, the novel would have been bereft of much of its narrational urge'[28]). Inside the space of adultery the women have little room to manoeuvre, and can exact, effectively, nothing from their men.

Mme de Vionnet is the skilled exponent of Balzac's *métier de femme*. And that phrase in the Balzac essay – women 'playing always, sooner or later, into the hands of man' – calls to mind the Prince in *The Golden Bowl*, who 'once more, as a man conscious of having known many women ... could assist, as he would have called it, at the recurrent, the predestined phenomenon, the thing always as certain as sunrise or the coming round of Saints' days, the doing by the woman of the thing that gave her away' (61). In his late fictions James is exploring a world of relations between men and women quite other than that safer and more protected space of courtship where the Anglo-Saxon novel tradition had mostly sited itself; and a great deal of what he has learned about it he has learned from the French novel tradition. But the difference between James's and Balzac's representations of the types and presumptions and power relations of these un-innocent men and women is that James, like Strether, is no more finally persuaded of, say, Chad's version of the story (or the Prince's) than he is by Woollett's. Into a world charged with a very masculine sexual energy and élan he intrudes qualities of gentleness and conscientiousness (Strether's 'enormous sense of responsibility about personal relationships') which read as coming rather from the Anglo-Saxon novel tradition: and his women perceive as well as being the objects of perception. When he writes that Balzac is not interested in women's *conscience*, the word need not only mean that his women are not *good*; it suggests that he is not interested in their *consciousness* of what they are at all.

In his critical writing James had from the beginning both complained about and celebrated the 'delicacy' of the English-language novel tradition. His ambivalent relationship with English literary proprieties reads very like the complex pained tenderness with which Strether feels the pressures, the claims, of Woollett:

'And yet Mrs Newsome ... *has* imagined, did, that is, imagine, and apparently still does, horrors about what I should have found. I was booked, by her

vision – extraordinarily intense, after all – to find them; and that I didn't, that
I couldn't, that, as she evidently felt, I wouldn't – this evidently didn't at all,
as they say, "suit" her book. It was more than she could bear. That was her
disappointment.'

'You mean you were to have found Chad horrible?' [asked Maria.]

'I was to have found the woman.'

'Horrible?'

'Found her as she imagined her.' And Strether paused as if for his own
expression of it he could add no touch to that picture.

His companion had meanwhile thought. 'She imagined stupidly – so it comes
to the same thing.'

'Stupidly? Oh!'

But she insisted. 'She imagined meanly.'

He had it, however, better. 'It couldn't but be ignorantly.'

'Well, intensity with ignorance – what do you want worse?'

This question might have held him, but he let it pass. (449)

His hesitations are not simply a residual loyalty to Mrs Newsome (although they are that too): he corrects Maria's too glib certainty, her
writing off Woollett. (Maria is angry with Woollett of course partly in his
defence – as well as for her own purposes.) He insists Mrs Newsome's
failure to imagine Mme de Vionnet is *not* stupidity. How was she, given
her culture, her circumstances, given her very imagination and its formation, to know? And he does not give his assent to Maria's contempt
for 'intensity with ignorance': we suspect that, for better or for worse,
intensity has come too close ever to be quite dismissed; it has impressed
its permanent high-water mark on him, left him forever with the taste of
its strong flavour, its peculiar conviction.

Even while the progress of his own 'seeing and facing' has made
relations with Woollett's 'intensity with ignorance' impossible, that is
only because Woollett will not go on understanding him. He can go on
understanding Woollett and Mrs Newsome, giving them his tribute of
appreciation which is almost deepened and made more resonant by its
non-reciprocity:

It struck him that he had never so lived with her as during this period of her
silence; the silence was a sacred hush, a finer clearer medium, in which her
idiosyncrasies showed. He walked about with her, sat with her, drove with
her and dined face-to-face with her – a rare treat 'in his life', as he could perhaps scarce have escaped phrasing it; and if he had never seen her so soundless
he had never, on the other hand, felt her so highly, so almost austerely, herself: pure and by the vulgar estimate 'cold', but deep devoted delicate sensitive
noble. (302)

'In his life' that treat of full appreciation of the things Mrs Newsome is was hard to come at, up too close. 'Out of his life', in that suspension of belonging Paris has produced in him, he can more generously take in her value, the complete picture of her type. The sonorous string of her qualities – 'deep devoted delicate sensitive noble' – is both meant and gently ironic; it is not that she is *not* those things, but just that they might be, all together like that, something too much for him ever to be adequate to (or for any man, certainly too much for a Waymarsh, a Jim Pocock, a Chad).[29]

It is significant that it is Sarah that Strether has to negotiate with and not her mother: Sarah is the blunt end of Woollett values, and James is able to render her righteous indignation with comic gusto while still leaving over for the mother who waits at home an aura of deeper solemnity, a power to affect that is only partly compromised and ironised (and at these moments we somehow feel her to be more like *Strether's* 'mother' than by any stretch of the imagination any sort of 'lover'[30]). But if Sarah is comic in the scenes of her confrontation with Strether then James is capable of a wry comedy at Strether's (and his own) expense too: he makes us hear how the mannered elaborations and hyperbole of Strether's (and his own) late style might sound in the decent ears of plain-speaking Woollett:

'You can sacrifice mothers and sisters to her without a blush, and can make them cross the ocean on purpose to feel the more, and take from you the straighter, *how* you do it?' [exclaimed Sarah.]

' . . . Your coming out belonged closely to my having come before you, and my having come was a result of our general state of mind. Our general state of mind had proceeded, on its side, from our queer ignorance, our queer misconceptions and confusions – from which, since then, an inexorable tide of light seems to have floated us into our perhaps still queerer knowledge . . . '

It put to her also, doubtless, his tone, too many things. (418)

In the end, any reading of the novel has to take the tone of its attitude towards Woollett from all that gentle tact Strether exercises on its behalf. However impossibly far he has left its narrow proprieties and certainties behind, and even if he cannot talk to it any more, Woollett is where his imagination was formed, and he has learned things from there that incapacitate him for the Parisian male 'jungle'. Some of Woollett's delicacy was prudery, and its decency the false 'optimism of ignorance', as James wrote of the Anglo-Saxon novel tradition. But delicacy has traditionally operated as a protection and a shelter *as well as* a blinkered conservatism: a protection for certain kinds of seriousness, a shelter for women (for 'good' women, anyway). In the gynocentric world James imagines for Woollett, the women are full (even too full) of a conviction of their rights and their privileges, and feel under no obligation to charm; and nor do they fear the loss of their youth, their looks, their men.[31] They are not afraid that they will be boring. In James's Paris there is more charm and less tedium all round, and even the women whose 'attachments' are not 'virtuous' have their share in the sun, but as he basks in its life-giving sensuality Strether cannot help his suffering sense that this happiness, this pleasure, is exposed and vulnerable, free from the protection of socially imposed conscience and responsibility.

Strether's suffering is most acute whenever he has to consider Jeanne, the daughter; it is as if she stands, rather impersonally realised as she is, for some sacrifice buried deep within Parisian sexual culture which he cannot bear to entertain nor to lend himself to, not in word nor even in imagination. Some instinct of refusal almost as if at an incestuousness (he is sure she loves her mother's lover, her mother's lover is going to marry her off to someone else; and the text makes repeated play of misunderstandings over Chad's relation to Jeanne) hurries the very mention of Jeanne's initiations out of Strether's conversation, out of his mind, as soon as they chance there. She represents some secret, final shame in the whole liaison which he *cannot* lend himself to – or even perhaps *has* lent himself to, innocently, involuntarily?

He had allowed for depths, but these were greater: and it was as if, oppressively – indeed absurdly – he was responsible for what they had now thrown up to the surface. It was – through something ancient and cold in it – what he would have called the real thing . . . He was prepared to suffer – before his own inner tribunal – for Chad; he was prepared to suffer even for Mme de Vionnet. But he wasn't prepared to suffer for the little girl. (364)

At the end of the novel, the liaison with Jeanne's mother has served its purpose for Chad in the time-honoured (Continental) tradition. Gallantly he acknowledges the inestimable gloss that only Mme de Vionnet's femininity could have bestowed upon him; he is improved and ready to move on. (We note Strether's and Maria's guess – how Strether is coming on in worldliness! – that there is another woman in London.) Mme de Vionnet cannot be indignant at his desertion – she has no rights, nor sense of her wrong, but only, to help her out, an old female wisdom, *vieille sagesse*, which unites her with a whole history of abandoned women in a gender commonality of powerlessness and emotional subjection. This transcends, James suggests, the divides of class and refinement, so that she cries in front of Strether 'as vulgarly troubled, in very truth, as a maidservant crying for her young man' (483). The *vieille sagesse* of these women makes Strether squeamish sometimes ('to deal with them was to walk on water', 482), with its currency of innuendo, gossip, secrets, betrayals. It is a female 'know-how', the counterpart of Chad's male bravado that first evening in the café; only, it reflects such a different spectrum of experience, and such a different experience of power in the relations between men and women. 'A man in trouble *must* be possessed somehow by a woman, if she doesn't come in one way she comes in another', (280); 'It's when one's old that it's worst . . . It's a doom – I know it; you can't see it more than I do myself. Things have to happen as they will' (484). Or from Maria, 'What woman was *ever* safe?' (492).

Mme de Vionnet's tears do not last too long; we suppose, Strether supposes, that they are after all, *as well as* being real and heartfelt, another part of the performance of this woman of many tones, 'like Cleopatra in the play, indeed various and multifold' (256). She is (like Cleopatra at the end of *her* play) both genuinely desperate, and calculating what she can do to help herself. In her last scene she never deplores or protests; it is her 'doom', and in a spirit that has nothing to do with being 'right' or 'good', and much to do with an aesthetic, a 'good form', she will carry it off. When Strether finally opens the door on the grown-up reality of the pleasures of passion, he also discovers how intimately pleasures are tangled with pain; that to take a step off the edge of the safeties of Woollett, to really take the risk he enjoins upon little Bilham with his 'live all you can!', is to step into the free fall of suffering, that 'great and constant suffering' which Benjamin says in his essay on Proust is what saved Proust's pleasures in 'life and the course of the world' from being merely 'ordinary indolent contentment'.[32]

There is a passage in the correspondence of Flaubert and George Sand which sets out starkly the ground plan, as it were, of sex and gender relations for the sophisticated classes in nineteenth-century France. Flaubert's remarks certainly suggest that it is not ridiculous to connect much of the energy and brilliance of the French nineteenth-century novel to a male sexual élan, to a whole system of permissive and exploitative male sexuality. And if we remember that the young James fresh from New England in 1876 was made welcome by Flaubert and spent time with him, then it might seem likely that the roots for the confrontation of cultural systems inside *The Ambassadors* lie far back in the shocks

and distastes and excitements of the young James responding to his first
freedom of the male jungle.

Flaubert and George Sand are discussing Saint-Beuve, who is 'plunged
in gloom at the thought that he can no longer haunt the Cyprian groves'.
Flaubert writes:

How hard you are on old Beuve. After all, he is neither a Jesuit nor a green
girl...Men will always be of the opinion that the one serious thing in life is
sexual enjoyment. Woman, for all the members of my sex, is a groined archway
opening on the infinite. That may not be a very elevated attitude, but it is
fundamental to the male...

George Sand replies:

I am *not* a Catholic, but I do draw the line at monstrosities! I maintain that the
old and ugly who buy young bodies for cash are not indulging in 'love', and that
what they do has nothing in common with the Cyprian Venus, with groined
arches or infinities or male or female! It is something wholly against nature,
since it is not desire that pushes the young girl into the arms of the ugly dotard,
and an act in which there is neither liberty nor reciprocity is an offence against
the sanctity of nature.[33]

That glimpse of a fundamental argument within French culture may also
help an understanding of why James persisted in his sympathetic criticisms of George Sand long after she had died and gone out of fashion.
Does her distinctiveness within the French novel tradition have something to do with an effort, not to moralise pleasure, or return it inside the
bourgeois fold, but to write a feminised version of it, so that male pleasure is no longer contingent upon female suffering? Is it possible to read
her as defending, protecting, the 'seriousness' of passion, against a cynicism which depended upon the impossibility of mutuality, reciprocity?
(It must have seemed very hard to write the seriousness of passion after *Madame Bovary*.[34]) If so, then it is hardly surprising that the author
of *The Ambassadors* should have felt an especial tenderness towards even
the inconsistencies of this particular predecessor, a loyalty even to what
seemed to him dated and dusty in her enterprise.

CHAPTER 5

Poor girls with their rent to pay: class in 'In the Cage' and The Wings of the Dove

James, like Strether, finally allows himself to imagine pleasure unbound from a moralising framework. The challenge is to find an expression for how the liberated late-Jamesian imagination of pleasure interacts with James's ever-sharpening perceptions of social class. The great love affairs in the late novels take all their colour and flavour from the rich medium of the privileged lives of their protagonists: the lovely rooms, the brilliant displays of clothes and jewels, the long leisured hours to play in, the stimulating discipline of an exquisitely cultivated good taste. John Goode in his chapter on *The Wings of the Dove* in *The Air of Reality* describes eloquently a James not only succumbed to the seductions of privilege but actually offering the possession of vast wealth as an opportunity for a kind of transcendence: 'James sets out to realize an unsentimental acceptance of the price of innocence by regranting money its mystery and its representativeness, by creating for the intellectual a relation to it which is not that of contract but of consent, as to a power greater than any this world by itself can show.' James is 'honest' in finding in 'the coffers of the millionaire . . . the root of innocence and the flower of imagination'.[1]

It is true, and important, that the opportunities for pleasure afforded by the possession of great wealth are never fudged or sentimentalised in the late writing.[2] But perhaps it is possible to make out a different reading of James's imaginative involvement in that writing with the pleasures of privilege; a reading that has him at once succumbed and equivocal, dependent for the imaginative richness of his fictions upon all the vivid difference money makes, and yet with an essentially tragic perception of the crushing social machinery that distributes it so inequitably.

Again, Benjamin's essay on Proust can help find a way to describe how the money in James's novels interacts with social and sexual behaviours;

Benjamin's Proust is neither complacently conservative nor banally homiletic about the 'economic aspect' of his world.

This disillusioned, merciless deglamorizer of the ego, of love, of morals – for this is how Proust liked to see himself – turns his whole limitless art into a veil for this one most vital mystery of his class: the economic aspect. He did not mean to do it a service. Here speaks Marcel Proust, the hardness of his work, the intransigence of a man who is ahead of his class. What he accomplishes he accomplishes as its master. And much of the greatness of this work will remain inaccessible or undiscovered until this class has revealed its most pronounced features in the final struggle.[3]

No criticism could be more empathetic with the convolutions of Proust's class consciousness, his minute snobberies, his surplus of material detail, his valetudinarianism. If Benjamin's is a 'revolutionary' reading of Proust, then whatever radical critique of the French nineteenth century he attributes to the *oeuvre* is at a level more entangled with its material than mere surface disapproval and detachment:

We do not always proclaim loudly the most important things we have to say. Nor do we always privately share it with those closest to us, our intimate friends, those who have been most devotedly ready to receive our confession. If it is true that not only people but also ages have such a chaste – that is, such a devious and frivolous – way of communicating what is most their own to a passing acquaintance, then the nineteenth century did not reveal itself to Zola or Anatole France, but to the young Proust, the insignificant snob, the playboy and socialite who snatched in passing the most astounding confidences from a declining age as from another, bone-weary Swann.[4]

What Benjamin suggests is that fundamental to the deepest critique literature can make of a society is a contamination, virtually, of that literature by its society: in order to penetrate society's deepest secrets, the writer needs to be an initiate, a skilled practitioner of all its appearances and disguises. Immunity and objectivity, for all their superficial appearance of being the right qualifications for authority, are not enough. It is Conrad's contamination with the mentality of the colonial exploiter that makes his rendering in *Heart of Darkness* of the damaged white psyche in search of its lost meaning so harrowingly plausible (while Chinua Achebe changed our reading of the novel forever when he pointed out how its rendering of *black* Africa is flawed and jejune). It is Jane Austen's contamination with the values of a conservative gentry class that makes her penetration of its economics and its finely nuanced social structure so coolly dissecting.

James's *The Princess Casamassima* (1885) offered one kind of answer to the 'economic' question. It reads very much as a novel exacted by conscience, produced under the pressure of the consciousness of suffering. James had seen the 'ragged slum children in London parks', gin mills, prostitutes, an old woman 'lying prone in a puddle of whiskey', and he had written about them in *Portraits of Places*.[5] He had read Dickens and Balzac and Zola. To Grace Norton in 1879 he wrote in a letter about 'that great total of labour and poverty on whose enormous base all the luxury and leisure of English country houses are built up'.[6] In *The Princess Casamassima* the pressure of that consciousness of suffering, that 'conscience', is both the source and the explicit subject of the novel. Hyacinth is destroyed because he cannot either silence his conscientious awareness *or* believe in a revolutionary solution to the inequity he sees. The argument of the novel, in the end, is apologetic for that impasse, presents it virtually as a tragic dialectic; Hyacinth cannot imagine the things that make life worth living without the social inequities which make their production possible (the revolutionist 'would cut up the ceilings of the Veronese in strips, so that everyone might have a little piece', 353).

The argument cannot silence, but *appeases* conscience; Hyacinth's death is a sacrifice to the unanswerable. And the argument is made too transparently – too glibly – in the novel to give it the mass and weight it requires to really drag the bottom of this social structure, which depends on 'the immense disparity, the difference and contrast, from class to class, of every instant and every motion'.[7] Not only does Hyacinth literally move too easily between these immense disparities, camouflaged rather improbably in smart circles by his 'air of aristocracy'; more importantly, the language of the novel itself fails to create for us the reality of disjunction. It *describes* irreconcilables and abysses of difference between classes but does not enact them. It seems rather by associating them in the seamlessness of its realist narrative to conjoin them in a mild irony.

The Princess Casamassima is (in Benjamin's phrase) 'devotedly ready to receive a confession' from its age. But the confession is too murky and ingrown a secret to yield itself up to the lucidity, the keen conscientiousness, of this prose of James's middle period.[8] That confession can only be bestowed at the end of a process analogous to (and in fact inseparable from) the one we have traced through the preceding chapters, where the progressive opacity and ingrowing irony of his prose have won James an independence from the proprieties and pieties of the English-language novel tradition. Those social structures which in the early and middle periods of his writing may be sometimes criticised head-on but none the less feel implicit in and essentially coextensive with his fictional worlds, seem to come alive with a new menace in the late Jamesian imagination. They loom immense, mobile, devouring.

Of the late novels, *The Wings of the Dove* (1902) is the one most manifestly interested in social class.[9] It is characteristic of *The Wings of the Dove* that at significant moments in its narrative individual consciousness tends to spill over the usual constraints of class and perceive a world outside itself. Where Milly pauses in Regents Park on her way home from the interview with her doctor, she shares the park with 'smutty sheep' and 'idle lads at games of ball'. In Venice on the day he sees Lord Mark Merton brushes shoulders with 'brown men with hats askew'. Kate watching from the balcony of Milly's hotel room sees 'a small public house, in front of which a fagged cab-horse was thrown into relief'. Kate and Merton fall in love, more or less, on the Underground, exchanging smiles and looks until they finally get seats, having to wait for this passenger and that to leave the train. When Merton walks Kate home they are 'for all the world, she said to herself, like the housemaid giggling to the baker'(40). Those moments of touch across class are small things in themselves; but they are significantly telling in this novel where Chirk Street (with its crumpled table-cloth, scraped dishes, and lingering odour of boiled food), or Leonard Croy's lodging house (with its slippery and sticky upholstery), are always just around the corner.

The Wings of the Dove contrasts, in this respect, with *The Golden Bowl*, where the hermetic seal of class and wealth is part of the subject of the novel. Those ranks of servants who attend the Prince and Princess from their carriage after their dinner engagements are never looked at (they are livery glimpsed out of the corner of an eye), let alone named. One might well read the houses in Portland Place and Eaton Square as filled with the servants' rustle, and intimacy in the novel as at every point shaped and constrained by the servants' omnipresence; yet the only subjects from outside a privileged élite ever pulled into actual focus or given voice in the novel are the two Jewish antique dealers in Brighton and Bloomsbury. Neither of these encounters suggests any breaking of the seal: on the contrary, the suggestions are all of the dealers' expertise and insight in ministering, almost sacerdotally, to the initiations of wealth and privilege. Their Jewishness makes their class ambivalent in the novel in any case; makes that latitude in which they are at once shopkeepers *and* the guardians of sophisticated mysteries.[10]

Chirk Street and the lodging house in *Wings of the Dove* may be what Kate dreads, and what makes her not so much *want* Milly's money as desperately *need* it: but they are certainly not part of an undifferentiated class-mass that is everything outside the closed doors of Lancaster Gate. The social structure represented in the novel consists of innumerable minute and precise differentiations.[11] (And of course the doors of Lancaster Gate are by no means the last doors in the novel's long vista of social hierarchy; Mrs Lowder – for example – cannot get her invitation for Matcham until Lord Mark chooses to manage it for her.) Mrs Condrip has a governess for her children, although only an Irish one (presumably cheaper), who cannot keep much control. Mrs Condrip does not wash up; but she sits at an uncleared table.

Mrs Condrip's status, of gentility pressed and threatened at every turn, haunted by the possibility of sliding into the abyss of exclusion which is all gentility can imagine below a certain social marker, is one James finds particularly rich for his representation of a finely stratified, striving, competitive, mobile social structure. The governess in 'The Turn of the Screw' is fraught with a similar status anxiety (we remember how she ignores and mistrusts and never names any servants below the housekeeper). The telegraph operator in 'In the Cage' guards her superiority to her co-workers fiercely and in suffering inside the cage of family memories of 'better times'. In 'Brooksmith' the intelligent butler cannot reconcile his servant status with the fatal taste he has had of the privilege of 'good conversation'; the story makes vivid the uncomfortable inadequacy of 'good conversation' in the face of the brute facts of the man's social exclusion. In 'The Bench of Desolation' Herbert Dodd comes to recognise the disastrous mistake he has made in preferring the signs of Nan's refinement and ladylikeness and taste (her 'natural elegance stamped on her as by a die . . . her dim and disinherited individual refinement of grace', her inability to 'abide vulgarity') to the signs of Kate's passionate and purposeful pragmatism (*Complete Tales* XII, 379).

It is in 'The Bench of Desolation' (1910) that James seems to shape most explicitly a suggestion which hovers in all these later stories, that actually the touch of that great world lying outside the boundary markers of the refined and the superior – outside the closed doors of 'good society' – is a healing touch. Brushing shoulders with Venetians in brown jackets, sharing a space of repose with those 'scattered, melancholy comrades – some of them so melancholy as to be down on their stomachs in the grass' (166) as Milly does in Regent's Park (and she deliberately sits on the common bench, eschewing the chair she would have to pay for and that would mark her apart from those 'comrades', as superior and privileged); these feel like moments of release from a class consciousness which excludes *both ways*. James has Strether imagine Mme de Vionnet weeping for Chad 'like any shopgirl weeping for her lover' (483), just as Kate and Merton are like the housemaid and the baker; the sharp particular angst of leisure-class *amours* opens up onto a commonality of experience which soothes and ironises at once. After all, nothing is so special under the sun. 'Their box, their great common anxiety, what was it, in this grim breathing space, but the practical question of life?'(163).

In 'In the Cage' (1898), James's representation of class values is richly ambivalent. The telegraphist herself, fatally infected with those intimations of 'superiority' which make her rage and suffer in her straitened circumstances, is no mere dupe of them. Her rage is not only at her 'inferiors', it is at a whole system based on inequitable accidents of distribution:

What twisted the knife in her vitals was the way the profligate rich scattered about them, in extravagant chatter over their extravagant pleasures and sins, an amount of money that would have held the stricken household of her frightened childhood, her poor pinched mother and tormented father and lost brother and starved sister, together for a lifetime. (153)

She sees and judges the inequity at the foundations of the system, but that cannot liberate her from recreating in her imagination and longings the very discriminations of taste and style through which the system perpetuates itself: the young telegraphist is ground inside this contradiction. It is something like the same contradiction as Hyacinth's in *The Princess Casamassima*, when he fears that a redress of the social inequity from which he has suffered will make impossible the art whose exclusivity he has loved (Veronese will have to be cut into strips). But in the girl's imagination the contradiction is realised much more opaquely and densely. It is the *same* passion of desire for the touch of superior possibilities which is also a passion of resentment at her exclusion, and it wrings her and wraps her up in the dark subjectivity of her imaginings; Hyacinth, by contrast, is capable of lucid companionships and free movements between the terms of his contradiction.

The metaphor around which the whole story is constructed, the girl's situation as the copyist and transmitter (her office does not *receive* telegrams) of messages and meanings she cannot actually participate in or alter, is fundamental to James's insight into how a class culture based on separation and exclusion perpetuates itself in imagination. The telegraphist is the sensitised receptor at the very point at which closed class-languages cross; she picks up the language of the extravagant telegram-senders whose 'much loves' and 'awful regrets' 'cost the price of a new pair of boots' (153); she also picks up the language of a Mr Mudge, whose reading of aristocratic extravagance in terms of petit bourgeois profit is as seamlessly untroubled, complete unto itself, as is the aristocratic unconsciousness of him. They are there for his profit just as he is there for their pickles and hams. But painfully, and unlike either Mr Mudge or his customers, the telegraphist can see both ways.

What she sees is not Mr Mudge's best of all possible smoothly synthesised social systems:

He couldn't have formulated his theory of the matter, but the exuberance of the aristocracy was the advantage of trade, and everything was knit together in a richness of pattern that it was good to follow with one's fingertips. (171)

She sees that the apparent equivalence of convenience between the grocer and the customer is not a real equivalence at all. 'Real justice was not of this world, yet, strangely, happiness was' (174). The difference in opportunities for happiness between those employed long hours in tedious work and those privileged leisured beings for whose pleasures the employed ones are merely instrumental, are vividly actual, factual, for this girl 'in whom the sense of the race for life was always acute' (160). When Lady Bradeen is contemptuous of the little corner where the customers have to write out their telegrams, the girl is in the same moment of recognition able both to be in sympathy with the discrimination and all the personal taste and refinement of sensibility it represents; *and* to see as Lady Bradeen cannot see the irony of her unquestioning assumption of her right – her right to pleasantness, to convenience, to *what she wants*. The girl knows – no-one could know better – that one might, after all, have all that discrimination and all that sensibility (and all that want) and yet discover there is no *right* at all. One might in fact, however one's taste and sensibility revolted, even have to spend a lifetime in a smaller and nastier space than the one Lady Bradeen is disgusted at having to use for a few minutes.

This real pain of social exclusion is passionate in the story; it drives that apprehension of injustice into consciousness much more cruelly than even conscience, even social responsibility, could drive it. (That is why the telegraphist's suffering is so much more intensely felt, intensely created, than Hyacinth's; his feels so much more like an *idea*.) It is because she feels in her own want the reality of the advantage of privilege that the girl understands its arbitrary inequitable basis. In the summer season the telegrams she has to send are full of names – Eastbourne, Folkestone, Cromer, Scarborough, Whitby – which torment her 'with something of the sound of the plash of water that haunts the traveller in the desert':

> She had not been out of London in a dozen years, and the only thing to give a taste to the present dead weeks was the spice of a chronic resentment. The sparse customers, the people she did see, were the people who were 'just off' – off on the decks of fluttered yachts, off to the uttermost point of rocky headlands where the very breeze was playing for the want of which she said to herself that she sickened. (183)

The power of the idea of an aristocratic 'superiority' builds upon the girl's unfulfilment; her dreams feed off her hunger and her hunger feeds off her dreams in a spiralling drama of intense interior awareness. It is interesting that in this story James has under his pen a material so close to the material of *Madame Bovary*; and that he treats it so significantly differently. The narrative perception, to begin with, is sited very differently in James's story. Flaubert's perception of Emma's want and of Emma's dreams is remote; the whole length of intelligence and self-consciousness yawns between the author and the character. Emma's story would sound quite differently, presumably, if she told it herself; presumably it would sound like one of those novels she reads.

In 'In the Cage' the narrative is intricately, inextricably meshed with the self-awareness of the girl; not because she is exceptional (she is not Flaubert) but because James's instinct is that whatever story there is in these dreams and this unfulfilment it is in the girl's own consciousness of it as story and dilemma. He never tries in his stories of petit bourgeois struggle for an imitation of class 'colour' or accent (there is nothing unfortunate like Katherine Mansfield's 'The Lady's Maid', say, or Septimus Smith in *Mrs Dalloway*, or the pub voices in *The Waste Land*).[12] But he lends his own complex opaque expression to the girl's complexity, rendering a state of fantasising need that is nothing like Emma Bovary's delusion, because it is so charged with sharp recognition of its own precariousness, and its fatality:

But she forbore as yet to speak; she had not spoken even to Mrs Jordan; and the hush that on her lips surrounded the Captain's name maintained itself as a kind of symbol of the success that, up to this time, had attended something or other – she couldn't have said what – that she humoured herself with calling, without words, her relation with him. (172)

The 'relation', in her own mind, defines itself through a series of with-holdings and negations. It exists, almost, because it does not exist; she protects the possibility of dreaming it by never naming it, not to anyone, not even, in words, to herself. Once named, the 'relation' would have to appear for the absurdity it is. The withholding his name in itself eroticises it; she surrounds his name with her lips but does not let it out. But the tenderness with which she protects the 'relation' also more or less ac-knowledges its extreme vulnerability; she can allow herself to surround it with consciousness just because she understands that she is 'humouring herself', cheating, practising a sleight of imagination, turning a nothing, by surrounding it with desire, into a something.

She would have admitted indeed that it consisted of little more than the fact that his absences, however frequent and however long, always ended with his turning up again. It was nobody's business in the world but her own if that fact continued to be enough for her. It was of course not enough just in itself; what it had taken on to make it so was the extraordinary possession of the elements of his life that memory and attention had at last given her. There came a day when this possession, on the girl's part, actually seemed to enjoy, between them, while their eyes met, a tacit recognition that was half a joke and half a deep solemnity. He bade her good morning always now; he quite often raised his hat to her. He passed a remark when there was time or room, and once she went so far as to say to him that she had not seen him for 'ages'. 'Ages' was the word she consciously and carefully, though a trifle tremulously, used; 'ages' was exactly what she meant. To this he replied in terms doubtless less anxiously selected, but perhaps on that account not the less remarkable, 'Oh yes, hasn't it been awfully wet?' That was a specimen of their give and take; it fed her fancy that no form of intercourse so transcendent and distilled had ever been established on earth. Everything, so far as they chose to consider it so, might mean almost anything. The want of margin in the cage, when he peeped through the bars, wholly ceased to be appreciable. It was a drawback only in superficial commerce. With Captain Everard she had simply the margin of the universe. (172)

This is a passage of absurd disproportions; between the minuteness of their real relations and the hugeness of the imaginative power they have for the girl; between the banality of their exchanges and the meaning she compresses into and reads out of them. There are two different experiential scales on which their moments of contact can be read; one in which the power of imagination and desire is so vast it delivers her momentarily, out of such insignificances, into the universe; another in which her very gesture of repletion ('the want of margin in her cage, when he peeped through the bars, wholly ceased to be appreciable') actually underscores for us the extreme of her constraint, reminds us of those bars and of that cage.

The real complexity in the passage is the problem of just how much of the consciousness of that disproportion, that experiential instability, is the telegraphist's own. Is she deluding herself that her fantasy of desire is reciprocal, in the real world of possibilities? Or is it in *her* consciousness that the perpetual play of irony indulges and exaggerates what it also undercuts and exposes? It seems likely that the clue is in the passage; the game is 'half a joke and half a deep solemnity'. Her imagination dances on a razor's edge between delusion and mockery. The Captain's comment on the weather both is (because it takes her breath away) and, hilariously, is not, 'remarkable', and she can sustain both those truths in the air at once. She knows the 'relation' is a nonsense in the very same moments that she is creating it as a reality. She never loses hold of the fact that the Captain 'was in love with a woman to whom . . . a lady-telegraphist, and especially one who passed a life among hams and cheeses, was as the sand on the floor' (174). But what she builds upon these insurmountables is a fragile fantastic structure of nuance upon nuance, intimation upon intimation, inference upon inference; it takes up no space in the real world, it exists only fluidly in the interstices between the solidities of real life and between the immense disparities 'from class to class, of every instant and every motion' (153).

Her dream creates and fills a fantastic classless uncomplicated now-here, a nowhere where their relations can be at once eroticised *and* innocent. It is a nowhere whose impossibility makes it resemble those novels the girl has filled her head with, and she knows it; the very language in which she imagines it touches so closely and playfully on pastiche:

He was in love with a woman to whom . . . a lady-telegraphist . . . was as the sand on the floor; and what her dreams desired was the possibility of its somehow coming to him that her own interest in him could take a pure and noble account of such an infatuation and even of such an impropriety. (174)

Not only the 'pure and noble' but the very syntax makes fun there; the girl as good as acknowledges the far-fetchedness of her fantasising in that cumulative twisting convolution which is characteristic of the story.

It bears a family resemblance, naturally, to any late Jamesian elaboration; but there is a disingenuous piling up of improbability on improbability with an appearance of artlessness which seems particularly telling here. (It is very unlike, for instance, the prose of 'The Turn of the Screw', with its different disingenuousness.)

They would never perhaps have grown half so intimate if he had not, by the blessing of heaven, formed some of his letters with a queerness – ! It was positive that the queerness could scarce have been greater if he had practised it for the very purpose of bringing their heads together over it as far as was possible to heads on different sides of a cage. It had taken her in reality but once or twice to master these tricks, but, at the cost of striking him perhaps as stupid, she could still challenge them when circumstances favoured. The great circumstance that favoured was that she sometimes actually believed he knew she only feigned perplexity. If he knew it, therefore, he tolerated it; if he tolerated it he came back; and if he came back he liked her. This was her seventh heaven. (175)

'She sometimes actually believed he knew she only feigned perplexity': the attenuated reasoning stretches syntax just as the hope strains probability. 'The queerness could scarce have been greater if he had practised it for the very purpose of bringing their heads together over it': the sweet possibility is kept at a tentative distance by that implicit negative ('but of course he *hadn't* practised it, for any purpose at all') whose irony hovers, unprecipitated. This is a reasoning tense with awareness of its own factitiousness.

The telegraphist is no louche fantasist addicted to her wish fulfilments. She dreams with rigour, sustaining impossible possibilities through the ingenious devices of her double thinking; and a sort of critical scrupulousness makes all her dreams stop short of actual fulfilments. Or rather, whenever they approach fulfilment, a fierce mocking realism intervenes, insisting upon raising the dark spectres of the only *real* relations possible, within this class system, between a man like Captain Everard and a girl like her. When she imagines confronting him with all she 'knows' about him, from somewhere a sordid picture distorted with ugly motives and sinister exchanges imposes itself even on her fantasy:

She quite thrilled herself with thinking what, with such a lot of material, a bad girl would do. It would be a scene better than many in her ha'penny novels, this going to him in the dusk of evening at Park Chambers and letting him at last have it. 'I know too much about a certain person now not to put it to you – excuse my being so lurid – that it's quite worth your while to buy me off. Come, therefore; buy me!' There was a point indeed at which such flights had to drop again – the point of unreadiness to name, when it came to that, the purchasing medium. It wouldn't, certainly, be anything so gross as money, and the matter accordingly remained rather vague, all the more that *she* was not a bad girl. (176)

Of course this is also the implicit acknowledgement of that part of her which *is* a bad girl. The 'thrill', the dusk, the unaccustomed fierce commanding language: these are the frank acknowledgements of hungers, of potential other selves. Then there is the daring of the hint that fantasy opaquely circles: if the purchasing medium is not going to be money, what is it to be then? But a great deal of the relish – and the conscious comedy – is in the sheer incongruous impossibility of the scene. She *knows herself*, how careful she is, and decent; even if she also knows she has it in her to at least *imagine* behaving differently, imagine talking the language, in a context crackling with sexual electricity, not of 'love', but of buying and selling.

The danger is a thrill, a glimpsed temptation. She dreads the dénouement of her fantasies, but also desires it; and it is essential to James's story that to a certain extent she gets it, her chance and her opportunity and her recognition, in the real world. There is another possible story, a poignantly ironic one, in which what we finally learn is how completely oblivious Captain Everard is to all the girl's dreams: he probably does not even recognise her, out of her cage. In that story the girl is a deluded fool. But instead, in James's story, the man and the girl really do talk, she really moves him, he really is drawn; the story asserts the power of imagination and dream to produce real, surprising, improbable effects in the real world. In *Madame Bovary* Emma's fantasies certainly produce real effects. But there remains a separation – a separation of delusion – between those effects and what Emma thinks they are; whereas in 'In the Cage' the telegraphist sustains even into the heady interview in the park with the Captain her own scrupulous realism, sustains her poise on that razor's edge between believing too much or believing nothing at all.

In the dusky park the girl has momentarily made the impossible thing happen, made real the impossible classless space in which she can speak to the Captain as an equal, and as if there really was a 'relation'. For a moment there *is* a relation. The man, here, is not simply the repository of her fantasies; we make out (and she does) through all the penumbra of her idea of him, and of his beauty and of the charming casual good manners of his class, a real attention to her; he is astonished at this little working girl suddenly so sharply in focus, and rather bewildered as to whether she is offering herself to him or not. His gentlemanly tact is at full stretch as he takes his lead from her; may he hold her hand? ask her to supper?

What, in it all, was visibly clear for him, none the less, was that he was tremendously glad he had met her. She held him, and he was astonished at the force of it; he was intent, immensely considerate. His elbow was on the back of the seat, and his head, with the pot-hat pushed quite back, in a boyish way, so that she really saw almost for the first time his forehead and hair, rested on the hand into which he had crumpled his gloves. 'Yes,' he assented, 'it's not a bit horrid or vulgar.' (193)

And she persists in her impossible juggling. She holds off the possibility of a 'relation' with him with the one hand, because it can only be one kind of relation: she sees and does not see the couples entwined in the dusk on the benches all around them. She invites it with the other, taking in a rush all the privileges of womanliness she knows about from the novels and from the telegrams; the tears, the touches, the dignities, the evasions.

She is almost too much for him: he means it when he says she is 'cleverer'. She is cleverer, he is thinking, than Lady Bradeen, but he is thinking that she is cleverer than him too; and of course that irony underpins all the complex power structures in the scene. She is cleverer, brighter, stronger than him, the scene is all hers, controlled by her initiative, her imagination, her intelligence; he is the comparative helpless spectator, or rather the *object*, of it all. And yet, because he is a man and even more because he is a *gentleman*, she is also powerless beside him, powerless to project anything forward out of this moment save one of those two polarities available to her, to them, in the real daylight world outside the impossible space. She can have him, and lose herself, and become at the same instant his lover and abjectly his social inferior – it is a touch away, and very tempting, and one afternoon weeks later she comes boldly close to abandoning everything for the sake of that touch. Or she can lose him, and preserve herself, in the 'time-honoured' gesture of renunciation which will close forever the impossible space her imagination has opened. The dilemma does not depend on any nineteenth-century moralising of the sexual act. It has to do with social control and the impossibility of separating sexual relations out from the nexus of political and class relations within which they occur.

The essential of the scene is that she has him *at a loss*; for as long as she holds open the impossible space for them and he has the good taste not to spoil it, we can glimpse the possibility that the social structure which holds them apart is as constraining and as limiting for him as for her. We glimpse, as it were, the *pain* of the whole experience of social class. The Captain is momentarily bereft of his privileged status – that privilege which has so completely wrapped him up again by the time he comes to Cocker's desperate to recover the compromising telegram. (He hardly sees the girl, then, as she saves him.) But in the park we do – just – seem to hear from the Captain those strains of class identity, that pressure of class performance, which would find their solace in the cross-class (out of class) 'relation' that momentarily seems a possibility. Lady Bradeen is exacting, their affair is fraught, he needs 'help', he is in 'danger'. There are things he 'can't' do. There are hungers *on the other side of privilege* for release, escape; the very world of those telegraphed indulgences the girl has so envied suddenly looms as the tangle it also has to be. The girl, so utterly out of that world, with her passionate desire to serve his privilege ('We must manage it for you somehow', 195) and soothe his complications ('I believe you like it – my always being there and our taking things up so familiarly and successfully', 195), cannot but seem an attractive possibility.

Such cross-class sexual relationships are everywhere, of course, in nineteenth-century European literature (perhaps less obviously apparent in the more 'proper' English tradition); like the dark undergrowth of a socio-sexual reality out of which the tall trees of the great leisure-class love stories flourish. It feels as though Thomas Mann is writing the very archetype itself in *Buddenbrooks*, in his poignant treatment of the affair between Thomas Buddenbrook and the flower-girl in Fisher's Lane. Nadine Gordimer updates the tradition, while gesturing to its European origins, in transposing it to twentieth-century South Africa and making it an issue of race as well, in her story 'Town and Country Lovers'.[3]

If 'In the Cage' is different from *Madame Bovary* in its sympathetic, interior treatment of female fantasy, and in its granting to the telegraphist herself her own grasp on her own delusion, it is also worth noting another quality in the story which marks it out decisively as belonging to the English rather than the French literary tradition. The treatment of Mr Mudge the grocer is surely tender and respectful in a way that would have been incompatible with that French anti-bourgeois presumption which James often takes issue with, here in an essay on Balzac:

it is impossible to believe that a chronicler with a scent a little less rabidly suspicious of Philistinism would not have shown us this field in a somewhat rosier light. Like all French artists and men of letters, Balzac hated the bourgeoisie with an immitigable hatred.[14]

Mr Mudge is not simply the ludicrous foil to the Captain's desirability; neither, in the end, is the girl's option simply a discrimination in favour of Mr Mudge's safety over the Captain's glamour, although it is that too. The 'immense disparity, the difference and contrast, from class to class, of every instant and every motion' (153), to be rendered with justice, will exact a relativity of treatment which will make Mr Mudge and the Captain *both* men, both representative of certain utterly different possibilities, both authoritatively, as it were, *themselves.* The telegraphist herself is a practised relativist; she actually does not have a position, she simply moves somewhere on the axis between those aristocratic values she loves and condemns (exuberant, profane, prodigal, improper, greedy) and those petit-bourgeois ones which are her refuge from poverty and inconsequence (non-conformist, materialist, decent, thrifty, continent).

No amount of sympathetic reading can find in Mr Mudge the power to move the girl's imagination that the Captain has. This is not personal, it belongs to the accident of the Captain's beauty and (much more) to all that heady perfume of leisure and pleasure and style and manner that drifts after the fact of his arbitrary privilege. And she will never have her chance to 'let down her hair' for any man's appreciation; we glimpse a longed-for fulfilment in that touching dreamy moment of self-display when she gestures Lady Bradeen's beauty to Mrs Jordan (233). Such a gesture, such a self-display, could never be for Mr Mudge. But there are places within the story where James makes us feel the telling weight of other possibilities, other ways of seeing than the Captain's, and other ways of seeing the Captain than the girl's. Mr Mudge casually calls Captain Everard a 'cad', and we're sure he might well be, given half a chance, a cad. Mr Mudge is numbingly unimaginative and predictable, but capable of suddenly surprising with an act of dignity, as when he saves his marriage proposal until the end of the holiday. His 'serenity of possession' is *and* is not, at once, what the girl wants. She needs *and* needles at his unshakeable confidence in her. The Captain is beautiful, but it is Mr Mudge who is willing to have her mother to live with them; and his generosity in that associates in her mind with the episode where he showed her another kind of manliness, putting out the drunken sailor from the shop.

In the final sentences of the story, we are made to wonder with the watching policeman for a moment whether the disappointed telegraphist is going to throw herself into the river: a gesture out of the vocabulary of ha'penny novels (and out of the same repertoire as 'bad girls' making their way alone to gentlemen's rooms). Then the story reproaches us for our suspicion. She was not thinking about any such thing. There would have been something tawdry – and, perhaps more important, something *second-hand* – about such a gesture. It would belong (the last words of the story place it there) rather with the choices of Mrs Jordan and Mr Drake, who, as servants, inhabit apologetically the hand-me-down refinements and gentilities of their masters and mistresses, than with the choices of the future wife of Mr Mudge, she who possesses with a sturdiness that truth of Milly Theale's, that she 'would live if she could' (163).

It might be interesting to think about the telegraphist's relationship with the world of 'superior' leisure-class *moeurs* in terms of a Girardian mimetic rivalry. The telegraphist learns to desire Captain Everard because the 'model' she both emulates and envies (Lady Bradeen) desires him, or perhaps – just as Girardian – because the heroines she reads about in her romances would desire him. She desires *him* because she wants to *be* them. In Girard's words:

The hero in the grip of some second-hand desire seeks to conquer the *being*, the essence, of his model by as faithful an imitation as possible. If the hero lived in the same world as the model instead of being distanced from him by myth or by history . . . he would necessarily come to desire the same object. The nearer the mediator, the more does the veneration that he inspires give way to hate and rivalry.[15]

What this suggestion opens up are two interesting ways of exploring the Girardian model of desire further. First, it is certainly worth thinking about class systems as perpetuating themselves within culture through Girardian mechanisms of imitative desire; and James's *oeuvre* offers all sorts of insights into the workings of such a social dynamic. Secondly, it is also worth thinking about how such a model might interact specifically with systems of imagining gender; how especially prone to sublimating rivalry into desire women might be. A Girardian reading might suggest that what the telegraphist really wants is power, is freedom. By a Girardian transference she ends up wanting Captain Everard; she comes in fact very close to ruining herself (losing her real self) through

mistaking him for the object of her desire. Is there something represen-
tatively feminine in this predicament? In terms of that great underworld
of transgressive cross-class sexual relationships which the telegraphist
feels herself approaching so scorchingly close to in the story, the pattern
certainly seems full of suggestion.

Can a Girardian reading help uncover patterns of intention in James's
late novels, in *Wings of the Dove* in particular, which stress his interest in class
division, social exclusion and the consequences of class in culture and in
consciousness? Such a reading of the late novels would be consistent with
an impression that those stories of the late nineties and the new century
which have petit-bourgeois protagonists are not by any means marginalia
in the *oeuvre*. They seem to represent on the contrary a significant part
of a whole enterprise of perception of class and of the mysteries of social
order, its rituals, its taboos, its sacrificial secrets. In attempting to read
James's late writing as such an enterprise, we would be addressing that
essential question raised by Alfred Habegger in *Henry James and the 'Woman
Business'*: is James in the late novels, as Habegger believes, 'engaged in
defending the costs the civilised order exacts' (235), or is he engaged
rather in *describing* those costs? It is a very Girardian distinction: Girard
writes – not *à propos* of James – that 'in the first case the obsession masters
the works, in the second the work masters the obsession'.[16]

A reading of *The Wings of the Dove* which *did* interpret it as *defending* the
costs the civilised order exacts would tend, following Girard, to scapegoat
one of the girls in this novel conveniently provided with two heroines; we
would expect a narrative closure in the expulsion of that scapegoat into
the desert, charged with all the sins of the social order, thereby purging
and renewing the collective (the 'civilisation') left behind. We can see why
Habegger suspects James of this purging through narrative closure. It is
true that at the end of all three of the late novels someone is abandoned,
rejected, or taken off to American City; and it is significant that every
time that 'scapegoat' is female.

But *The Wings of the Dove* has two heroines, and complicatingly both of
them are in a sense cast out at the end of the novel: Milly dies, and Kate
loses Merton. Readings of the novel have tended to scapegoat one or the
other of them; either, straightforwardly, accusing Kate of corruption and
delusion and vindicating Milly, or (sometimes reading 'against' James,
as Leavis did) finding Milly insufferable and at least indirectly guilty of
spoiling the more 'authentic' life of Kate and Merton. But there have of
course also been readings which have registered the real importance for
James's fiction of the difficulty in deciding between them, notably Oliver

Elton's insightful appreciation in 1903:

And – chief alteration of all – the sympathies are entangled with both sides. The puritan dualism, so to call it, of the older books is greatly blunted; and the artist, borne along by his own discoveries, comes to bend his intensest and finest light upon the arch-conspirator, who nearly supplants the intended victim in tragic and intellectual interest.[17]

Elton reads the conflict between the girls as a 'conflict between the world and the spirit' which ends 'drawn'. Building on the suggestion that James is working through and beyond a 'puritan dualism' in the novel, we may be able to uncover the extent to which the novel is in fact also *about* that dualism, about the process which establishes the rivalry which locks the girls in competition.

Of course *The Wings of the Dove* is by no means the first English novel which has two 'heroines'. Milly and Kate are created out of a stock of such contrasting pairs: Fanny and Mary, Emma and Jane, Hetty and Dinah, Becky and Amelia, Maggie and Lucy. A distinct pattern emerges; one girl is dark and one fair, one vivacious and one compliant, one dangerous and one 'good'. They are often friends; but their relationship is vitiated by an uneasy apprehension on one side at least that they will somehow do one another harm. Fanny Price finds Mary Crawford 'careless as a woman and a friend'. There is no acceptable mould into which their 'competition' can be cast, as there might be if they were young men; it is not a part of the apparatus and expectation of femininity that girls should even playfully spar together. Therefore their concealed competition – their sense, often, that one has what the other wants – is dissimulated under all the appearances of a feminine cosy communion, the innocent sharing of shopping and confidences. But this in turn makes the anticipated betrayal loom all the more oppressively (we remember those last sour days of Maggie's in Lucy's house before she elopes with Stephen, or Emma's miserable consciousness of the cheating games she has played with Jane Fairfax).

The early days of Kate's and Milly's friendship are full of just such concealments and suppressions:

Milly's range was thus immense; she had to ask nobody for anything, to refer nothing to anyone; her freedom, her fortune and her fancy were the law; an obsequious world surrounded her, she could sniff up at every step its fumes. And Kate, in these days, was altogether in the phase of forgiving her such bliss; in the phase, moreover, of believing that, should they continue to go on together, she would abide in that generosity. She had, at such a point as this, no suspicion of a rift within the lute. (116)

Susan Shepherd at least bored [Kate] – that was plain; this young woman saw nothing in her – nothing to account for anything, not even for Milly's own indulgence: which little fact became in turn to the latter's mind a fact of significance. It was a light on the handsome girl – representing more than merely showed – that poor Susan was simply as nought to her. This was, in a manner too, a general admonition to poor Susie's companion, who seemed to see marked by it the direction in which she had best most look out. It just faintly rankled in her that a person who was good enough and to spare for Milly Theale shouldn't be good enough for another girl. (120)

The two girls – and through them the two archetypes, dark and light, of tradition – are distinctive even in their mode of apprehending the 'rift within the lute' of their communion. Kate is chaffing and attacking, naming the worst to herself in her robust elastic ironies: how generous it is in her to forgive Milly her wealth! One might so easily have been jealous, unforgiving: except that finally one is at least intelligent enough to laugh! The passage rings with that arrogance of health and beauty whose acute survival instincts pick up even at this early stage something 'wrong' in Milly, some vulnerability that makes Kate sure that in spite of everything she would not want to 'change places, to change even chances' with her (116). At this stage of course one does not know – Kate does not know – whether the upshot of that quick intuition will be sympathetic-protective or exploitative. Perhaps it disturbs us that the intuition of vulnerability helps Kate with the 'forgiving' of everything else.

Milly's apprehensions feel quite different. They loom out of a white mist of hopeful anticipations and thinking the best of everyone. Her doubts are involuntary and reluctant, rather than embraced, like Kate's, on principle and in anticipation of the worst. Sharp and dark objects emerge from out of the mist and Milly winces, but concentrates on them, takes them slowly privately in, drinks down whatever bitterness they have in them as if she is used to taking medicines because they will be 'good for her'. 'It rankles' with her that Susan is not good enough for Kate; but she dwells on it long enough to come round to understanding it as something more to appreciate in her; 'the handsome girl was, with twenty other splendid qualities, the least bit brutal too, and didn't she suggest, as no one yet had ever done for her new friend, that there might be a wild beauty in that, and even a strange grace?' (120).

The pattern is established between them. Kate with her instincts for what she can 'use' has fastened on to Milly's weakness and can be kind to her because of it. Milly has already learned to fear a 'brutality' in Kate, and yet admires her because of it. And while Kate has not noticed that Milly has noticed anything, Milly, for all she is less 'clever', has more 'consciousness': she actually knows what is missing from Kate's conversation (Merton Densher), while Kate does not know that Milly is aware. James wraps up this whole nexus of relationship with its inequities (Kate's health, Milly's wealth), its needs, its dissimulations, in a striking image:

> Milly was the wandering princess: so what could be more in harmony now than to see the princess waited upon at the city gate by the worthiest maiden, the chosen daughter of the burgesses? It was the real again, evidently, the amusement of the meeting for the princess too; princesses living for the most part, in such an appeased way, on the plane of merely elegant representation. That was why they pounced, at city gates, on deputed flower-strewing damsels; that was why, after effigies, processions, and other stately games, frank human company was pleasant to them. (113)

It is Susan's image: and superficially it has Susan's innocence, as well as her 'Boston quaintness'. But it has a resonance beyond what Susan thinks she means by it. To begin with, it defines the girls and their relationship in terms of social function and status. Milly is the 'princess' with its aristocratic implications of unearned privilege, its greatness that is innate, 'in the blood', genealogical. Kate is the representative of the burgesses whose sphere is probably in some sense inferior but certainly *separate*: that is, the city they welcome the princess to is theirs, independent of her. Presumably the welcome is a kind of permission as well as a courtesy. The importance of the burgesses, we presume (and of their daughters), rests rather upon bricks and mortar, on the solidities of material accumulation through effort, than on genealogy. Although we note that the burgesses' daughters do the strewing, there is the implication of an equality in separateness, a fittingness to the companionship.

What this clearly *cannot* represent is any sociological or historical reality in the novel: if anything, English Kate is more likely to have aristocratic 'blood' than Milly; Milly's princess-like fortune was amassed in a democratic America where her ancestors must at some stage have been (at best) burgesses. But here the imagery, the taxonomy of social class or caste is used as a sort of flexible transparency to be overlaid, deliberately, on incongruous material. It is the essential *process* of caste differentiation James wants us to feel here; how in custom and perception, and in naming and in language, functions of status and place are assigned to individuals, and individuals are interpreted as *representative* of particular arrangements of place, and particular forms of power. Latent in those arrangements, too, are elements of competition, of rivalry. The charming ideal form of the flower-strewing welcome is surely a civilised, *feminised* replaying of an alternative possibility, where the invading noble is met at the closed gate by the burgesses' militia.

In a sense what James is drawing our conscious attention to here is that process of *making representative* which is the one that has produced, to begin with, the two girls set up in opposition (dark and fair) within the patterning of the novel. It is a process we see continually at work on both Kate and Milly. Kate is required to represent the female object of desire, and this responsibility is far from being a passive one. She 'earns' her role, her value, at Lancaster Gate by a constant, conscious effort:

This was the story that she was always, for her beneficent dragon, under arms; living up, every hour, but especially at festal hours, to the 'value' Mrs Lowder had attached to her. High and fixed, this estimate ruled, on each occasion, at Lancaster Gate, the social scene; so that our young man now recognised in it something like the artistic idea, the plastic substance, imposed by tradition, by genius, by criticism, in respect to a given character, on a distinguished actress. As such a person was to dress the part, to walk, to look, to speak, in every way to express, the part, so all this was what Kate was to do for the character she had undertaken, under her aunt's roof, to represent. It was made up, the character, of definite elements and touches – things all perfectly ponderable to criticism; and the way for her to meet criticism was evidently at the start to be sure her make-up was exact and that she looked at least no worse than usual. Aunt Maud's appreciation of that tonight was indeed managerial, and Kate's own contribution fairly that of the faultless soldier on parade. Densher saw himself for the moment as in his purchased stall at the play; the watchful manager was in the depths of a box and the poor actress in the glare of the footlights. But she *passed*, the poor actress – he could see how she always passed; her wig, her paint, her jewels, every mark of her expression impeccable, and her entrance accordingly greeted with the proper round of applause. (217)

Here the analogy between a social process and the processes of representation in art is explicit; beyond analogy, in fact, the two processes are really interrelated. Like an actress, Kate is really 'earning her living' by her performance; as for an actress, of course, there is élan as well as sacrifice involved in the huge effort of performing well, perhaps élan in the very exhilaration of sacrifice.

All the stress of the passage is upon the production of the female object of desire as a process in the hands of collaborating women; Merton's misery in the face of this sacrificial ritual of charm is partly at his helplessness – his irrelevance – in a procedure ostensibly intended for male audience and male gratification. He finds himself paying – and dearly – to participate in a fixed (and fundamentally commercial) ritual of female performance for male appreciation which is nothing like what he wants.[18] Both sexes are locked into models of performance and desire which may not answer to what either actually *wants*. Of course this is just Mrs Lowder's point; she insists on the fixed pattern of male connoisseurship of female performance precisely in order to assert the impossibility – the commercial unviability – of that alternative which Merton and Kate are clandestinely pursuing, outside the 'theatre'.

Mrs Lowder's collaboration with her niece in the 'production' of Kate's charm is felt ambivalently in the novel. If Kate in James's analogy is an 'actress', with all that has implied both in terms of genuine stage skills and commercial sexual availability, then Mrs Lowder is both the procuress *and* the experienced stage practitioner, past her prime, to whom the talented and promising girl is apprenticed. Mrs Lowder is genuinely looking after Kate (even to the extent eventually of collaborating in her scheme to deceive Milly) as well as realising the assets of her beauty and her intelligence. But the collaboration is constructed upon premises of a social existence whose fundamental dynamic is conflictual differentiation, perpetual rivalry for place, a 'you-win-I-lose' process of inclusion through exclusion. In a sense, the only way Mrs Lowder knows to help Kate is to use her.

James does not casually employ the analogy with the actress to express Kate's entanglement in the social process. Like Kate's thought that she and Merton are like the baker and the housemaid, or like Susan's idea that Kate represents the burgesses' daughter greeting a princess, or like Milly in the Park comparing herself to 'a poor girl' with 'her rent to pay, her rent for the future' (165), the novel characteristically borrows from a vocabulary of class differentiation to express complications of leisure-class relationships.[19] In other words, the complications of leisure-class relationships do not exist independently from the large social systems of which the leisure class are beneficiaries. Leisure-class relationships will on the contrary reproduce in their processes, in whatever complex disguises, the sacrifices and the pains, the struggles and the losses, the exclusions, on which their privilege is founded.

This is Benjamin's 'class struggle'; a struggle not only between classes, but intrinsic to the very mobile, competitive processes of class identity itself. Kate's talk to Merton, the same evening of her 'performance' at the dinner party at Lancaster Gate, reproduces these underlying structures of loss and gain both ironically *and* with relishing expertise: a mobile and pressured and ever self-reconstructing frame of social 'value' and social hierarchy based upon social exclusion:

Yet he stuck a minute to the subject. 'You scarcely call [Lord Mark], I suppose, one of the dukes.'

'Mercy, no – far from it. He's not, compared with other possibilities, 'in' it. Milly, it's true,' she said, to be exact, 'has no natural sense of social values, doesn't in the least understand our differences or know who's who or what's what.'

'I see. That,' Densher laughed, 'is her reason for liking me.'

'Precisely. She doesn't resemble me,' said Kate, 'who at least know what I lose.'

Well, it had all risen for Densher to a considerable interest. 'And Aunt Maud – why shouldn't *she* know? I mean, that your friend there isn't really anything. Does she suppose him of ducal value?'

'Scarcely; save in the sense of being uncle to a duke. That's undeniably something. He's the best moreover we can get.' (235)

She sounds very reminiscent of Mary Crawford gamely ironising her problem in falling for an Edmund who is not only younger son but even a clergyman. And just as Mary is capable, out of the same irony, of admitting how convenient it would be if the elder son died of his fever; so Merton even as he marvels at Kate's ironising grasp also experiences a pang of fear at its potential for cruelty (expressing his admiration too, perhaps only half-consciously taking his note from Kate, in terms borrowed from the language of competition and struggle and surpassing):

'No marvel Aunt Maud builds on you – except that you're much too good for what she builds *for*. Even "society" won't know how good for it you are; it's too stupid, and you're beyond it. You'd have to pull it uphill – it's you yourself who are at the top . . . '

. . . It had been, however, as if the thrill of their association itself pressed in him, as great felicities do, the sharp spring of fear. 'See here, you know: don't, *don't* . . .'

'Don't what?'

'Don't fail me. It would kill me.'

She looked at him a minute with no response but her eyes. 'So you think you'll kill *me*, in time, to prevent it?' She smiled, but he saw her the next instant as smiling through tears. (235)

In the logic of competition, every felicity must be twinned with a corresponding fear; every gain must represent a loss somewhere along the logical sequence. Of course just what they anticipate for a moment here is what *will* happen; Kate will 'fail' him; or rather, he will 'kill' her, first, so that he does not have to see it. The playful, eroticised vocabulary of violence gives covert expression to the latent antagonism in their

relationship. And, at moments like this, it is their half-articulated awareness of that antagonism which is the very material of their special sympathy, their exhilarated, appreciative hyper-consciousness of one another.

That same evening at Lancaster Gate, Merton is also the reluctant witness to another kind of performance-production than Kate's as the female object of desire: he watches the production of Milly in her absence
as a social phenomenon, a success, a 'feature of the season's end'. The
dinner guests, spurred on by Kate and Mrs Lowder, who both have their
ulterior motives, work Milly up in a way that makes both Susan, her
real friend, and Merton, reluctantly 'paying dear' for his spectator seat,
uneasy and slightly appalled:

> the young man had, by an odd impression, throughout the meal, not been wholly
> deprived of Miss Theale's participation. Mrs Lowder had made dear Milly the
> topic, and it proved, on the spot, a topic as familiar to the enthusiastic younger
> as to the sagacious older man. Any knowledge they might lack Mrs Lowder's
> niece was moreover alert to supply, while Densher himself was freely appealed to
> as the most privileged, after all, of the group. Wasn't it he who had in a manner
> invented the wonderful creature – through having seen her first, caught her in
> her native jungle? Hadn't he more or less paved the way for her by his prompt
> recognition of her rarity?
> ... What touched him most nearly was that the occasion took on some-
> how the air of a commemorative banquet, a feast to celebrate a brilliant if
> brief career. There was of course more said about the heroine than if she had
> not been absent, and he found himself rather stupefied at the range of Milly's
> triumph. Mrs Lowder had wonders to tell of it; the two wearers of the waistcoat,
> either with sincerity or with hypocrisy, professed in the matter an equal expert-
> ness; and Densher at last seemed to know himself in the presence of a social
> 'case'. (219)

Again, as with Kate's performance, we see the *women* collaborating
through their social modes – making conversation, being charming, promoting values in the social currency of talk – to produce the feminine
spectacle (this time Milly). Everyone at the dinner table is aware, more
or less consciously, more or less uncomfortably, that Milly is 'weird',
'wonderful', 'rare', 'brilliant', because she is fabulously rich. It is not
that they are lying when they eulogise her; her wealth really does transform her for them, the wealth in itself really does excite their awe, their
aesthetic appreciation, their imagination of her type. But Merton's, and
Susan's, deep unease at Milly's canonisation in this secular church recognises that there is unmistakeably a sacrificial element in the process.
Milly, absent, is being sacrificed to an idea of Milly: an idea that cannot

be separated from her 'economic aspect'. Even as they begin to produce their 'idea' of her, Merton hears in it a premonition of its end: the dinner sounds to him like 'a commemorative banquet, a feast to celebrate a brilliant if brief career'. What Milly 'represents' will be privileged far over what she 'is'; and what she represents can only end by consuming her. What she represents for this social machinery is not a stable value, but a value that is mobile, cumulative, devouring: a value defined by the others' need of her, that is, of her money. The very qualities the guests eulogise in (or *onto*) Milly put them in fact invisibly, essentially, in conflict with her.

Milly herself is very well aware of this sacrificial element in the 'representativeness' that is pressed upon her at every turn: it is one reason she is so upset when at Matcham Lord Mark shows her the Bronzino portrait. As well as her shock at mortality ('she was dead, dead, dead', 144) the shock is at the possibility that a dead, finished, beautiful *version* of oneself might end by being substituted for the sacrificed live thing.[20] Milly is in fact hyper-sensitive to other people's versions of her. She is wryly sorry she cannot be more of a Byzantine 'princess' for Susan (167). She takes on board the whole apparatus and implications of the 'dove' imagery the others invent for her with a private sceptical detachment. She half-embraces the simplifications of the role, and the shelter it seems to afford her from confrontation: the 'dove' first comes up at a moment when Kate has made her sharply afraid with one of her half-franknesses, half-confessions, as the girls talk. 'Oh, you may well loathe me yet!' Kate says. 'Why do you say such things to me?', Milly asks, and Kate replies, inspired, 'Because you're a dove'.

She met it on the instant as she would have met the revealed truth; it lighted up the strange dusk in which she lately had walked. *That* was what was the matter with her. She was a dove. Oh, *wasn't* she? – it echoed within her as she became aware of the sound, outside, of the return of their friends. (184)

But this shelter – this privacy – behind an idea of oneself can be an equivocal advantage: her being a dove is not only 'the revealed truth', it is also 'what was the matter with her'. Milly finds her friends address themselves in fact safely and simplifyingly to the dove and the princess and she becomes increasingly isolated behind her double privilege (of rank and innocence):

Her heart could none the less sink a little on feeling how much his [Merton's] view of her was destined to have in common with – as she now sighed over it – *the* view. She could have dreamed of his not having *the* view, of his having something or other, if need be quite viewless, of his own; but he might have what he could with the least trouble, and *the* view wouldn't be, after all, a positive bar to her seeing him. The defect of it in general – if she might so ungraciously criticize – was that, by its sweet universality, it made relations rather prosaically a matter of course. It anticipated and superseded the – likewise sweet – operation of real affinities. (196)

Both girls are partly complicit in the production of *views* of themselves.[21] Kate energetically performs and competes.[22] That habit of self-conceal-ment behind compliance in Milly (she does not want to 'ungraciously criticize'), that reluctance to owe anyone any 'trouble' (Merton 'might have what he could with the least trouble'), perpetuate and license the princess and the dove.

The dove of course is chaste, too. In James's sketches for the novel in his notebooks, there are two strong emphases to Milly's story both of which are complicated, diffused, almost dissimulated in the completed novel. First, Milly in the notebooks reacts with violent incontinent protest to her death sentence: 'She is in love with life, her dreams of it have been immense, and she clings to it with passion, with supplication. "I don't want to die – I won't, I won't, oh, let me live; oh, save me! . . . " She is like a creature dragged shrieking to the guillotine – to the shambles.' And secondly, it is explicit in the notebooks that Milly's appetite to live – her fear that she will have missed out on life – is focused on a sexual passion. James deliberates at some length on the problems for decorum in representing this sexuality of a sick girl:

The young man, in his pity, wishes he could make her taste of happiness, give her something that it breaks her heart to go without having known. That 'something' can only be – of course – the chance to love and be loved. The poor girl, even if he loved her, has no life to give him in return: no life and no personal, no physical surrender, for it seems to me that one must represent her as too ill for *that* particular case. It has bothered me thinking of the little picture – this idea of the physical possession, the brief physical, passional rapture which at first appeared essential to it; bothered me on account of the ugliness, the incongruity, the nastiness *en somme*, of the man's 'having' a sick girl: also on account of something rather pitifully obvious and vulgar in the presentation of such a remedy for her despair – and such a remedy only. 'Oh, she's dying without having had it? Give it to her and let her die' – that strikes me as sufficiently second rate.[23]

The 'brief physical, passional rapture' at first 'appeared essential'; and of course that essential thing is not lost in the finished novel, it is only that in a final tragic twist of the rivalry that binds them to one an-other's insufficiency, Milly's 'physical passional rapture' is displaced onto

Kate. Kate has the sexual consummation that Milly wanted, the sexual consummation that James wanted for Milly but could not find means to express within the vocabularies of representation, within his contemporary aesthetic. What has prevented Milly is that she has to be a 'dove', she is the fair girl and not the dark one, she cannot be allowed to be sexual, or sexually desiring.

In the light of this transferral of sexuality from the one girl to the other, the whole issue of Merton's room in Venice, Kate's visit there, the visit Milly asks for, Merton's reluctance to let her come there, then his changing his mind but too late, is poignantly suggestive.[24] Both these themes in the notebook – Milly's incontinent unseemly rage at dying young, and the focus of that rage on her dread of missing out on sexual passion – *remain*, in fact, central within the finished novel, and their dissimulation is not a matter of James's squeamishness, but is in a sense a *representation*, even, of a social processing which continually dissimulates certain realities, deflects and disallows them, renames and redescribes them. Reading the space between the dove and Milly, observing Milly negotiating with the dove idea how it will both shelter and constrain her, we read the pain – the sacrificial element, to borrow from the Girardian vocabulary – in social identity and social function, social becoming.

When Merton is made uneasy by the processing of the two girls at the Lancaster Gate dinner party, this distorting performance in talk and manner of their social value, he is able to put some distance between himself and the process:

So he judged, at least, within his limits, and the idea that what he had thus caught in the fact was the trick of fashion and the tone of society went so far as to make him take up again his sense of independence. He had supposed himself civilised; but if this was civilisation – ! One could smoke one's pipe outside when twaddle was within. He had rather avoided, as we have remarked, Kate's eyes, but there came a moment when he would fairly have liked to put it, across the table, to her: 'I say, light of my life, is *this* the great world?' (224)

The 'process' is a kind of stupidity ('twaddle'), an unreality; at this point Merton is still able to keep it firmly outside himself (or, as his image has it, the 'twaddle' is inside, and freedom outside it). But by the end of the novel, Merton's definitional boundaries are collapsed, and he is compromised, contaminated. When he meets Mrs Lowder on Christmas morning and they talk about the news of Milly's death, he finds himself assenting in paralysed self-disgust to the falsity of the exchange:

'Our dear dove then, as Kate calls her, has folded her wonderful wings.'
    'Yes – folded them.'
    It rather racked him, but he tried to receive it as she intended, and she
evidently took his formal assent for self-control. 'Unless it's true,' she accordingly
added, 'that she has spread them the wider.'
    He again but formally assented, though, strangely enough, the words fitted
an image deep in his own consciousness. 'Rather, yes – spread them the wider.'
    'For a flight, I trust, to some happiness greater – '
    'Exactly. Greater.' Densher broke in; but now with a look, he feared, that did,
a little, warn her off. (427)

He has lost his power to dissent, to find a different version of his own.
Earlier, he was able to oppose to the smothering dove imagery his own impression that talking to Milly was 'as simple as sitting with his sister might
have been, and not, if the point were urged, very much more thrilling'
(308).[25] Now he even, disconcertingly, finds congruencies between his
imaginings and Mrs Lowder's: his new involvement with Milly comes
to him in images entangled with *their* ambiguous imagery of dove-grace,
and dove-sacrifice.

This progressive contamination of Merton by that 'civilisation' he
ironises earlier in the novel is embodied particularly acutely in the evolution of his relationship with Lord Mark. To begin with – at the dinner
party at Lancaster Gate – Merton's irony is watertight, his contempt
secure:

'Oh!' said the other party [Lord Mark], while Densher said nothing – occu-
pied as he mainly was on the spot with weighing the sound in question . . . It
wasn't . . . , he knew, the 'Oh!' of the idiot, however great the superficial resemblance: it was that of the clever, the accomplished man; it was the very specialty
of the speaker, and a great deal of expensive training and experience had gone
to producing it. (232)

The 'Oh!' represents some essence of class codification; communication
and expression in it are atrophied to the point where Lord Mark is all sign,
and all belittling, placing judgement. The man is so lost in the manner
that he is indistinguishable from it. 'What has the brute to do with us
anyway?' Merton asks. ('What indeed?' replies Kate.) But his indifference
to the 'Oh!', the judgement, of a Lord Mark, is eroded as he lets himself
progressively farther in to the deep games of Lord Mark's world. On
Christmas Day when Merton peers into Mrs Lowder's carriage expecting

Kate it is Lord Mark who is startlingly, disconcertingly in her place:

Densher felt his own look a gaping arrest – which, he disgustedly remembered, his back as quickly turned, appeared to repeat itself as his special privilege. He mounted the steps of the house and touched the bell with a keen consciousness of being habitually looked at by Kate's friend from positions of almost insolent vantage . . . Densher was thinking that *he* seemed to show as vagrant while another was ensconced. He was thinking of the other as . . . more ensconced than ever; he was thinking of him above all as the friend of the person with whom his recognition had, the minute previous, associated him. The man was seated in the very place in which, beside Mrs Lowder's, he had looked to find Kate, and that was a sufficient identity. (424)

Merton can no longer count on the 'independence' he felt at the dinner party from 'twaddle' and 'the great world'. He is helplessly in relationship – humiliating and abject relationship – with this almost *grand guignol* representative of the great social machine who sits significantly in the place he looks for Kate; Lord Mark's presence there, 'ensconced', makes a mockery of any superiority Merton ever imagined he had, makes an irony of Merton's irony. The distinction between 'inside' and 'outside' which had seemed to constitute his independence, finally (when Lord Mark is *in* Florian's, or *inside* the carriage) only leaves him abjectly excluded.

The girls are to an extent complicit in their representations, and Merton is progressively contaminated by his complicity in their rivalry. This is not a novel about the mere victims of social process, or indeed about social process as something existing outside of and independent of those individuals who enact it. It is not a novel, even, which protests at social process, or subverts it. The novel itself in fact enacts the complicity, the involvement, the dissimulation, the incompletion of its subjects; it renders at their maximum power-to-move those social identities bound in to rivalry (male, female; dark girl, light girl; old woman, young woman) whose social construction it *also* renders. But what James wants primarily to record – as in 'In the Cage', in his other 'petit bourgeois' stories and in the whole *oeuvre* – is the *pain* of social process, the suffering entailed in class identity. The characteristic of this suffering in the *oeuvre* is that as it is imposed in one place (that is, in the simple inequity of privilege, so that Lady Bradeen can disdain to spend a minute in the little office where the telegraphist must spend her lifetime, or the telegraphed surplus effusions of the leisured class would be enough to buy boots and dinners for the class that serves them) it takes its subterranean course and resurfaces in another. (Is Captain Everard 'happy'? Is Milly? Above all, is Kate?)

This is not a system of compensations which somehow balances out the imposition of privilege by 'paying back' winners and losers in the struggle, spoiling their triumphs or 'making up for' their losses. On the contrary, one of the things James is strongest on is the reality and the amorality, the undeservedness, of happiness. As the telegraphist puts it, 'Real justice was not of this world, yet, strangely, happiness was.' James's novels all centre upon 'real things', real happinesses rendered precious, beautiful, desirable precisely by their difficulty of achievement in a dizzyingly inequitable society, in a competitive 'race for life' ('In the Cage', 160). Milly is really lucky to be rich; only a sentimental reading could discount her opportunity, her scope, her freedom, the whole glorious temptation of the kingdoms of the world. And Kate is really lucky to have her 'physical possession, the brief physical, passional rapture' (James's words from his notebooks). All the late novels make *that* chance weigh – for joy, for poetry – in any scale against any sounder, more solid, longer happiness. The reality of the luck of each girl is made sharp, is made poignant, is made into the very essence of the desirable, by how much each would have given for the luck of the other. Each would have given everything: this is the last twist of that rivalrous process of co-definition that binds the girls fatally to one another's loss.

That system in the novels which registers the pain of social process is a system, then, of accumulations, not of compensations; it is not moralised. All acts, all complicities, all mere involuntary participations in this inequitable social process add to the sum of hurt, because its inclusion works through exclusion, and in its long chain of connectedness all its happinesses are also losses somewhere. For Lady Bradeen to arrange her dinner engagements with facility, the telegraphist must be paid to sit day in, day out in her cramped hole. For Kate to triumph in the role which is the only way she – and we – can imagine her fulfilment – as dazzling society beauty – Milly has to die, so that Kate can have her money. For Milly to have what she wants – to make Merton *see* her, and not merely the dove in her place – Kate has to be spoiled in Merton's eyes. This sacrificial element in happiness is of the essence of a society arranged to privilege a leisured, segregated élite; and it is of the essence of an aristocratic vision of life and of pleasure.

James is not interested in imagining alternatives.[26] His critique of that late, threatened, declining leisure-class world of Western Europe is not a polemic. He is interested rather in discovering deep within the imagination of that world – its imagination of itself – the dynamics of identity, rivalry, fulfilment and loss.[27] And he is interested too in 'doing justice' (the only kind of justice there is in the novels) to the aesthetic of that leisure-class world, to its 'style'. That essential aristocratic elegance, tensed over its foundations in sacrifice and exclusion, consists in the good form, the panache, the style, with which the inevitable pain is carried off; so that Milly will never 'smell of sickness' and Kate will cover her eventual defeat with a performance of high-mindedness in magnificent good taste. They will both in the end thoroughly and spectacularly *be* that which they have been required to represent.

Milan Kundera writes about Stravinsky's *Le Sacre du Printemps*:

Until Stravinsky, music was never able to give barbaric rites a grand form. We could not imagine them musically. Which means: we could not imagine the *beauty* of the barbaric. Without its beauty, the barbaric would remain incomprehensible. (I stress this: to know any phenomenon deeply requires understanding its beauty, actual or potential.) Saying that a bloody rite does possess some beauty – there's the scandal, unbearable, unacceptable. And yet, unless we understand this scandal, unless we get to the very bottom of it, we cannot understand much about man . . .

It is all the more interesting in that [Stravinsky] had always, and explicitly, declared himself a partisan of the Apollonian principle, an adversary of the Dionysian: *Le Sacre du Printemps* (particularly in its ritual dances) is the Apollonian portrayal of Dionysiac ecstasy: in this portrayal, the ecstatic elements (the aggressively beating rhythm, the few extremely short melodic motifs, many times repeated and never developed, and sounding like shrieks) are transformed into great, refined art (for instance, despite its aggressive quality, the rhythm grows so complex through the rapid alternation of measures with different time signatures that it creates an artificial, unreal, completely stylized beat); still, the Apollonian beauty of this portrayal of barbarity does not obscure its horror; it makes us see that at the very bottom point of the ecstasy there is only the harsh rhythm, the sharp blows of percussion, an extreme numbness, death.[28]

In order to discuss further James's interest in aristocratic 'style' – the beauty of the barbaric – and also the complex relationships within the late work between the Apollonian and the Dionysiac, it makes sense to move forward into a reading of that most stylised and most enigmatic of James's novels, *The Golden Bowl*.

CHAPTER 6

'A house of quiet': privileges and pleasures in
The Golden Bowl

James's fascination with privilege and the privileged predicament culmi-
nates in his last completed novel, *The Golden Bowl* (1904). His protagonists
and his plot and the late Jamesian manner are all tensed up to an improbable ultimate high pitch of performance; from all of them the novel
exacts extreme demonstrations of elegance, of complexity, of rarity. The
novel is emptied of any significant life outside the Ververs' rarefied oxygen tent, pitched at the pinnacle of social amenity and exempt from all
the ordinary pains and mess of material struggle. (Nicola Bradbury calls
it the 'goldfish bowl'.[1]) The ranks of servants that attend everywhere are
mute as furniture. There are no Venetians in brown jackets, no comrades
sleeping off sorrows in the dusty grass of the park. Only occasionally, with
Charlotte, a moment's breeze blows in from a world outside: she first ar-
rives in the novel fresh from 'winds and waves and custom-houses . . . far
countries and long journeys' (58); later she comes to the Prince from a
day spent wandering in London streets and lunching 'on some strange
nastiness, at a cookshop in Holborn' (231); and then there are the train
timetables and the inn at Gloucester.

James's subjects are the vacancy that follows on that exemption from
material struggle – what to do? what to be? where to go? when there
is no need – and the resulting intensifications of attraction, angst and
antagonism inside the narrowness of the privileged space. The novel is
not, of course, a naturalistic representation of the real transactions of
a European / North Atlantic turn-of-the-century leisure class. James's
exaggerated and mannered imagination of class and privilege, with its
concentration on good form, its self-regarding stylishness, its disdain for
humdrum concrete detail and its implied contempt for any 'ordinary'
reading of its situation, is absolutely in keeping with his subject. If he
invents an impossibly sophisticated aristocracy, he invents it out of a
material that is to hand. His style mimics characteristics – the drawl of
initiated knowledge, the high patina of charm, the overstatement of a

perpetual ironising concealment – which convince us as representing something of how that turn-of-the-century leisure class imagined itself. Part of the authenticity of the novel is in the intense period feel of its vocabulary and imagery, with its 'wonderfuls' and 'beautifuls', its 'ahs', its 'poor dears' and its 'funks'.

Rather than that habit of realism which counters and unpicks the ideas a culture has of itself (Tolstoy in *Anna Karenina*, say), James is exploiting realism's other potential: to build its reality out of the material of a culture's own image of itself, within, as it were, the culture's own *mystique*. Kipling both invents and imitates (impossible to say which movement of the double pulse comes first) the mystique of the Raj. Borges both imitates and invents the mystique of the Buenos Aires neighbourhoods. In his dream of an impossibly rarefied upper-class entanglement James is both imitating and creating a *fin-de-siècle* European / North Atlantic 'aristocracy'.[2]

If it is an 'aristocracy', then it is a complex transnational composite: the Prince lends to it his (European) genealogy, Charlotte her (American) individual distinction (we never learn anything of her antecedents) and the Ververs their (American) money. The old aristocratic association with land and buildings is severed; the wealth that sustains the oxygen tent of this leisure was created in the insubstantial transactions of high finance. The Ververs do not build homes, or even buy them, they rent houses. Their very relationship with the substantial symbols of their wealth is different. Adam Verver's precious material items were commissioned by other aristocrats in other eras, but Adam does not commission them or even use them, he collects and collates them, he puts them away in his museum.[3] To borrow Yeats's symbol from 'Ancestral Houses', he merely has his ear to the exotic shell that is all that is left of a life once lived in the 'rich streams'.

> though now it seems
> As if some marvellous empty sea-shell flung
> Out of the obscure dark of the rich streams,
> And not a fountain, were the symbol which
> Shadows the inherited glory of the rich.
>
> Some violent bitter man, some powerful man
> Called architect and artist in, that they,
> Bitter and violent men, might rear in stone
> The sweetness that all longed for night and day,
> The gentleness none there had ever known;
> But when the master's buried mice can play,

And maybe the great-grandson of that house,
For all its bronze and marble, 's but a mouse.

O what if gardens where the peacock strays
With delicate feet upon old terraces,
Or else old Juno from an urn displays
Before the indifferent garden deities;
O what if levelled lawns and gravelled ways
Where slippered Contemplation finds his ease
And Childhood a delight for every sense,
But take our greatness with our violence?[4]

The pretty shell is easy to handle and admire; the creature whose
biology it once was part of would have been disconcertingly alien. Yeats's
definition in 'Ancestral Houses' of successive phases of aristocracy is
surely relevant to the analysis of *fin-de-siècle* privilege in *The Golden Bowl*.
In Yeats's poem the 'violent bitter' man who sponsors artists to create
that 'sweetness' he longs for, is succeeded by a 'mouse', by 'slippered
Contemplation', whose greatness has been taken along with his violence.
James's novel could be read as an interestingly complicating account of
that 'gentle' phase of privilege. Strictly speaking, it is the Prince who is
the real heir to the genealogies of 'violent bitter men', and certainly he
represents the tradition of European nobility tamed. The last vestige of
'violence' that breaks out in him – the last violence that is left available
to him – is chastened and brought to heel by the end of the novel. But
the actual contemporary tenant of the ancestral house does not belong
to the aristocratic bloodline at all: it is Adam Verver with his New World
wealth who 'finds his ease' in 'levelled lawns and gravelled ways', and
enjoys his 'slippered', domesticated Contemplation. By the standards of
the old aristocratic code, he is certainly a 'mouse', this man who cannot
father a child with his new young wife (Charlotte's certainty (233), can
presumably only mean that she and her husband no longer have sexual
relations), who never actually speaks a word to accuse his son-in-law
who cuckolds him nor his wife who dishonours him; whose reply to
their insult is to enfold himself in an ever less penetrable white fog of
seeming innocence and ignorance. And yet in James's configuration it
is the mouse at last, and for his very appearance of innocence, that all
the others most fear. (In Yeats's poem too the mouse is – triumphant? It
seems the wrong word. Like Adam Verver he quietly and complacently
possesses.)

Within the dispossessed space of the ancestral house of *The Golden Bowl*,
two ideas – two ideals – of aristocracy contend. It would be absolutely

a mistake to read Maggie and Adam's cosy domesticity – 'like children playing at paying visits, playing at "Mr Thompson" and "Mrs Fane", each hoping that the other would really stay to tea' (196) – as bourgeois. Maggie herself, before the last tea-time of all with the other pair, uses to her husband the vocabulary of class differentiation to ironise the anxiousness with which they wait:

'We're distinctly bourgeois!' she a trifle grimly threw off . . . though to a spectator sufficiently detached they might have been quite the privileged pair they were reputed, granted only they were taken as awaiting the visit of Royalty. (537)

It is ironic, and she is grim, of course, because 'bourgeois' is so far from the reality of how they perceive themselves. We should not be surprised to discover that Maggie has her class pride, just because she has been so little interested in the invitations to the Foreign Office or to Matcham, and so indifferent, until piqued into jealous curiosity, to the opinion of, say, a Lady Castledean. Maggie's class pride is a very different thing to Charlotte's; it does not feed upon knowing 'what it was to look "well"' (191), or feeling herself 'in truth crowned' (192) at grand public occasions. It perhaps consists rather in turning down grand occasions with genuine indifference, preferring the privacy of a home whose status in the ranked order of social priority is beyond question. The suggestion in the passage above, that the bourgeois appearance of eagerness is redeemed by the possibility that it is royalty the couple await, feels just right; there has always been a latitude for royalty and its close connections to be little and modest and domestic without jeopardising their position at the apex of a great system of leisure-class display and surplus consumption.

Adam and Maggie's ultimate class privilege expresses itself as indifference to the very parade and apparatus of that privilege. And this is only one of the many notes in *The Golden Bowl* which touch off significant reminiscences of *The Portrait of a Lady*: only, as so often, what was exposed as spurious and faked in the earlier novel is presented at face value in the later one. One of the ways Isabel learned to 'see through' Gilbert Osmond was in discovering that his indifference to opinion was only pretended; in fact his whole life was an attitude struck in order to be admired. In Adam and Maggie the indifference is quite authentic.

The 'aristocratic' in Maggie's consciousness is at first experienced primarily not as entailing consequences (the need to 'appear', the need to 'live up') but as exempting her from them. Her 'aristocracy' is sentimental (in the older sense of the word and perhaps – we will come round to discussing this – in its newer sense too), private, conscientious, innocent. She buys with her privilege, or so she believes, a fairy-tale clearing in the dark forest. And it comes into conflict in the novel with an opposite kind of 'aristocracy'; Charlotte and the Prince know they have been bought for their 'value', and to prove they have been worth their high price they can only imagine that they must perform the superior man and woman that they are. Their aristocracy resides not in exemption from responsibility, but in the responsibility to live out their 'type' to its fullest possibility, its fullest expression in romance and glamour: what other use can they have? That responsibility had always been part of an old aristocratic ideal; the presumption of precious, superior qualities intrinsic to the blood-line entailed the 'proof' of superiority in more striking behaviour, in stronger passions and larger needs.[5]

At Matcham, just before the Prince and Charlotte consummate their adulterous affair at Gloucester, this question of the function of privilege and the 'proof' of superiority comes up with particular urgency:[6]

All of which, besides, in Lady Castledean as in Maggie, in Fanny Assingham as in Charlotte herself, was working for him [the Prince] without provocation or pressure, by the mere play of some vague sense on their part – definite and conscious at most only in Charlotte – that he was not, as a nature, as a character, as a gentleman, in fine, below his remarkable fortune . . . the Prince had the sense, all good-humouredly, of being happily chosen, and it was not spoiled for him even by another sense that followed in its train and with which, during his life in England, he had more than once had reflectively to deal: the state of being reminded how, after all, as an outsider, a foreigner, and even as a mere representative husband and son-in-law, he was so irrelevant to the working of affairs that he could be bent on occasion to uses comparatively trivial. No other of her guests would have been thus convenient for their hostess; affairs, of whatever sorts, had claimed, by early trains, every active, easy, smoothly-working man, each in his way a lubricated item of the great social, political, administrative *engrenage* – claimed most of all Castledean himself, who was so very oddly, given the personage and the type, rather a large item. If he, on the other hand, had an affair, it was not of that order; it was of the order, verily, that he had been reduced to as a not quite glorious substitute.

It marked, however, the feeling of the hour with him that this vision of being 'reduced' interfered not at all with the measure of his actual ease. It kept before him again, at moments, the so familiar fact of his sacrifices – down to the idea of the very relinquishment, for his wife's convenience, of his real situation in the world; with the consequence, thus, that he was, in the last analysis, among all these so often inferior people, practically held cheap and made light of. But though all this was sensible enough there was a spirit in him that could rise above it, a spirit that positively played with the facts, with all of them; from that of the droll ambiguity of English relations to that of his having in his mind something quite beautiful and independent and harmonious, something wholly his own. (264–5)

'As a nature, as a character, as a gentleman, in fine': the narrative is interior to the very process of the Prince imagining himself, imagining his identity; his sequence of selves, in ascending order of exhaustiveness, begins with blood and ends, subsuming all those others inside it, with caste, with the privilege and the exigencies of aristocracy. The privilege is his 'great fortune', the exigency is that he will earn his 'great fortune' by living up to it. His sense of being 'happily chosen' is of the essence of aristocratic identity; in a complex reconciliation the accident of birth, of privilege, conspires with and is justified by individual distinction. Luck and desert gratifyingly fulfil one another.

But the Prince's sense of himself as a gentleman is reworking itself carefully in the passage here around certain difficulties, around alternative versions of caste definition. All the English gentlemen with whom he has spent the weekend – and other weekends – dining, hunting and shooting, have gone back up to town by early trains, claimed by 'the great social, political, administrative *engrenage*'. There is a nineteenth-century British version of aristocracy whose justification has displaced itself from fulfilment in individual distinction onto fulfilment in self-sacrifice to a greater social good. It is the type of English aristocracy which James so enjoyed representing at its maximum possibility (the maximum possibility as expressed, say, in Lawrence's portraits) in Lord Warburton in *The Portrait of a Lady*. But even the generosity of that portrait is interestingly qualified: Isabel refuses to marry Lord Warburton because she sees his so consummately representing a social ideal as essentially, personally limiting. His eyes 'burned with a passion that had sifted itself clear of the baser parts of emotion – the heat, the violence, the unreason – and that burned as steadily as a lamp in a windless place' (105). In James images of stillness are usually images of qualification; in the end, it is Caspar Goodwood, whose passion is full of heat and violence, and not Lord Warburton, who comes closest to convincing Isabel.

By the time he comes to write Lord Castledean, James's way with the British aristocratic type is less respectful, more offhand (in the meantime he has also 'done' Lord Mark). The qualification of Castledean's importance in the 'great social, political, administrative *engrenage*' is there in the Prince's all-but-imperceptibly raised eyebrow, at 'Castledean himself, who was so very oddly, given the personage and the type, rather a large item'. We do not need to know anything more about the 'personage' and the 'type' except that for the Prince, confident in his own nature and character, it makes his greatness odd; that, and the fact that while the Lord goes off to his kind of affairs, his Lady amuses herself with a Mr Blint. It is what the Prince puzzles over in these English gentlemen, it is what makes their 'gentleman' count so differently to his. The 'nature' where his sense of himself as justified in being a gentleman is centred does not count with them. He has no problem with recognising their gentility; but they do not convince him, according to *his* idea of a gentleman, as being *men* enough. Tied up with competing ideals of aristocracy here are competing versions of masculinity.

Competing versions, because of course what the Prince is reacting to in so carefully reimagining himself in relation to these Englishmen here, is a version of manliness which would emasculate *him*, not by impugning his sexuality or his sexual honour but by relegating him through his lack of function in the social *engrenage* to that margin where he is *merely*, decoratively, irrelevantly sexual (that margin in the British imagination where, at the other end of the social scale, are the gigolo and the warbling Italian tenor in tights). It could sting; the Prince is quick to register how he is 'held cheap and made light of' (265), how he is being 'placed' on the British scale. His thoughts revisit for some moments the 'sacrifices' that have left him open to such implications. There are Italian responsibilities, we gather, a 'real situation in the world' which the Prince has more or less relinquished 'for his wife's convenience' (265); although we learn elsewhere that rather than a role in any 'social, political, administrative *engrenage*', these are matters of property and family. The Continental aristocracy which the Prince represents has never displaced its responsibility from the 'tribe' onto the general good, any more than it has displaced its blood-borne superiority from the splendid male individual onto the collective or the ideal of service.

The Prince is a barbarian; with all that has always implied both of essential limitation and especial sensuality and strength. We know that he is a barbarian, for example, from his fundamental absolute assumption, swaddled under however many paddings of exquisite courtesy and consideration, that woman's 'nature' exists in an intrinsically dependent and abject position in relation to man's:

Once more, as a man conscious of having known many women, he could assist, as he would have called it, at the recurrent, the predestined phenomenon, the thing always as certain as sunrise or the coming round of Saints' days, the doing by the woman of the thing that gave her away. She did it, ever, inevitably, infallibly – she couldn't possibly not do it. It was her nature, it was her life, and the man could always expect it without lifting a finger. This was *his*, the man's, any man's, position and advantage, that he only had to wait, with a decent patience, to be placed, in spite of himself, it might really be said, in the right. Just so the punctuality of performance on the part of the other creature was her weakness and her deep misfortune – not less, no doubt, than her beauty. (61)

(One reading of the novel would have the Prince learning his lesson, his fundamental assumptions broken by the one woman who *does not* 'do the thing that gave her away'.) We know he is a barbarian, because he is – quite seriously – superstitious; because there is more than a tinge of anti-Semitism in his contempt for the Jew in the Bloomsbury shop. We know he is, because (as Charlotte, who is so different, notes) 'below a certain social plane, he never *saw*', he 'took the meaner sort for granted – the night of their meanness or whatever name one might give it for him made all cats grey' (99).

It is out of his 'barbarism', his unbounded faith in his own 'nature', his belief in a superiority based, after all, not on a bureaucracy or on a 'post' but in his blood, his *body*, that in the very instant of registering the implied slight from the self-importantly preoccupied Englishmen the Prince reasserts an alternative scale of importance, through a personal irony, through the raised eyebrow of his tone, through the smile (at the 'droll ambiguity of English relations') on the beautiful face. For its great moment – whatever happens in the long run – the splendid male creature so sure of his 'nature' as the basis of his breeding owes no apology to mere 'lubricated items' of the social machine. This *is* the Prince's moment:

sunny, gusty, lusty English April, all panting and heaving with impatience, or kicking and crying, even, at moments, like some infant Hercules who wouldn't be dressed ... the bravery of youth and beauty, the insolence of fortune and appetite ... Every voice in the great bright house was a call to the ingenuities and impunities of pleasure; every echo was a defiance of difficulty, doubt, or danger; every aspect of the picture, a glowing plea for the immediate ... a world so constituted was governed by a spell, that of the smile of the gods and the favour of the powers; the only handsome, the only gallant, in fact the only intelligent acceptance of which was a faith in its guarantees and a high spirit for its chances. (251)

His taking advantage of the moment is no mere opportunism, it is rather his assertion of his idea of himself in the face of other ways of imagining him. His idea of himself as a gentleman is so bound up with himself as a *man*, that Maggie and Adam's trust in his sexual abstinence is virtually insulting:

Being thrust, systematically, with another woman, and a woman one happened, by the same token, exceedingly to like, and being so thrust that the theory of it seemed to publish one as idiotic or incapable – this was a predicament of which the dignity depended all on one's own handling. (252)

It is not only out of privilege – luck – that he takes Charlotte off to Gloucester; it is almost out of responsibility too, responsibility to his nature, his identity as gentleman, his princeliness.[7]

It is poignant, somehow, that in creating in *The Golden Bowl* his sensual Continental male with a touch of barbarism (out of that typology that has developed from the Count Gemini who beat his wife in *The Portrait of a Lady* to Gloriani the male tiger in the jungle in *The Ambassadors*), James has made his Prince Italian and not French. James has used the Italian reference in his human typology much less; here in the Prince we have our idea of what he means it to evoke.[8] Sensual Frenchmen in James are intellectually sensual (Gloriani is an artist); what the Prince has above all is personal, the charm of the person, of the body: beauty.

Charlotte's function in the novel, and in the little world of the novel, links her to those other performing and displaying women in the late works, Mme de Vionnet and Kate Croy. Rather than reading like a theme of James's, the sequence of these women reads like a theme of the era; a theme expressed, say, in contemporary fashion, those turn-of-the-century dresses with their bold gestures, flaunting sexuality, crippling constraints.[9] It is interesting that James experiments with this typology across nationality: the French, the English and the American are all, in a sense, the more or less doomed counterparts to the Prince's assumption of advantage, his presumption upon 'the doing by the woman of the thing that gave her away'. (In the final scenes of *The Wings of the Dove* even Merton, uncomfortably, reluctantly, finds himself at an impasse where he cannot help using his advantage, *the* advantage, against Kate.) This is the old sexual relation, the one that belongs with the old idea of aristocracy based on the ideal of the splendid male individual, on the male sexual *élan*.

Buried deep under the sophisticated courtesies of that ideal, the dissimulations of its elaborate homage to female refinement, somewhere the man seeks the right female *animal* to match with. She must reflect his nature, in its special superiority, she must absorb his superiority and re-radiate it out of a superiority of her own that matches his. All these three women work so hard at absorbing and radiating, at *charming*. Their very lightness and grace, the very pleasure of their company, how they soothe and facilitate and entertain, even (or above all) how they are beautiful, is all, paradoxically, the result of an effort the strain of which James meticulously records. Kate is an actress dressed and painted for the footlights; Mme de Vionnet, mother of a marriageable daughter, can make herself seem a twenty-year-old girl. Maggie imagines Charlotte, 'always on the rampart, erect and elegant, with her lace-flounced parasol now folded and now shouldered, march to and fro against a gold-coloured east or west' (397). Like Mme de Vionnet with Chad, Charlotte must 'never, on any pretext' bore her Prince (280). And all three women will be sacrificed, at the end of their novels, in spite of (or because of) all their efforts. In the Prince's formulation, it is indeed the very busy-ness of the women's charm which will eventually 'give them away': 'the punctuality of performance on the part of the other creature was her weakness and her deep misfortune'. Their very efforts will put them at an intrinsic disadvantage with the man who will simply wait while they perform: the essence of *his* charm is that he does not 'lift a finger' for it. (It is interesting, for example, that even Chad's great transformation in *The Ambassadors* from rude American to smooth cosmopolite is never discussed in terms of *his* efforts in achieving it; they are always Mme de Vionnet's efforts and successes, she did it *for* him.)

The novels, of course, do not only record the sacrifice: they also enact the romance. If one merely reads the novels as chains of causation, then they certainly do have that story to tell, that sacrifice of the female buried deep within a certain masculine ideal. But, to re-use the spatial metaphor formulated in other chapters, because the late novels are essentially dialogic and not monologic, in the same movement of imagination which sees through and round such a phenomenon, they also imagine its bottomlessness, its persuasive beauties, its pleasures. The 'truth' of *The Golden Bowl* does not only lie along that trajectory of *chronos*, linear time, which delivers as its last word Charlotte's defeat and Maggie's victory. In fact one of the models of consciousness being contested within the ancestral house of privilege by the two pairs of subjects (the Ververs, here, against the lovers) might be precisely this issue of meaning in time; meaning which is either linear and progressive and delivers triumph at its ending, or circular and fatalistic, shaped around a centre of climactic realisation. The reconciliations of comedy are opposed to the irrevocable losses of tragedy; it is the dialogue between these models inside *The Golden Bowl* which has led to the primary critical quarrel over it, over whether James is writing to justify the Ververs or the lovers, whether he is giving us a happy or a tragic ending. It helps defuse the quarrel to suggest that he is creating a world in which both readings co-exist: not reconciled, but in a perpetual tension.

In Charlotte's – tragic – novel, there is triumph, happiness, fulfilment, completion of a sort; only of a different shape to Maggie's. Ignoring the power of the pleasure in the novel is like hearing *Don Giovanni* without the music; to merely read the adulterous affair as a transgression which the narrative will, for better or for worse, eventually purge, is to miss what it *sounds* like as James writes it. Even critics who give persuasive accounts of James's narrative commitment *against* the Ververs' version of events are often dismissive – disapproving, even – of the love affair. For example, Michiel Heyns, whose analysis of the Ververs' acquisitiveness in terms of Veblen's *The Theory of the Leisure Class* is very fine, describes the Prince and Charlotte as 'all too evidently parading their contempt for the "sweet simplicity" of the Ververs as "sacred" solicitude', and writes: 'The comic discrepancy between the Prince and Charlotte's dialogue and their actions is merely an extreme form of the manipulations of language, whereby bedizened description does duty for moral definition.'[10] But that simple opposition between 'true' action and 'false' bedizened description simply does not seem to answer to the late Jamesian manner: if we are to mistrust bedizened description as mere cover for real actions, what in the late novels *can* we trust?[11] James's own narratives demonstrate surely how bedizened description enacts, and becomes, its own reality. And then, would we prefer lovers who *did* exchange 'moral definitions'? And if the Prince and Charlotte are this shabby – this 'comic' – then how can we readers be made to mind their being bought by the Ververs anyway?

The novel is engaged in scrupulously defining just what kind of arrangement the Prince and Charlotte negotiate, and just how it is founded in inequity, in male advantage and female sacrifice, in male freedom and female abject need. The novel is also engaged in defining how that arrangement has to compete against the Ververs' different values, against a reading which finds the lovers, precisely, shabby and immoral. But that match between the splendid male animal and the splendid female animal is not only set up in order to be deplored and seen through; it moves James, surely? And surely he means it to move us, to seduce us, just as when Strether finally allows himself to imagine Chad with Mme de Vionnet he finds himself, somewhere beyond all his anxieties and qualifications, consenting to the inevitability and the beauty of the idea of their embraces, 'supposing innumerable and wonderful things'. He is not supposing that they exchange moral definitions (or answer any of his anxieties); any more than Zerlina is seduced by Don Giovanni's morality when he sings to her. What Giovanni promises Zerlina is not anything she can have permanently, to defeat anxieties and qualifications. It is the erotic secret space inside the anxious world, not extended into chronological real time and real futures; just as the telegraphist in 'In the Cage' dreams up the impossible space in which she can love Captain Everard. The erotic is the secret space where the very material of inequality (seigneur and peasant, gentleman and working girl, or just male and female) can be transformed, can dissolve in a new fluidity. Reciprocities and equalities impossible to establish in the real structures of a world in time (or inverted inequalities, like Swann abjecting himself before the *demi-mondaine* Odette) can be invented and enacted and played out in the alternative world of the body, they can become the very material of touch and exchange:

They were silent at first, only facing and faced, only grasping and grasped, only meeting and met. 'It's sacred', he said at last.

'It's sacred,' she breathed back to him. They vowed it, gave it out and took it in, drawn, by their intensity, more closely together. Then of a sudden, through this tightened circle, as at the issue of a narrow strait into the sea beyond, everything broke up, broke down, gave way, melted and mingled. Their lips sought their lips, their pressure their response and their response their pressure; with a violence that had sighed itself the next moment to the longest and deepest of stillnesses they passionately sealed their pledge. (237)

This in *The Golden Bowl* is the very description of that loss of self, that confusion of the boundaries between self and other, literally, on the skin and in the body, that Isabel feared and fled from in *The Portrait of a Lady*. When Caspar kisses her Isabel's sensation is that she has lost her footing: 'it wrapped her about; it lifted her off her feet', and 'she seemed to beat with her feet, in order to catch herself, to feel something to rest on' (598, 90). Later in *The Golden Bowl* Maggie is also described as feeling for her feet – and then, like Isabel, finding them – in a sea of sensations: 'She had her feet somewhere, through it all – it was her companion, absolutely, who was at sea. And she kept her feet; she pressed them to what was beneath her' (438). What is different in *The Golden Bowl* from the earlier novel is that James can create with sympathy both the woman who – saving herself – resists the strange flood of the erotic *and* the woman whose genius is to give herself to it. Isabel no longer has the novel to herself; it is almost as if Mme Merle were given back her youth and beauty to weigh in the scale with her rival, the bright good girl.

The metaphors of space and time in James's account of the Prince's and Charlotte's kiss describe an erotic space exempt from linearity, provisionally free. The space begins as a circle of reciprocity: ('facing and faced, grasping and grasped, meeting and met'); then the 'tightened circle', self-completing, reaching out nowhere, inverts itself and becomes instead a passage, a 'narrow strait', through which the very self-containedness, completion, of the circle of two becomes paradoxically an opening onto boundless fluid space: 'the sea beyond'.[12] The metaphor imitates and suggests sexual penetration just as the kiss does, in a realm of infinite correspondences, where all definitional boundaries 'broke up, broke down, gave way'. The violence of entry from one dimension, linear narrative, to this circular surrounding of the sea, changes, after the 'narrow strait', to 'the longest and deepest of stillnesses'; the minute ('moment') and the infinite ('longest and deepest') are experienced alongside one another in a time that defies counting by any standard of linear extension.

There are two places in the novel where these two alternative shapes of experience, of narrative – the linear and the circular – are placed side by side, quite explicitly. The first is where Charlotte persuades the Prince to come out with her to buy Maggie's present:

'Well, now I must tell you, for I want to be absolutely honest.' So Charlotte spoke, a little ominously, after they had got into the Park. 'I don't want to pretend, and I can't pretend a moment longer. You may think of me what you will, but I don't care. I knew I shouldn't and I find out how little. I came back for this. Not really for anything else. For this,' she repeated as, under the influence of her tone, the Prince had already come to a pause.

'For "this"?' He spoke as if the particular thing she indicated were vague to him – or were, rather, a quantity that couldn't at the most, be much.

It would be as much, however, as she should be able to make it. 'To have one hour alone with you.'

It had rained heavily in the night, and though the pavements were now dry, thanks to a cleansing breeze, the August morning, with its hovering, thick-drifting clouds and freshened air, was cool and grey. (88)

'This', in one way of reckoning, cannot be 'much'; the Prince is about to marry Charlotte's friend for a lifetime, and the one hour she has managed to contrive with him for herself (and at the cost of giving herself away to him absolutely) does not seem in any ordinary reckoning like any kind of compensation. But it has been enough in Charlotte's imagination for her to travel half way round the world for it; and in the long run it will indeed turn out to be 'much', in the sense that the golden bowl they find on this expedition will be the key to Maggie's uncovering the secret of their liaison. Charlotte has put, as it were, all the rest of the time in which she cannot have the Prince in a scale against the one hour ('or say two') in which she can, and found they weigh equally.

The language of disproportion, of the extreme relativity of values, is picked up and played with in the Prince's and Charlotte's talk about Maggie's present in the chapter; he hates 'to encourage her – and for such a purpose, after all – to spend your money'. She replies 'Because you think I have so little? I've enough, at any rate – enough to take us one hour' (90).

'I'm too poor for some things,' she had said – yet, strange as she was, lightly enough; 'but I'm not too poor for others.' And she had paused again at the top. 'I've been saving up.' (91)

She is weighing Maggie's purchasing power against her own; Maggie can 'buy' the Prince in extension, for permanence; all Charlotte can 'buy' is this hour out of time, whose worth is not in its duration but in its intensity, in its density of meaning. And the intensity accumulates precisely through Charlotte's deprivation; she cannot have duration, permanence, so the short moment she can have will be all the more freighted with a lifetime's importance: 'I've been saving up'. The connection between this language of relative value here and their adulteries later is obvious; the intense short hours and afternoons stolen by the lovers in the secret erotic space will be bargained against the long extensions of time on the surface of life where they obediently appear as husbands and wives.

One of the ways James makes us experience in the very texture of the novel the intensity – the relative value – of the 'hour' of pleasure is in that easy movement in the prose from Charlotte's announcing she has come back to have her hour alone with the Prince to the vividly individuated August day: 'It had rained heavily in the night, and though the pavements were now dry, thanks to a cleansing breeze, the August morning, with its hovering, thick-drifting clouds and freshened air, was cool and grey.' Our reading consciousness is released from speculation into motives and futures and pasts into a different temporal awareness, of the *now* of the novel, felt on the skin and breathed in: the description is given in terms of sensations and scents rather than primarily in visuals. The weather itself has cleared a space of freshness and opportunity after heavy rain, just as Charlotte is taking possession of her moment amidst all her difficulties and disappointments: the 'heavy rain' suggests tactfully and eloquently for us (and perhaps for the Prince too, if we take his as the narrative register of the passage) the sorrows she will not complain about. The sensuality of the moment and the appreciative leap of responsiveness to its appeal in Charlotte create an excitement in the text that escapes the linear sequencing of plot: what is going to 'happen next', however short, is also infinite in possibility. And James's description here invokes a natural, pagan magic; just as it will in another erotically charged context, later, at Matcham, with its April like an infant Hercules; just as it did in the French countryside on the day Strether met Chad and Mme de Vionnet. The rain has cleansed the odours of the city and its civilisation and through them 'a wholesome smell of irrigation . . . rose from the earth'.

The other place in the novel where the two alternative shapings of experience (an 'hour' as opposed to a lifetime; the moment's intensity of the circle as opposed to *chronos*, the projection of linear time) are explicitly contrasted is near the very end, when Maggie imagines Charlotte's desperation in the weeks before she leaves for America.

Behind the glass lurked the whole history of the relation she had so fairly flattened her nose against it to penetrate – the glass Mrs Verver might, at this stage, have been frantically tapping, from within, by way of supreme, irrepressible entreaty . . . She could thus have translated Mrs Verver's tap against the glass, as I have called it, into fifty forms; could perhaps have translated it most into the form of a reminder that would pierce deep. 'You don't know what it is to have been loved and broken with. You haven't been broken with, because in *your* relation what can there have been, worth speaking of, to break? Ours was everything a relation could be, filled to the brim with the wine of consciousness; and if it was to have no meaning, no better meaning than that such a creature as you could breathe upon it, at your hour, for blight, why was I myself dealt with all for deception? Why condemned after a couple of short years to find the golden flame – oh the golden flame! – a mere handful of black ashes?' (521)

The two women are separated by the glass that first seems to exclude one way, then the other. Once it shut Maggie out, and she registers how she demeaned herself, seemed childish ('flattened her nose against it'), in her first efforts to see what was on the other side; now it traps Charlotte, leaves her – and foolishly – at the mercy of Maggie's interpretations, Maggie's charity. The glass separates two ideas, two versions of life and value. Its transparency represents their mutual awareness, their mutual dependency, even; its impermeable hardness represents their irreconcilable opposition.

This passage exists in a relationship to Charlotte's 'hour' with the Prince that is like the before and after of fulfilment. It is in the very nature of 'romance' that it does not last; the 'hour' of the erotic choice, the choice out of responsibility, out of consequences, will end, in linear time, and will be succeeded by loss and diminishment. That pattern – of desire for a fulfilment that promises exemption from linear time, succeeded *in linear time* by emptiness, doubt, decay, is of course the shape of sexual pleasure itself (*post coitum omni animali tristi sunt*); and it is the classic dualism of love-in-poetry. Poetry promises – and, within its own space, delivers – exemption from all laws outside the charmed circle of the erotic; but in its very hyperbole of assertion it also acknowledges its own vulnerability *in time* to all those laws (Donne's 'The Sunne Rising' – 'Love, all alike, no season knowes, nor clyme, / Nor houres, dayes, moneths, which are the rags of time'; or Marvell's 'To His Coy Mistress'). This 'before and after' shape is in fact the 'shape' of the European novel of adultery (*Elective Affinities, Mme Bovary, Anna Karenina*); while Maggie's story represents something more like the English novel tradition, with its gradually and problematically progressing love story ending in the fulfilment of marriage, projected into a linear future full of the unknown. The European novel-shape is a steep curve, a pinnacle of fulfilment, then a falling off as steep and sharp, *an ending*, as opposed to the English winding, thwarted slow approach to a threshold.[13] Both shapes co-exist inside *The Golden Bowl*.

It is difficult to resist reading the whole intrusive hyper-elaborated commentary by the Assinghams in the novel as playing out James's explicit interest in how the story revolves around these two polarised possibilities in novelistic structure, the European and the English. The invention of Fanny and the Colonel, characters whose only function in the action is their agitated and fascinated consciousness of it, is not characteristic of James's method elsewhere in the *oeuvre*. Fanny, surely, is the female English – or American – novelist, irrepressibly match-making, unstoppably imagining, feverishly romanticising: hence her 'exotic' colouring and dress. But under the exoticism – the romance – of her surface, as she herself often jokes, there shelters a highly respectable lady; moralising, shockable, conscientious, frightened and guilty at the wild improprieties her naive dabblings in romance have set in train. The comedy here is at the expense of those anomalies in the English-language novel tradition exemplified by, say, *Jane Eyre* or *Mill on the Floss*; those anomalies which owe everything to the preponderance in the tradition of women,

both as writers and readers, women sufferingly juggling the irreconcilables of contemporary femininity. Fanny is trapped inside a 'novel'
whose romance will not stay inside the boundaries of the proper where
she wants it; will not end with marriage, but spills over, out of the very
energies of passion she responds to so quiveringly, into the improper
territory of the European novel. At the end of *The Golden Bowl* Fanny
is even punitive, vengefully and relishingly (and apparently without any
of Maggie's ambivalent feelings about it) expelling Charlotte, who had
so threatened to spoil the happy ending she had planned, to the ends
of the earth; rehearsing that familiar scapegoating device by which so
many English-language novelists had purged and made safe the passions
conjured in their fictions.

'Ah, make no sacrifice,' said Maggie. 'See me through.'
  'That's it – that's all I want. I should be too base –! Besides,' Fanny went on,
'you're too splendid.'
  'Splendid?'
  'Splendid. Also, you know, you are all but "through". You've done it,' said
Mrs Assingham.
  But Maggie only half took it from her. 'What does it strike you that I've done?'
  'What you wanted. They're going.'
  Maggie continued to look at her. 'Is that what I wanted?' . . . Her companion
smiled superior. '*I* don't need to be told – either! I see something, thank God,
every day.' And then as Maggie might appear to be wondering what, for instance:
'I see the long miles of ocean and the dreadful great country, State after State –
which have never seemed to me so big or so terrible. I see *them* at last, day by day
and step by step, at the far end – and I see them never come back. But *never* –
simply.' (505)

  It would be absurd to stretch a point and have James make the Colonel
represent Flaubert or Tolstoy. But his less moralising *laisser faire*, his
man-of-the-world's unflappable realism (when Fanny convinces herself
that the Prince and Charlotte did not have time to consummate their
relationship in Italy, he wonders, 'Does it take so much time?', 76) do
represent within the novel a different way, and a male way, of reading
what happens. It is interesting that, unlike his wife's, his sympathy is often
with Charlotte; he often gives voice to shades of hesitation in response
to his wife's unqualified talking up of Adam and Maggie:

'In the first place Mr Verver isn't aged.'
  The Colonel just hung fire – but it came. 'Then why the deuce does he – oh,
poor dear man! – behave as if he were?'
  She took a moment to meet it. 'How do you know how he behaves?'

'Well, my own love, we see how Charlotte does!'

Again, at this, she faltered; but again she rose. 'Ah, isn't it my own point that he's charming to her?'

'Doesn't it depend a bit on what she regards as charming?' (292)

It is almost at moments like these as if they write the story between them, demonstrating its incompleteness and the impossibility of finalising it, of reconciling their versions, as they dispute one by one – hesitating, doubting, ironising – the very terms in which it is told. The Colonel challenges the pattern through which Fanny reads Adam's innocence and Charlotte's defection; he inserts instead into the story Charlotte's need and Adam's defection. Her frame of reference is moralising and in terms of female duty; his is sexual and in terms of male responsibility. Until a long way into the novel Fanny dissimulates and denies the adultery; the Colonel realistically estimates its likelihood from the start, out of that male tradition of frank and unagonised recognition that could be said to connect him with Maupassant and Balzac, and that has something to do with a wider male experience (his wife with characteristic feminine hyperbole says he has 'taken part in the sack of cities', 84). 'What in the world did you ever suppose was going to happen?' (213) he asks, like Strether's 'what in the world else would one have wished it to be like?'. The Colonel responds to Charlotte with a kind of wistful sympathy: he likes Charlotte's 'knowing what she wants' (84) and her 'instincts that made against waste' (73); he feels she is 'much more of his own sort than his wife' (73). Both the sympathy and its wistfulness, its essential ineffectiveness to save her, could be thought of as characteristic of the treatment of the adulterous woman in the European novel tradition.

Charlotte's instincts make against waste: to borrow from her own vocabulary of economy, she 'spends' her life where Maggie 'saves' hers. It is characteristic of the anti-Puritan frame of reference of the late novels that here it is the spender, and not the saver, who does not 'waste'. All Maggie's long struggle to recover her husband is expressed to herself in terms of abstinence. Over and over again her syntax defines the almost-said that is held back, the almost-done that is restrained. 'Had he but uttered . . . she would have found herself . . . voluble almost to eloquence' (318); she might 'sound out their doom in a sentence' (457), but she does not. Her first impulse, or at least her second, is always to preserve the bridge game, not to allow the 'cry to pierce the stillness of peaceful sleep' (352). Her 'high undertaking' is 'to prove there was nothing the matter with her' (354), she practises a 'passionate prudence' (357). Her triumph on the very last page of the novel is in preventing her husband from telling her the truth he is at last ready to tell her. 'All she now knew . . . was that she should be ashamed to listen to the uttered word' (547); she seals it up in silence with her kiss.[14]

It is 'bad' Charlotte and not 'nice' Maggie, who is the truth teller in this novel. Wherever all that is unspoken and dissimulated in the novel comes closest to utterance, it is in Charlotte's mouth. When Adam proposes to her, for instance, she does not speak one word in her reply that is not painfully, painstakingly truthful:

'I won't pretend it won't be good for me to marry. Good for me, I mean,' she pursued, 'because I'm so awfully unattached. I should like to be a little less adrift. I should like to have a home. I should like to have an existence. I should like to have a motive for one thing more than another – a motive outside of myself. 'In fact,' she said, so sincerely that it almost showed pain, yet so lucidly that it almost showed humour, 'in fact, you know, I want to *be* married.' (175)

When Adam says that he has known her 'long and from far back', she asks him, 'Do you think you've "known" me?', and 'I mean when it's a question of learning, one learns sometimes too late' (176, 177). She does not of course actually offer him the salient fact, of her past relationship, whatever it was, with his son-in-law. Her truth telling is not of this kind: it is not moralised. Her utterances are not confessions: they represent, rather, proffered openings into the seamlessness of Ververesque certainty and safety. She rends the fabric of the linear unfolding of their imperturbability. Maggie's defeat of her in the linear unfolding of the novel consists in her repairing, sewing up that fabric as fast as Charlotte's open-ended utterance gashes it open.

It is perhaps this 'truth-telling' that distinguishes Charlotte the American and Kate the English girl from their Continental counterpart in Marie de Vionnet. The *vieille sagesse* Mme de Vionnet falls back on in her crisis has very little, we know from Marie herself, to do with telling the truth; on the contrary, all her hopes of keeping Chad, or, failing that, of best protecting her own future, depend on her traditionally feminine skills of dissimulation. Kate and Charlotte can be skilled dissimulators too, but their real, rare pedigree, their special attraction, consists in how frankly and with what intelligence they can describe – so long as they are never boring – their situation to their lovers. Mme de Vionnet plays out a role, knows from a common stock of women's wisdom on such matters what the older mistress of a young man must eventually expect. Kate and Charlotte, within a culture that (the famous English hypocrisy) has no stock of gestures for sustaining and explaining their improper and illegitimate roles, are inventing as they go along, offering analysis from the very frontiers of possibility.

There is some advantage for Charlotte in her frankness. It is the advantage she names herself, when she takes her hour with the Prince:

'I wanted you to understand. I wanted you, that is, to hear. I don't care, I think, whether you understand or not. If I ask nothing of you I don't – I mayn't – ask even so much as that. What you may think of me – that doesn't in the least matter. What I want is that it shall always be with you – so that you'll never be able quite to get rid of it – that I *did*. I won't say that *you* did – you may make as little of that as you like. But that I was here with you where we are and *as* we are – I just saying this. Giving myself, in other words, away – and perfectly willing to do it for nothing. That's all.' (94)

It is impossible to imagine Mme de Vionnet clearing that space for her own motives to be articulated aloud – or wanting to. Of course, as Charlotte says herself, speaking them aloud cannot help her, is not even intended to make any difference in how the Prince thinks of her. All she is able to articulate, in fact, is that she at least knows and can freely name her own abjectness, her own 'giving herself away' to him. Her articulation is essentially for herself. It is a small, an equivocal freedom, it only exists provisionally and in relation to the Prince's encompassing larger one; but for her moment Charlotte is able to transform it into a generous breathing space, and to find a paradoxical self-possession in the very naming of her helplessness.

In the scene on the terrace the night of the bridge game, the same pattern of rending freedom and repairing reticence is played out in the speech between Maggie and Charlotte. Charlotte appears to assert herself – and violently (as in the relationship between Kate and Milly, one of things James is interested in showing us is how women, even working within the codes of charming appeasing femininity, threaten and fear one another) – as the offerer of candour, the clearer of an air 'heavy with thunder' (463).

'Have you any ground of complaint of me? Is there any wrong you consider I've done you? I feel at last that I've a right to ask you.' (466)

The risk she takes is characteristic; bravely she brings the novel to the brink of plain statement. Maggie has only to reply with the same candour for all the 'high decorum' of the bridge game to fail and collapse in an instant. But equally characteristically Maggie falters back from that brink, denying, with her usual protective reticence, that there is any 'complaint'. And Charlotte's appearance of candour here is not in fact quite candid: she is presuming upon Maggie's reticence, gambling on Maggie's *not* answering her, on Maggie's refusing to say that she knows what Charlotte is talking about. She offers the truth, but in order for Maggie to deny it for her. The rent she proffers in the fabric no longer opens onto any real world of possibilities outside. Or perhaps – if the possibility that Maggie will answer is, for its moment, real – they both look through the rent into the howling storm, and both, each momentarily dependent on the other, the dissimulator on the impasse of the truth-teller, the truth-teller on the persistence of the dissimulator, step back from that brink. So that in the end Charlotte's candour as her story winds down into her collapse and defeat dwindles to only representing a very limited kind of openness: all she can do, finally, is force a situation in which both women will, explicitly and directly, and each knowing the other knows she is doing it, lie to one another, in full view of their little world. In the end the truth-teller can only compel an inverted anti-truth. By the end of the novel Charlotte has forced open Maggie's eyes; Maggie has forced shut Charlotte's mouth. The kiss seals the reciprocity of the exchange.

Maggie and Charlotte's rivalry in the novel *is* reciprocal. It is not only Charlotte who offends against Maggie's 'right'; there is another offence, Maggie's offence, written into the novel, more submerged and covert, a sin whose appearance is all innocence and daylight (the Prince calls it a 'thickness of white air that was like a dazzling curtain of light, concealing as darkness conceals', 42), counterpoint to the more old-fashioned night-time sin of Charlotte's and the Prince's adultery. Maggie's 'sin' reminds us of Isabel Archer too, the Isabel Alfred Habegger writes so percipiently about in *Henry James and the 'Woman Business'*, who, watching Osmond with his 'obedient, porcelain-like daughter', waits 'with a certain unuttered contentedness, to have her movements directed'.[15]

As in so many other places, that which was mere hypocrisy in *The Portrait of a Lady* is translated into the authentic thing-in-itself in the later novel. James in *The Portrait* could not fully explore that proneness to filial abjection in Isabel because Osmond is not really a good father. We are meant to be in no doubt in *The Golden Bowl* that Adam is completely the father Maggie believes he is. All that tenderly proud appreciation she has for his modesty, that painful sensitivity to his vulnerability, that responsible protectiveness which provisionally inverts their relationship so that she often refers to Adam as if he were her child and not she his; these are real values, not founded on any 'mistake'. When Maggie finds Adam with Mrs Rance he sees 'the look in his daughter's eyes – the look with which he saw her take in exactly what had occurred' (130); and indeed, just as Maggie has intuited, Adam has been victim of the predatory conversationalist just because of his inability to be anything but gentle and generous socially. When Maggie agonises (and exults) at the irony that her father 'did it all for *me* . . . did it all for me and only for me' (415) she is right; we are privy to Adam's 'discovery' that he might 'put his child at peace' by his own marriage, that Charlotte might 'contribute to' this 'service to his daughter' (168). When Maggie wails to Fanny over the adulterers' betrayal, it does not surprise us that it is the betrayal of the father that has for her the second, weightier emphasis: 'They pretended to love me . . . And they pretended to love *him*' (416).

The whole plot of the second part of the novel is structured around the father's and daughter's hyper-considerateness towards one another. The mainspring of Maggie's great effort at first is to protect her father from knowledge of the adulterous affair by her own appearance of seamless contentment. Later that effort seems to transform into an effort to appear not to know (again through demonstrating her contentment) what she now presumes her father knows, because she does not want him made unhappy by knowing she is unhappy. By the end of the novel what we seem to make out is that both father and daughter not only know about the affair, but presume the other knows about it too, and that the other knows they know. Yet the actual fact of the separation is as close as they get to an admission to one another of what both know. They continue to dissimulate that knowledge from one another almost as a kind of inverted mutual reassurance; their refusal to even once ever candidly *name* what has happened amounts to a denial of its power in the face of their power. At the end their collaborative dissimulation is victorious, even: it demonstrates that nothing the adulterers have done can break the sacred rules between father and daughter ('full as she was of little rules, considerations, provisions', 139) in which such possibilities have no names.

Deep in the very language James uses to piece out the relationship of father and daughter there is an ambivalence: the contradiction of their innocence and their concealments, their transparency and their denial. Maggie's own articulated version of this contradiction is that the innocence was real until the intrusion upon their innocence of the sin-bearing Charlotte. Repeatedly her imagination in its soreness returns to an iconic, yearning, familial Eden before the father and daughter, intact in their self-sufficiency, were intruded upon (an Eden in which somehow both of them are the parents and both the children; one of her repeated tender jokes with her father is that he is much younger than she is):

> the treasured past, which hung there behind them like a framed picture in a museum, a high watermark for the history of their old fortune; the summer evening, in the park at Fawns, when, side by side under the trees just as now, they had let their happy confidence lull them with its most golden tone. (357)

The absolute contrasts between the innocent then and the experienced now are expressed in Maggie's imagination in terms of various oppositions: a temperate summer is opposed to an overheated tropicalism ('husbands and wives, luxuriant complications, made the air too tropical', 471); young America is opposed to old Europe; images of the sacred are opposed to the profane; and above all the seemliness and decorum of a chaste reticence are opposed to the floridity and indecency of frank talk:

> The fractions of occasions, the chance minutes that put them face to face had, as yet, of late, contrived to count but little, between them, either for the sense of opportunity or for that of exposure; inasmuch as the lifelong rhythm of their intercourse made against all cursory handling of deep things. They had never availed themselves of any given quarter of an hour to gossip about fundamentals; they moved slowly through large still spaces; they could be silent together, at any time, with much more comfort than hurriedly expressive. It appeared indeed to have become true that their common appeal measured itself, for vividness, just by this economy of sound. (352)

Consistently, for Maggie, for Fanny, it is Charlotte and not Amerigo who is the serpent in this Eden, the scapegoat who must be expelled from it in order to decontaminate its original happiness. We watch the process of the scapegoating of Charlotte in the novel by all its characters (but not by James: this nice distinction is carefully made by Michiel Heyns[16]) including the Prince, that barbarian, whose gentleman's honour, towards the end of the novel, seems to consist in the unflinchingness with which he sacrifices she-who-had-been his match, his mate: 'He had to turn away, but he wasn't in the least a coward; he would wait on the spot for the issue of what he had done on the spot' (499). It is a sacrifice licensed, of course, by Charlotte's having from the beginning 'given herself away'. The Prince's phrase has folds upon folds of implication: of Charlotte's generosity; of her exposure; and of a contract, almost, in which she has dispossessed herself of herself, and of her right to exact anything, as a woman, from the gentleman in him. The scapegoating of Charlotte by the characters in the novel is essentially a gendered process. It is a familiar cultural pattern, of course, that in the sexual crime against propriety, or against Eden, it is the woman's act that profanes the trust of innocence, which was invested in her and not in the man.

In the light of this scapegoating of Charlotte, it is striking that the only time when the scapegoat is mentioned explicitly is when Maggie makes reference to herself in the role:

They thus tacitly put it upon her to be disposed of, the whole complexity of their peril, and she promptly saw why: because she was there, and just *as* she was, to lift it off them and take it; to charge herself with it as the scapegoat of old, of whom she had once seen a terrible picture, had been charged with the sins of the people and had gone forth into the desert to sink under his burden and die. That indeed wasn't *their* design and their interest, that she should sink under hers; it wouldn't be their feeling that she should do anything but live, live on somehow for their benefit, and even as much as possible in their company, to keep proving to them that they had indeed escaped and that she was still there to simplify. (457)

We need to ask what the significance of this transference is, and what makes Maggie see herself as the scapegoat even as she is engaged in the process of shedding Charlotte and recovering her husband. Associated with this transference are all those other moments when Maggie's iden-tification with Charlotte's suffering is so intense that she even voices to herself, ventriloquising for Charlotte, how it feels to be deprived, like Charlotte, of 'the golden flame' and left with 'a mere handful of black ashes' (521). Is this sympathetic identification disingenuous in Maggie, a sort of sublimated gloating over her rival?

There is certainly a way of reading a degree of disingenuousness as psychologically consistent with that Maggie whose precise history and persona are vivid in the novel; that plucky bright-faced convent-school girl whose natural mode is a shy playful irony. When the Prince in their courtship asks her to believe he is not 'a hypocrite', Maggie stares and blushes: 'duplicity, like "love", had to be joked about' (37). Much later on, and in the face of the Prince's 'duplicity', she thinks of the lovers as 'high-Wagnerian', with whatever little touch of private contempt. When she discovers 'high-Wagnerian' passion ensconsed at her very hearth, she is not merely overwhelmed by it, she has her own mockery of it, her insightful spiky guesses at its stumbles, its foolishnesses (as when she catches the Prince out misunderstanding what she means by 'two' relations with Charlotte, 429). At dinner with Maggie, Lady Castledean no doubt believes she is with 'a smaller social insect'; but it is Maggie's private irony that in fact the 'smaller insect' with its 'little protuberant eyes' is at that moment seeing more than her Ladyship (334).

In other words, there is in Maggie's very timidity a kind of stubbornness, a quiet presumption; something rather like how her father's unassuming social persona covers his huge ambition for American City, his imperturbable belief in himself. We are given sudden glimpses of Maggie's temper, her sheer indignation at being crossed; this little rich girl, after all, has always had everything she wanted. There is the revealing passing flash, for instance, while she is sticking her hatpin in, at the new maid who 'she had lately found herself thinking of as abysmal' (355); of course the fury and the pin are meant for Charlotte, but it seems telling too that this little vent of rage is one of the few places in the novel where James suddenly opens up for us an impression of how every least domestic gesture, every private twist of feeling in the two households, is afloat on the support of numberless, nameless, voiceless 'inferiors'.

That quietly opinionated Maggie, fighting her corner, we can imagine permitting herself some dissimulated satisfactions at Charlotte's defeat; nice convent-educated girls will not gloat – they are 'full of the superstition of not "hurting"' (135) – but may not be beyond dwelling, with every appearance of meek feelingness, on the abasement of Wagnerian tragic heroines. But the timbre of the late passages of the novel must convince us, surely, that James means there to be more to Maggie's identification with Charlotte's suffering than merely the sneaking triumph of the 'protuberant-eyed' social insect. There are moments in the last drawnout weeks at Fawns when the tensions between the protagonists feel more vexed and complex than can be explained by anyone's straightforward 'victory'.

Or, to put the problem the other way round, Maggie's triumph in having her husband finally all to herself in the last pages of the novel is too unalloyed not to make us ask some questions of it: would we not expect it to be mixed up with some sense of loss of that father she has been almost inseparable from in all that 'treasured past', that father the preservation of whose well-being has been the paramount law of her life? Maggie has lost her fantasy companion, her child-parent in that Eden relationship of innocence which has been at the heart of her imagination of value. But the huge relief at the departure of the senior Ververs for American City does not only feel like a relief at getting rid finally of the scapegoated Charlotte. Some other trouble, some other weight, has been lifted out of Maggie's life to liberate her for the final soaring reconciliation with her husband. She and the Prince agree to postpone their reconciliation, their reckoning, not until *Charlotte* has gone, but until *they* have gone, the mistress and the father both; 'till they're away . . . till they've left the country . . . Till we've ceased to see them – for as long as God may grant! Till we're really alone' (535).

In those last weeks at Fawns when Maggie weeps at Charlotte's torment there are glimpses in her narrative, flashed in the interstices of perception rather than seen head-on, of her father as something other than child-companion and put-upon innocent. His very neutrality, his mouse-likeness, his withholding of his utterance and verdict from everyone, loom suddenly, even to Maggie, as terrible in their own unaccusable way:

Charlotte hung behind, with emphasized attention; she stopped when her husband stopped, but at the distance of a case or two, or of whatever other succession of objects; and the likeness of their connexion would not have been wrongly figured if he had been thought of as holding in one of his pocketed hands the end of a long silken halter looped around her beautiful neck. He didn't twitch it, yet it was there; he didn't drag her, but she came; and those indications that I have described the Princess as finding extraordinary in him were two or three mute facial intimations which his wife's presence didn't prevent his addressing his daughter – nor prevent his daughter, as she passed, it was doubtless to be added, from flushing a little at the receipt of. They amounted perhaps only to a wordless, wordless smile, but the smile was the soft shake of the twisted silken rope, and Maggie's translation of it, held in her breast till she got well away, came out only, as if it might have been overheard, when some door was closed behind her. 'Yes, you see – I lead her now by the neck, I lead her to her doom, and she doesn't so much as know what it is, though she has a fear in her heart which, if you had the chances to apply your ear there that I, as a husband, have, you would hear thump and thump and thump.' (493–4)

The apparent innocence of silence and inaction (Adam has *done* nothing) might after all, Maggie suddenly intuits, cover such brutalities, such a cold relish at his so cruelly withholding himself. In Maggie's imagination the flutter in her own breast, where she conceals in shame what she has heard (shame at herself for recognising it, shame at Charlotte's abjection, shame at her father's exposure of a secret self?) sympathetically becomes the thump of fear in Charlotte's breast, the breast where Adam, taking his rights as a husband, may lay his head exultingly to listen to the fear he causes. The sexual charge of that imagery (the wife's breast where he listens is for a moment so close to the daughter's) is a part, surely, of Maggie's flutter of shame.

The image of Adam's leading Charlotte by a silken halter explicitly reverses that image Maggie has earlier entertained of him as a lamb sacrificed to the wickedness of the others (356). It also revisits Maggie's perpetual fallacy of the parent–child inversion: in fact her father is not a lamb, led, not a child, minded. It is he who leads and controls. In one of their long tête-à-têtes in the grounds at Fawns, Maggie had exclaimed, in the kind of sentimental hyperbole characteristic of her filial piety: 'Everything that touches you, everything that surrounds you, goes on – by your splendid indifference and your incredible permission – at your expense' (479). Maggie's mode as daughter has been mostly to bask in the all-powerfulness, the 'permission', of the father; reading it as a generosity by which they all live, as a power characterised, as it were, negatively, by its not exercising itself. But towards the end of the novel, as she is witness to Charlotte's punishment, that mode falters, and with an ambivalence that could almost be that of an Emily Dickinson poem (and the discomforting merging of father and lover imagery belongs in Dickinson territory too) she glances obliquely, through her moments of identification with Charlotte, at the real effects of the all-beneficence of that 'Papa above', wrapped around concealingly in his philanthropic white mist.[17] Does he suddenly frighten her; does she suddenly feel the silken halter of his devotion to her, his immense investment in her (her stupidity at bridge had ever been 'his small, his sole despair', 456) around her own neck?[18] That that ambivalence might in fact extend outside the familial into the social and political is of course quite explicit in *The Golden Bowl*. The inhabitants of American City clearly want nothing to do with Adam Verver's philanthropy; which can either be read as their 'horrible vulgar' philistinism (479), or as his unwanted imposition upon them of his willed fulfilment.[19]

Maggie's own image for the discovery she makes in the course of the novel – or rather, one of many images she tries out on what she discovers – is that she finds a sinister stranger in her home:

She saw at all events why horror itself had almost failed her; the horror that, foreshadowed in advance, would, by her thought, have made everything that was unaccustomed in her cry out with pain; the horror of finding evil seated, all at its ease, where she had only dreamed of good; the horror of the thing hideously *behind*, behind so much trusted, so much pretended, nobleness, cleverness, tenderness. It was the first sharp falsity she had known in her life, to touch at all, or be touched by; it had met her like some bad-faced stranger surprised in one of the thick-carpeted corridors of a house of quiet on a Sunday afternoon; and yet, yes, amazingly, she had been able to look at terror and disgust only to know that she must put away from her the bitter-sweet of their freshness. (459)

Ostensibly, this only reiterates that version of her experience which has an intrusion, brought by the adulterers, contaminating an Eden perfect before their transgression. But in the interstices of this account (or looking, like Maggie, *behind* it) can we not uncover something else? Because of the high decorum exacted of her as '*her* husband's wife . . . *her* father's daughter', Maggie has asked whether she has not been cheated of 'the protests of passion', 'the rages of jealousy'. We are concentrated absolutely here on what 'the civilised order exacts'; we are experiencing the learned movement of Maggie's reticence from the inside. It was not only bridge her father schooled her in; and perhaps all her lapses were met like her failure at bridge with his undemonstrative but definite disappointment. Or perhaps, in anticipation of his disappointment, she never lapsed.

Because of her learned high decorum, Maggie has had to put away the terror and disgust that came with her discovery of the adultery; she has had to put away 'the bitter-sweet of their freshness'. We remember how the susceptible governess in 'The Turn of the Screw' not only dreaded her ghosts but began to dread the possibility of their absence. There is an ambivalence, to begin with, about that thick-carpeted house of quiet, an ambivalence we do not perhaps quite focus upon until we read to the end of the sentence. Was the thick-carpeted quiet of the house stale, so that Maggie found even terror and disgust fresh? Why were those strong emotions of repulsion bitter-sweet and not just bitter; and why was even their bitterness part of their freshness? And although Maggie has always wanted to tell herself that the 'evil' came from outside and contaminated the house, does this ambivalent thrill at the astringency of 'seeing and facing more' (James's phrase from his review of Stevenson) not suggest that there was something wrong, something false, in the hermetic seal of the house before the stranger came?

In dreams, the mean-faced stranger met in the corridors of home turns out as often as not to be a family member, an intimate there (this recalls James's pursuing-fleeing ghosts in his story 'The Jolly Corner' and in his dream of an encounter in the Galérie d'Apollon, recounted in the *Autobiography*[20]). In the corridors of Fawns in those last weeks Maggie often surprises 'a little quiet gentleman' who 'presented a somewhat meditative back', leading Charlotte by her halter: he is her dear father, and he is at the same time a man capable of bringing a woman's 'heart in[to] her throat' and compelling her to follow him around with her shame and her defeat 'done up' in a 'napkin'. That image of the napkin, borrowed nightmarishly from dinner-table niceties, is particularly telling. The thing you carry round in a napkin, looking vainly for 'some corner' to put it down in, so that it cannot be traced to you, is something spat out, humiliating, unswallowable (491). The adjacent mention of Charlotte's (and / or Maggie's) heart in her throat inevitably interacts with the napkin idea; the heart, instead of the high-Wagnerian vessel of passion, is become a piece of choking gristle. (Is it making too explicit a nuance of suggestion to point out too that for women, carrying around shaming secrets hidden in awkward-to-dispose-of-napkins has usually to do with menstruation? Part of Charlotte's humiliation is that she will be the mother of no-one's children.)

In her own words, Maggie had only *dreamed* of finding 'good' behind 'so much pretended, nobleness, cleverness, tenderness'. The sharp, painful, bitter-sweet discovery of the stranger in the house wakes her up out of that dream; her own imagery makes the change sound less like innocence outraged (these things *were* real, and now they are spoiled) than innocence growing up into experience (these things were not real, and I was ignorant and deluded).[21] In retrospect, all the idealism and all the trust were not only misplaced, but were also intrinsically inadequate to the grown-up truth. The adultery in the novel is not the only wrong thing lurking in the Eden of this privilege.

Charlotte really has something to complain about; the ferocity with which she turns on Maggie in the garden temple at Fawns ('I want to have him [Adam] at last a little to myself; I want, strange as it may seem to you ... to *keep* the man I've married', 512) is not merely a dissimulation of the rage she feels at the loss of her lover. It has also simply been true that the relationship of father and daughter *has* prevented her having that marriage with her husband she thought she was agreeing to in Brighton. She protests, with a vehemence as if she really feels herself justified, as at a trick played on her, at something crooked and unclean in the bargain she accepted when she told Adam then that she thought it would be good for her to be married: 'I should like to have a home. I should like to have ... a motive outside of myself.' But she has not had the home, or the marriage, or the motive. When Fanny, flustered and reproachful, interrogates Charlotte on why she has come out with the Prince to the Foreign Office squash, Charlotte is neither appeasing nor defensive; she candidly, although never expecting Fanny to appreciate her point, *explains*. She is being as much wife as her husband is making space for her to be:

'I accepted Adam's preference that I should come tonight without him; just as I accept, absolutely, as a fixed rule, all his preferences. But that doesn't alter the fact, of course, that my husband's daughter, rather than his wife, should have felt that *she* could, after all, be the one to stay with him, the one to make the sacrifice of this hour.' (199)

When Charlotte finally makes her way to the Prince that rainy March tea-time, her explanation that she is there in the end more or less because she has nothing else to do, is not, after all, mere pretext, or mere 'bedizened description'. Somewhere between amusement and exasperation (never falling into the complaint which would fatally bore him) she spells out for the Prince fragment by banal fragment – timings, domestic details – the baffling crime against them that is not a crime, the innocence that blocks them and thwarts them and yields to them nowhere; channels them, effectively, into the inevitability of committing their own dark ordinary crime, the counterpoint to this bright unaccusable childish one:

'I can't help wondering when you must have last laid eyes on them.' And then as it had apparently for her companion an effect of abruptness: 'Maggie, I mean, and the child. For I suppose you know he's with her.'

'Oh yes, I know he's with her. I saw them this morning.'

'And did they then announce their programme?'

'She told me she was taking him, as usual, *da nonno*.'

'And for the whole day?'

He hesitated, but it was as if his attitude had slowly shifted. 'She didn't say. And I didn't ask.'

'Well,' she went on, 'it can't have been later than half past ten – I mean when you saw them. They had got to Eaton Square before eleven. You know we don't formally breakfast, Adam and I; we have tea in our rooms – at least I have; but luncheon is early, and I saw my husband, this morning, by twelve; he was showing the child a picture book. Maggie had been there with him, had left them settled together. Then she had gone out – taking the carriage for something he had been intending but that she offered to do instead.'

The Prince appeared to confess, at this, to his interest. 'Taking, you mean, *your* carriage?'

'I don't know which, and it doesn't matter. It's not a question,' she smiled, 'of a carriage the more or less.' (231)

Charlotte has been back to Eaton Square – her home – three times in the course of her day, to find Maggie still there, to slip away again, unnoticed. 'What do they really suppose', she asks, 'becomes of one? – not so much sentimentally or morally, so to call it, since that doesn't matter;

but even just physically, materially, as a mere wandering woman' (232). At Portland Place the Prince is *waiting for* his wife, feeling her absence obscurely wrong, obscurely significant, in a way that is a mirror-image of how Maggie will wait for *him*, later, on his return from Matcham. 'He could have named to himself no pressing reason for seeing her at this moment, and her not coming in, as the half-hour elapsed, became in fact quite positively, however perversely, the circumstance that kept him on the spot' (224).

Amerigo and Charlotte, for all their trying, are not *married enough*; the primary, the precedent bond between parent and child, that needs to be broken in order to make way for these grown-up marriages, remains inviolable, intact, takes up all the human space. 'For Mrs Verver to be known to people so intensively and exclusively as her husband's wife', the Prince says to Fanny, 'he should manage to be known – or at least to be seen – a little more as his wife's husband' (209). The Prince and Charlotte's conversation circles what is wrong, in a sort of incredulous confirmation of what both recognise. Maggie's and Adam's relationship is the very incarnation of innocence: a grandfather looks at a picture book with his grandchild. Yet when Charlotte and the Prince spell over all the apparently insignificant signs that somehow add up to the significant problem, the very idiom, the rhythm, of their fascination is just the same as the way Maggie, later, will rehearse and re-rehearse the innocent appearances between the lovers in order to uncover the secret crime beneath.[22]

Even Fanny wavers momentarily over something *wrong* in the Verver dolls-house of familial contentment, 'children playing at paying visits, playing at "Mr Thompson" and "Mrs Fane", each hoping that the other would really stay to tea' (196):

'He and Charlotte must have arrived – if they have arrived – expecting to drive together to Eaton Square and keep Maggie on to dinner there. She has everything there, you know – she has clothes.'

The Colonel didn't in fact know, but he gave it his apprehension. 'Oh, you mean a change?'

'Twenty changes, if you like – all sorts of things. She dresses, really, Maggie does, as much for her father – and she always did – as for her husband or herself. She has her room in his house very much as she had it before she was married – and just as the boy has a second nursery there, in which Mrs Noble, when she comes with him, makes herself, I assure you, at home. *Si bien* that if Charlotte, in her own house, so to speak, should wish a friend or two to stay with her, she really would be scarce able to put them up.'

It was a picture into which, as a thrifty entertainer himself, Bob Assingham could more or less enter. 'Maggie and the child spread so?'

'Maggie and the child spread so.'

Well, he considered. 'It *is* rather rum.'

'That's all I claim' – she seemed thankful for the word. 'I don't say it's anything more – but it *is*, distinctly, rum.' (279)

This 'rum' oblivious innocence of the filial pair, as if nothing could ever happen in the blue sky of their privileged Eden, cannot easily be accused; and yet it is as responsible for skewing and perverting the two marriages as the adultery of the others. Adam Verver, the inheritor of the wealth of the nations, is indeed Yeats's 'mouse'; and the maintenance of his childlikeness turns out to entail twists and abuses as convoluted as those in the behaviour of any violent and bitter ancestor. Fanny, catching him out early on in the novel in the most innocent of social evasions, sees 'the touching, confessing eyes of a man of forty-seven caught in the act of handling a relic of infancy – sticking on the head of a wooden soldier or trying the lock of a wooden gun' (112): the mixture in the image of Adam's innocence with something disconcerting – the man of peace caught out playing with mock-violence – is characteristic of James's representation of him. And Maggie, the daughter of this child-man who plays with expensive toys, schooled at the convent in worship of her 'Papa above!', is doubly bound: as his daughter fulfilling in her spotless happiness the great investment he has made in her, and as the parent of the child in him, keeping clean and sacrosanct that space in which he is not to be contaminated by what blows in from the 'horrid, vulgar' world outside. Just as he holds Charlotte on his silken halter he keeps Maggie, as it were, *sentimental*; for as long as he remains the centre of her emotional life she can only persist in being, or at least, latterly, pretending to be, that pert, sweet girl-child who jiggles his neck-tie and rubs noses with her Daddy 'according to the tradition of their frankest levity' (356).[23] It is only when her father and Charlotte are 'away . . . they've left the country . . . we've ceased to see them – for as long as God may grant! . . . we're really alone' (535), that Maggie can touch a man with gravity instead, having painfully unlearned her father's lesson that '"love", had to be joked about' (37).

Maggie is James's further exploration of that abjection which he first touched upon in Isabel in *The Portrait of a Lady*, and then evaded wholly following through by writing Osmond as only a pseudo-father-figure. Maggie is, though, defined differently from the virginal Isabel. She may suspect the high-Wagnerian, and have painfully to unlearn certain senti-mental innocences. But it is made clear that her passion for her husband is sexual, even that she is sexually subjected to him, from the very beginning of their relationship, from the innocent first days of their marriage, in their shared play-fantasy of his cruelty;

One of the comfortable things between the husband and wife meanwhile – one of these easy certitudes they could be merely gay about – was that she never admired him so much, or so found him heart-breakingly handsome, clever, irresistible, in the very degree in which he had fatally and originally dawned upon her, as when she saw other women reduced to the same passive pulp that had then begun, once for all, to constitute *her* substance. There was really nothing they had talked of together with more intimate and familiar pleasantry than of the license and the privilege, the boundless happy margin, thus established for each; she going so far as to put it that, even should he some day get drunk and beat her, the spectacle of him with hated rivals would, after no matter what extremity, always, for the sovereign charm of it, charm of it in itself and at the exhibition of him that most deeply moved her, suffice to bring her round. (138–9)

Maggie proceeds in the course of the novel to get exactly what she wants: the rival, the passive pulp, the (metaphoric) beating, and so on; notoriously, of course, in novels as well as fairy tales, getting exactly what you want involves painful discoveries about exactly what it costs. No doubt this founding fantasy in their relationship is a part of Maggie's need, at the very end of the novel, to hand back to the Prince intact at least the appearance of his power over her which his confession might have jeopardised. It is an open question whether in the closing moments we are glad of the silence, or miss too much the intelligent explanation of the truth-telling Charlotte.

The novel ends with a kiss, and it is punctuated by kisses, the Prince's with Maggie, Maggie's with Charlotte, Charlotte's with the Prince, Maggie's with her father, Maggie's with Fanny, Fanny's with the Colonel: these embraces weave a musical pattern of touch, electric, attractive, re-pulsive, through all the novel and around its polarities of innocence and experience. The novel is structured as a dance of changing partners, suf-fused with eroticism.[24] In its involved concentration upon the erotic *The Golden Bowl* does not really seem quite representative of the nineteenth-century novel, either English or European: novels are usu-ally 'about' so much 'more'. Even Jane Austen's seem to occupy a much larger social space than this. A search for antecedents for James's late love tangle might come up with something as improbable as *Liaisons Dangereuses*, which Ian Watt excludes from his mainline novel tradition of formal realism because it is 'too stylish to be authentic', its elegance and concision the opposite to the 'diffuseness' more characteristic of the novel form, the diffuseness of 'le réel écrit'.[25]

In order to characterise *The Golden Bowl* we may even be tempted to make reference outside the novelistic tradition itself. It feels rather as though it belongs in a tradition of erotic tragi-comedy, which would include, say, *Much Ado about Nothing* and *Così Fan Tutte*. Or with Jean Renoir's film *Les Règles du Jeu*; there too, in order to represent a late phase in a declining leisure-class civilisation, the artist deploys a style that imitates and exaggerates the laconic elegance, the 'good form', the oblivious privileges and aching voids and lurking violences of that class. In these comedies, as in *The Golden Bowl*, dark and light stories co-exist; happy endings are imposed with much music of reconciliation and resolution onto material that has repeatedly come near to forming itself into the threatening darker shapes of danger, waste and loss. *The Golden Bowl*, like the others, is full of suffering and sacrifice; sacrifice involuntary, resisting, unresigned. But that is not all: the music, the writing, also makes actual in these erotic comedies the momentary boundless possibilities of play and pleasure.

Notes

INTRODUCTION

1 Eve Kosovsky Sedgwick, *Epistemology of the Closet* (Stamford: University of California Press, 1990). Hugh Stevens, *Henry James and Sexuality* (Cambridge University Press, 1998), p. 173.

2 Ross Posnock, *The Trial of Curiosity: Henry James, William James, and the Challenge of Modernity* (New York: Oxford University Press, 1991), pp. 204, 242.

3 'Definitional frames' is from Stevens, *Henry James and Sexuality*, p. 125.

4 That Max Beerbohm cartoon of James examining the shoes outside the bedroom door seems to have had an extraordinary suggestiveness and staying power.

5 Even Ruth Bernard Yeazell, in her most percipient and sympathetic reading of the late novels, arguing for the importance in them of sexual passion, wrote about James's 'sexual reticence', said his characters 'repress and evade' sexual knowledge, and described the late style as the 'recording of the mind's effort to walk the tightrope between that fascination and that fear [of sexuality]'. *Language and Knowledge in the Late Novels of Henry James* (Chicago University Press, 1976), p. 20.

6 David McWhirter gives an account of James 'changing his mind', too, only he puts the pivotal moment later: 'I discovered an unexpected yet unmistakable movement towards a more affirmative vision of life, a movement crowned in the unprecedented embrace of enacted love which he attains with the renewal of Maggie Verver's marriage in *The Golden Bowl*.' He reads the *oeuvre* as an 'adventure in sustained frustration' up to that point and separates *The Golden Bowl* as unique in its 'affirmation of love', as against the 'thwarted and renounced passion' in *The Wings of the Dove* and *The Ambassadors*. See *Desire and Love in Henry James* (Cambridge University Press, 1989), pp. xi, 3. In another place he follows through this sense of a late 'change of mind' in seeing the 'fourth [post *Golden Bowl*] phase as charged with an exemplary 'revisionary energy'. '"A provision full of responsibilities": senses of the past in Henry James's fourth phase', in Gert Buelens (ed.), *Enacting History in Henry James: Narrative, Power and Ethics* (Cambridge University Press, 1997), p. 152.

7 For convenience, all page references to James's full-length novels unless otherwise stated are to the readily available Penguin editions. Where different editions are used, this will be indicated in the footnotes. For indications of which versions of the texts the Penguin edition uses, see Bibliography.

8 Posnock, *Trial of Curiosity*, p. vii. He also writes, 'My focusing upon Strether's pleasure seeks to challenge the critical tendency to immerse James's protagonist in a rhetoric of sterile negativity that portrays him as vicarious, renunciatory, prissy, fearful, and ascetic,' p. 222.

9 J. M. Coetzee, *Doubling the Point: Essays and Interviews*, ed. David Atwell (Cambridge, Mass: Harvard University Press, 1992), p. 159.

10 Ian Watt, *The Rise of the Novel* (London: The Hogarth Press, 1987), p. 30.

11 Coetzee, *Doubling the Point*, p. 180.

12 Thomas Mann, *Essays of Three Decades*, trans. H. T. Lowe-Porter. (London: Secker and Warburg, n.d.), p. 437.

13 As Peter Brooks has it: 'The unspeakable horrors of the unspecified French novel have moved through the group like a tracer dye, revealing relations, making clear positions and motives.' *The Melodramatic Imagination* (New York: Columbia University Press, 1985), p. 164.

14 Edmund Gosse, 'Editor's Note', in Mathilde Serao, *Fantasia* (Heinemann International Library, 1890).

15 To William James (1876). *Henry James: Letters*, ed. Leon Edel (London: Macmillan, 1974–84), vol. II, p. 58.

16 To Thomas Sergeant Perry (1876). *Letters*, vol. II, p. 44.

17 To W. D. Howells (1876). *Letters*, vol. II, p. 23.

18 Leon Edel, *The Life of Henry James* (Harmondsworth: Penguin, 1977), p. 445.

19 Edel, *The Life*, p. 226. Posnock makes an analogy with how Santayana thinks of the 'genteel American tradition' as simply a 'curious habit of mind . . . to be compared with other habits of mind'. Richard Lyon (ed.), *Santayana on America: Essays, Notes and Letters on American Life, Literature and Philosophy* (New York: Harcourt, 1968), p. 48.

20 M. M. Bakhtin, *The Dialogic Imagination*, trans. Caryl Emerson and Michael Holquist, ed. Michael Holquist (Austin: Texas University Press, 1981), p. 288.

21 Bakhtin, *Dialogic Imagination*, p. 292. Dorothy J. Hale makes an important distinction, though, between Bakhtin's ideas and James's on the representation of language: 'For Bakhtin the novelist's representation of language ultimately allows him a subjective freedom that has no equivalent in James's aesthetic theory. James asserts that the connection between representor and represented is determined . . . by the essential and inescapable quality of the artist's interests; the artwork represents the artistic subject in and through representing this relation. By contrast, Bakhtin believes that, once the novelist learns to objectify language, to display it and not simply to speak through it, his relation to the object of representation becomes contingent: as a novelist, he by definition will necessarily choose to represent language, but he can, it turns out, remain only partially identified with, and thus expressed by,

any particular language he represents.' 'James and the Invention of Novel Theory', in Jonathan Freedman (ed.), *The Cambridge Companion to Henry James* (Cambridge University Press, 1998), p. 98.

22 Edel, *The Life*, p. 448.

23 Shoshana Felman expresses this idea effectively: 'language discreetly dictates to its users – in an invisible manner – self-evident assumptions and proscriptions that are inscribed in its grammar (which is, by definition, imperceptible from inside the language). In order for grammar to appear as such, one must dislodge one's language from its self-presence, from its assumptions and proscriptions, by subjecting them to the otherness of a different grammar, by putting them in question through the medium of a foreign language.' *Writing and Madness*, trans. Martha Noel Evans and the author with Brian Massumi (Ithaca, NY: Cornell University Press, 1985), p. 19. Sara Blair in *Henry James and the Writing of Race and Nation* (Cambridge University Press, 1996) has James 'constructing a cultural position from which otherness can be more pleasurably and freely experienced' (p. 58).

24 'Guy de Maupassant' (1888), in *Henry James: Selected Literary Criticism*, ed. Morris Shapira (London: Heinemann, 1963), p. 93.

25 To W. D. Howells (1884). *Letters*, vol. III, p. 29.

26 'Guy de Maupassant' (1888), in Shapira (ed.), *Selected Literary Criticism*, p. 93.

27 While it is important in the context of this argument to follow through the positive emphases in James's critical discussions of the predominance of women writers in the English tradition, it is of course also important to remember another component of his attitude: his often irritated perception, as Richard Salmon puts it, that 'there is an affinity, or even identity, between the facility of women writers and the "wants" of the reading public'. Richard Salmon, *Henry James and the Culture of Publicity* (Cambridge University Press, 1997), p. 54.

28 'Mathilde Serao' (1902), in Henry James, *Notes on Novelists* (London: J. M. Dent, 1914), p. 236.

29 'Guy de Maupassant' (1888), in Shapira (ed.), *Selected Literary Criticism*, p. 103.

30 To W. D. Howells (1884). *Letters*, vol. III, p. 29.

31 'Guy de Maupassant' (1888), in Shapira (ed.), *Selected Literary Criticism*, p. 103.

32 'Mathilde Serao' (1902), in *Notes on Novelists*, p. 237.

33 'Mathilde Serao' (1902), in *Notes on Novelists*, p. 237.

34 Naomi Lebowitz writes: 'At its best, the genuine feminine sensibility can give us two things in the novel: personal relationships as a moral centre and the freedom that developing character demands from the bondage of society, ideology, and the picturesque.' *The Imagination of Loving: Henry James's Legacy to the Novel* (Detroit: Wayne State University Press, 1965), p. 64.

35 William W. Stowe gives a detailed account of James's debt to Balzac in *Balzac, James and the Realist Novel* (Princeton University Press, 1983).

36 It seems important to make out a relationship between James's work and the work of these less iconoclastic novelists of the first decades of the twentieth century; although Freedman is surely also right when he suggests

that James 'had much to do with the shaping' of the 'aesthetic agendas of high modernism'. Jonathan Freedman, *Professions of Taste: Henry James, British Aestheticism and Commodity Culture* (Stanford University Press, 1990), p. xviii. Undoubtedly James's influence on Joyce's aesthetic (of which Daniel Mark Fogel gives an account in *Covert Relations: James Joyce, Virginia Woolf and Henry James* (Charlottesville: University Press of Virginia, 1990)) is as telling in relation to James's own work as is his influence on Bowen's.

37 But see David Gervais in *Flaubert and Henry James: A Study in Contrasts* (London: Macmillan, 1978): 'Flaubert was fond of telling his friends that one must try not to live in the self. For Emma too the self is an embarrassment and a clog. Her dreamland has obvious affinities with Flaubert's own self-purging conception of art and is the expression of a similar self-absorption' (p. 129).

38 Stevens writes: 'Rather than asking whether James is or is not "homosexual", criticism might examine how his writing examines the workings of sexual identity within culture, without the assumption that James's own identity might be so simply uncovered.' 'Queer Henry in the Cage', in Freedman (ed.), *The Cambridge Companion*, p. 124.

39 Stevens, *Henry James and Sexuality*, p. x.

40 Leo Bersani writes: 'It could be said . . . that the very nature of the novel she appears in determines Isabel's return to Osmond at the end of *The Portrait of a Lady*; her dream of freedom has been defeated by the limited range of possibilities for being free available to the realistic imagination. Isabel *and* James can no longer imagine to what concrete use her desire to be free might be put.' *A Future for Astyanax: Character and Desire in Literature* (London: Marion Boyars, 1978), p. 67.

41 Perhaps Sallie Sears is even right to put it as strongly as this: 'The number of "aggressive" males he depicts can be counted on the fingers of one hand . . . But the number of aggressive females is considerable: there is scarcely a novel in which the extreme weight of possibility and responsibility is not placed on the women, for good or ill . . . James's fictional world is dominated by females.' *The Negative Imagination: Form and Perspective in the Novels of Henry James* (Ithaca, New York: Cornell University Press, 1968), p. 133.

42 Nancy Armstrong, *Desire and Domestic Fiction: A Political History of the Novel* (Oxford University Press, 1987), pp. 185, 253.

43 Michiel W. Heyns, 'The double narrative of "The Beast in the Jungle": ethical plot, ironical plot, and the play of power', in Buelens (ed.), *Enacting History*, pp. 114, 121. Sears says something similar about the 'toughness' of James's imagination, calling him 'the most unsentimental of our great romanticists' (*The Negative Imagination*, p. 151).

44 'In short, James does not limit Strether's awakening in Paris to homoerotic fascination but opens it to embrace heterosexual desire and, ultimately, pleasure itself as violent sensation without a fixed referent.' Posnock, *Trial of Curiosity*, p. 215.

45 Sears writes this about the three 'dark ladies', Madame de Vionnet, Kate Croy and Charlotte Verver: 'in their bravery, beauty, and magnificent

sexuality the former group of women dominate their respective worlds in spite of their "immorality" ... In the end each of them is expelled from the collective social organism like some noxious foreign body that by mistake gained entrance ... Yet even in spite of this they dominate in the possibilities they have represented for energy and passion, and in the strength of their suffering' (*The Negative Imagination*, p. 209).

46 Walter Benjamin, *Illuminations*, trans. Harry Zohn (London: Fontana, 1992), p. 199.

47 'Real justice was not of this world, yet, strangely, happiness was.' 'In the Cage', p. 174. Reference to James's short stories will be to *The Complete Tales*, ed. Leon Edel (London: Rupert Hart-Davis, 1962–4).

1 'JUST YOU WAIT!': REFLECTIONS ON THE LAST CHAPTERS OF *THE PORTRAIT OF A LADY*

1 November 1882. In *Henry James: The Critical Heritage*, ed. Roger Gard (London: Routledge and Kegan Paul, 1968), pp. 126–34.

2 The revision here in the New York Edition from the 1881 edition, from 'a scene that will last always' to 'a scene of the rest of my life' seems to make Isabel's meaning less ambiguous: she has to be implying to Henrietta here that she will go back *to resume her marriage with Osmond*. Of course the fact that she implies it to Henrietta does not necessarily mean she is not entertaining other possibilities.

3 Mostly in this chapter references will be to the 1881 edition (London: Macmillan), indicated by the letter M before the page number. I have worked from this edition because it is important to my argument to address the exact language James used to describe Isabel's dilemma in 1881; the changes made for the New York Edition reflect the changes in the later James's thinking. Page numbers without letters are to the Penguin imprint of the New York Edition, as usual.

4 From an unsigned review, *Saturday Review*, December 1881. In Gard (ed.), *Critical Heritage*, p. 98.

5 I have borrowed this formulation from J. M. Coetzee, in *White Writing: On the Culture of Letters in South Africa* (New Haven: Yale University Press, 1988), p. 113.

6 Notably of course in Tony Tanner's *Adultery in the Novel: Contract and Transgression* (Baltimore: Johns Hopkins University Press, 1979).

7 Tanner, *Adultery in the Novel*, p. 14.

8 R. H. Hutton, Nov. 1881. In Gard (ed.), *Critical Heritage*, p. 96.

9 As Alfred Habegger puts it: 'The freedom that interests James is the internal kind, where the manacles do not get taken off the hands but the spirit – somehow – spreads its wings'. *Henry James and the 'Woman Business'* (Cambridge University Press, 1989), p. 180.

10 Fred Kaplan, *Henry James: The Imagination of Genius* (London: Hodder and Stoughton, 1992), p. 239; Bonnie L. Heron, 'Substantive Sexuality, Henry

James constructs Isabel Archer as a Complete Woman in his Revised Version of Portrait of a Lady', *Henry James Review* 16. 2 (1995), 139. F. R. Leavis seems to think James does not punish Isabel *enough*: 'that she shouldn't be led by their unanimity to question her own valuation convicts her of a notable lack of sense, not to say extremely unintelligent obstinacy . . . but James doesn't let us suppose that he shares this view'. *The Great Tradition* (London: Chatto and Windus, 1948), p. 127.

11 H. E. Scudder, from an unsigned review, *Atlantic* 49 (1882). In Gard (ed.), *Critical Heritage*, pp. 126–30.

12 For a suggestion that George Eliot's portrait of Gwendolen Harleth in *Daniel Deronda* is in contrast disturbingly retributive, see Michiel Heyns, *Expulsion and the Nineteenth-Century Novel: Scapegoats in English Fiction* (Cambridge University Press, 1984).

13 Sallie Sears's account of the 'determined' nature of the Jamesian drama displaces the blame for the 'bitter farce' away from Isabel's mistake and onto the 'very nature of the situations he constructs'. 'The concept of "freedom" is the pivotal point of Isabel Archer's character, for example, but the book is about how, thinking she is freely making the choice that will bring her the most freedom, she has in fact been beguiled into making the one that will bring her the least.' *The Negative Imagination: Form and Perspective in the Novels of Henry James* (Ithaca, New York: Cornell University Press, 1963), p. 83.

14 Millicent Bell, in a generous and non-retributive account of the character, has James 'tenderly permissive of Isabel's self-contradictions'. Millicent Bell, *Meaning in Henry James* (Cambridge, Mass.: Harvard University Press, 1991), p. 89.

15 Ruth Bernard Yeazell's suggestion that Isabel, like Maggie later, 'reverses the look', that is, looks at herself rather than being looked at, seems relevant in the context of this suggestion that the novel is written from inside the formation of Isabel's psychology. Ruth Bernard Yeazell (ed.), *Henry James: A Collection of Critical Essays* (New Jersey: Prentice Hall, 1994), p. 4.

16 The question of Isabel's money is an interesting one. The impression we have from the novel is that she has retained control over it after her marriage: at some point she wishes she could give it all to Osmond in return for her freedom, and then the Countess Gemini talks about Isabel's power to give or not give Pansy a dowry. There had been in England Married Women's Property Acts in 1870 and 1874; in any case the 'top 10% of society were already marrying under the settlement arrangement, by which the wife kept control over her property through trustees'. Lawrence Stone, *Road to Divorce* (Oxford University Press, 1990), p. 375. We do not know for certain, of course, which law Osmond and Isabel were married under.

17 Habegger, *The 'Woman Business'*, p. 156.

18 Habegger, *The 'Woman Business'*, p. 157.

19 Naomi Lebowitz traces both the optimistic rhetoric ('the dogma of romance') and the 'great hope and leaven for personal wholeness' back to 'too much

freedom in the library rooms of Albany houses'. *The Imagination of Loving: Henry James's Legacy to the Novel* (Detroit: Wayne State, 1965), p. 115.

20 David McWhirter in his essay '"A provision full of responsibilities": senses of the past in Henry James's fourth phase' explores the importance in James's novels of 'keeping one's word'. Gert Buelens (ed.), *Enacting History in Henry James: Narrative, Power and Ethics* (Cambridge University Press, 1997), p. 156.

21 Criticism remains divided over Isabel's return to Rome. Winfried Fluck, for example, calls it a 'triumph over her melodramatic impulses', and sees it as a sign that she has developed from a 'passive, incompetent reader of reality to a reader of heightened awareness' (in Buelens (ed.), *Enacting History*, p. 26). But Peter Brooks feels that the decision is 'freighted with lurid connotations of sacrifice, torture, penance, claustration' (*The Melodramatic Imagination*, p. 157). This is the same essential divergence as between, say, Naomi Lebowitz and Sallie Sears in the 1960s. Lebowitz is positive about the return, and sees it as Isabel's opportunity to 'work to infuse [the aesthetic idea of marriage] with moral life' (*Imagination of Loving*, p. 69). Sears calls it 'a return to spiritual destitution' (*The Negative Imagination*, p. 131).

22 Habegger, *The 'Woman Business'*, p. 153.

23 Sallie Sears writes: 'Her narcissism, her frigidity, and the profound sexual terror she exhibits when Goodwood succeeds in arousing her remain undealt with, unrelated to the philosophical and moral motifs of the novel, yet the relation is in fact integral if not crucial . . . It is made very clear in the novel that she is afraid of Goodwood's sexuality, and her decision to return to Osmond is not definite until after the scene where Goodwood kisses her in the garden. Whatever James's conscious intentions, the effect is to suggest a connection between these two things. James's evasion of the implications here is one of the few lapses in an otherwise superb novel.' *The Negative Imagination*, pp. 130–1.

24 Mann, *Essays of Three Decades*, trans. H. Lowe-Porter (London: Secker and Warburg, n.d.), p. 184.

25 *Anna Karenina*, trans. Aylmer Maude (Oxford University Press, 1965), p. 169; *Le Rouge et le Noir* (Paris: Garnier-Flammarion, 1964), p. 93 (my translation); *Lady with a Lapdog*, trans. David Magarshack (Harmondsworth: Penguin, 1970), p. 268.

26 See, for example, 'Souls Belated' and 'Autres Temps', reprinted in *Roman Fever* (London: Virago Modern Classics, 1983).

27 To W. D. Howells (1884). *Letters*, vol. III, p. 29.

2 'AS CHARMING AS A CHARMING STORY': GOVERNESSES IN *WHAT MAISIE KNEW* AND 'THE TURN OF THE SCREW'

1 The book reviewed is *Eight Cousins: or, The Aunt-Hill* by Louisa May Alcott (Boston, 1875). Quoted from Henry James, *Literary Reviews and Essays*, ed. Albert Mordell (New York: Grove Press, 1957), p. 245.

2 James, *Literary Reviews*, pp. 246–7.

3 Nancy Armstrong gives a characteristic slant to her striking account of the power of the governess/teacher in the formation of 'authority': 'those cultural functions which we automatically attribute to and embody as women – those, for example, of mother, nurse, teacher, social worker, and general overseer of service institutions – have been just as instrumental in bringing the new middle classes into power and maintaining their dominance as all the economic take-offs and political breakthroughs we automatically attribute to men'. *Desire and Domestic Fiction: A Political History of the Novel* (Oxford University Press, 1987), p. 26.

4 *French Writers and American Women Essays*, ed. Peter Buitenhuis (Branford, Conn.: Compass, 1960).

5 Tanner, *Adultery in the Novel* (Baltimore: Johns Hopkins University Press, 1979), p. 14.

6 *The Notebooks of Henry James*, ed. F. O. Matthiessen and Kenneth B. Murdock (New York: Oxford University Press, 1961), p. 257.

7 *The Spoils of Poynton*, 1897 is an exception here.

8 Armstrong, *Desire and Domestic Fiction*, p. 6.

9 Millicent Bell, in her magisterial chapter on 'Turn of the Screw' in *Meaning in Henry James* (Cambridge, Mass.: Harvard University Press, 1991), calls it 'the romantic improbability of Charlotte Brontë's dream of feminine self-realisation and wish-fulfillment' (p. 224).

10 '[Mrs Wix's] view of Sir Claude is straight out of romantic fiction'. Bell, *Meaning in Henry James*, p. 246.

11 'Her self-contemplation in the mirror, along with the somewhat frenzied scopic activity in which she sees things not seen by other people or alternatively, imagines herself being seen, may be partially understood as responses to this crisis of identity . . . [the] governess's wish to be seen [is] a wish powerful enough to influence almost everything she says, does, and thinks.' Beth Newman, 'Getting Fixed: Feminine Identity and Scopic Crisis in *The Turn of the Screw*' in Neil Cornwell and Maggie Malone (eds.), *New Casebooks: The Turn of the Screw and What Maisie Knew* (Basingstoke: Macmillan, 1998), pp. 121, 125.

12 References are to *The Complete Tales of Henry James*, ed. Leon Edel (London: Rupert Hart-Davis, 1962–4), vol. x.

13 Ezra Pound's phrase. 'Henry James', in *Literary Essays of Ezra Pound*, ed. T. S. Eliot (London: Faber, 1974), p. 323.

14 '[S]uch sacrificial gains are common to James's female characters, whose very identities in a patriarchal society compel them to interpret sacrifice as reward and fetishise surrender or self-denial as their own property.' John Carlos Rowe, *The Theoretical Dimensions of Henry James* (London: Methuen, 1985), (p. 138).

15 The transformation is reminiscent of the transformation of the little girl in Svidrigailov's sin-burdened dream at the end of *Crime and Punishment*; and one remembers Dostoevsky's comments on the numbers of child prostitutes in London.

16 'Miles can only be angelic or satanic, like Satan himself for whom there could have been no halfway halting place between Heaven and the Hell to which he fell. If she surrenders her belief in his perfection she must insist upon his capacity for some unspeakable act of wickedness.' Bell, *Meaning in Henry James*, p. 236.

17 This rather literal way of putting things bypasses, brutally perhaps, a great deal of critical discussion of whether the governess is sick or not, or whether the ghosts are 'real' or not. Shoshana Felman's work on the story in *Writing and Madness* (Ithaca, N.Y.: Cornell University Press, 1985) makes out a subtle case that the story does not invite us to come down on one side rather than another; and she is unsympathetic to any interpretative process which 'strives . . . to eliminate from language its inherent silence, anything that misses the specific way in which a text *actively* "won't tell"' (p. 153). Even critical work which professes to work within this 'undecidability', however, usually seems to go on to deal, in fact, with the governess's pathology in one version or another, and to show little interest in the possibility of the solicitings of supernatural evil (which perhaps interested James's Victorian readers more). Felman's account of the governess, although complex and not easily summarised, makes her part of precisely this same epistemological problem about knowing and certainty, and is not much interested in the specifics of her particular history as lady and governess.

18 'The existence of the story is thus assured only through the constitution of a *narrative chain*, in which the narrators relay the story from one to the other. The story's origin is therefore not assigned to any one voice which would assume responsibility for the tale, but to the deferred action of a sort of *echoing effect*.' Felman, *Writing and Madness*, p. 167.

19 It seems appropriate that James's idea for 'The Turn of the Screw' originated with an anecdote told him by Edward Benson, Archbishop of Canterbury, himself by all accounts a stern and distant patriarch, pillar of church and state. The archbishop, of course, told the story 'straight', believed in the children's depravity and in an evil which beckoned and solicited them from dangerous places. See the article on Benson by Penelope Fitzgerald, 'Reviewing the Struggle', *London Review of Books* 20.12 (June 1998), 17.

20 In Vivian R. Pollak, ed., *New Essays on Daisy Miller and The Turn of the Screw* (Cambridge University Press, 1993), p. 91.

21 'Invisible to everyone but the governess, Miss Jessel as apparition monstrously exaggerates not only the governess's own social invisibility but also the unremitting surveillance that all governesses were expected to exercise.' Newman, 'Getting Fixed', p. 132.

21 '[T]he ghosts . . . are projections of the governess herself and of her imagination of the Master, suggesting a once-enacted story she might have relived if she had been seduced and abandoned by him.' Bell, *Meaning in Henry James*, p. 27.

23 Felman writes: 'far from implying the simplicity of a self-present literal meaning, sexuality points rather to a multiplicity of conflicting forces, to the

complexity of its own divisiveness and contradiction'. *Writing and Madness*, p. 158.

24 Felman's account has something of the right chill about it: 'For each of the people who receive and keep the manuscript of the story, that manuscript constitutes, well beyond the death of the addressor – the person who bequeathed it to them –, the survival of the giver's language and the giver's own survival *in* his language: a *return* of the dead *within the text.' Writing and Madness*, p. 174.

25 'She, too, is to be abandoned by Miles for the education and future career which are not open to her.' Bell, *Meaning in Henry James*, p. 236.

3 'THE SACRED TERROR': *THE AWKWARD AGE* AND JAMES'S MEN OF THE WORLD

1 Perhaps the belief in the possibility of 'talk' is as important in *The Awkward Age* as the reconciliation with the sexual facts; perhaps the 'talk' is fundamental to the reconciliation. Leo Bersani describes James's 'optimistic view of how speech and thought can, in time, diversify desires and break up rigid structures of character'. *Future for Astyanax: Character and Desire in Literature* (London: Marion Boyars, 1978), pp. 129–130. Elizabeth Deeds Ermath writes: 'Consensus is a matter of the greatest difficulty in James. He can show us what goes on inside a single mind interestingly, enthrallingly; but the exchange between minds, the meetings that establish a common discourse or a common medium of exchange, are centres of strain and difficulty.' The difficulty is certainly one of James's subjects; and the achievement of 'exchange' and the 'meetings' that 'establish common discourse' are the essential story of *The Awkward Age*. Elizabeth Deeds Ermath, *Realism and Consensus in the English Novel* (Princeton University Press, 1983), p. 258.

2 *The Notebooks of Henry James*, ed. F. O. Matthiesson and Kenneth B. Murdock (New York: Oxford University Press, 1947), pp. 192, 194, 195.

3 Martha Banta writes: 'There is little or nothing going on in Henry James's mind that is not about social relations between women and men; every issue is ultimately gendered.' 'Men, Women, and the American Way', in Jonathan Freedman (ed.), *The Cambridge Companion to Henry James* (Cambridge University Press, 1998), p. 21.

4 Ezra Pound, *Literary Essays*, ed. T. S. Eliot (London: Faber and Faber, 1974), p. 325.

5 Salutary to recall the careful balance struck by Jonathan Freedman in his introduction to *The Cambridge Companion to Henry James* (pp. 18–19): 'We miss the real importance of James, however, if we attempt to turn him into one of our contemporaries – even if . . . James gives a range of subversive or alternative readings to the dominant cultural commonplaces of his moment in such a way as to offer our hypercritical age a critical leverage on those perceptions. But James's chief usefulness for the contemporary reader is not to identify subversive potentials in his own culture for our complacent

approval. Rather, it is that he foregrounds the sheer range of possibilities that circulated through his own time, and suggests the difficulty of navigating among them.'

6 William W. Stowe writes: 'Mr Longdon is the novel's great success because he interprets a strange world boldly, discarding an outdated set of proprieties and recognising the true value behind Nanda's "modern principles"'. *Balzac, James, and the Realist Novel* (Princeton University Press, 1983), p. 17.

7 Stowe comments on how 'the first few lines of the book humourously depict him [Van] "interpreting" the weather according to a set of fixed principles'. *Realist Novel*, p. 17.

8 'George Sand' (1899), in *Notes on Novelists* (London: J. M. Dent, 1914), p. 167.

9 *Autobiography*, ed. Frederick W. Dupee. (Princeton University Press, 1983), p. 213.

10 Leon Edel, *The Life of Henry James* (Harmondsworth: Penguin, 1977), p. 511.

11 '"Meridian manhood" lived on the bachelor plan.' Freedman, *The Cambridge Companion*, p. 15.

12 Walter Benjamin, *Illuminations*, ed. Hannah Arendt, trans. Harry Zohn (London: Fontana, 1992), p. 203.

13 Pierre A. Walker points out that the episode with the French novel in *The Awkward Age* is interestingly reminiscent of an episode in Gyp's 1884 novel, *Autour du Mariage*, where the bridegroom brings out an 'unseemly' book and is appalled to find his very young convent-educated wife has already read it. (Gyp is the French countess who wrote dialogue novels in the 1880s and 1890s, and whose approach is mentioned as a model in James's preface.) Walker stresses how well-worked a 'type' the too-knowing adolescent girl was in French fiction. *Reading Henry James in French Cultural Contexts* (Northern Illinois University Press, 1995), p. 109.

14 The names have *Jane Eyre* resonances, of course.

15 *Essays in London and Elsewhere* (London: Osgood, 1893), p. 252.

16 Michael Egan puts his stress on the influence of Ibsen's symbolism: 'the golden bowl was struck in Norway', and 'it was Ibsen who showed James how to use Hawthorne'. *Henry James: the Ibsen Years* (London: Vision Press, 1972), p. 29. Laurence B. Holland describes the relevance for James of Ibsen's work, given James's aim in the late 1890s for 'an extension of scale and moral urgency beyond what the meagre appearances, the ostensibly bare materials, suggest; a pressure towards symbolic extension so strong that customary "signs" are abandoned or remade, and the very foundations of the art, its structure, becomes symbolic'. *The Expense of Vision: Essays on the Craft of Henry James* (Baltimore: Johns Hopkins University Press, 1982), p. 87.

17 *Notes on Novelists*, pp. 337–8.

18 N. H. Reeve in an essay on 'Mora Montravers' suggests that at the very end of 'the last work of fiction James was ever to complete' the heroine turns her back on the world of dingy proprieties and sexual taints with an insouciance that is 'strangely and powerfully liberating'. It is perhaps as if James has come in sight of the possibility of simply taking no further serious notice of

that social machinery predicated upon women's sexual innocence. 'One can sense for an instant, beyond Traffle's dismay, the presence of an anarchic, vengeful, utopian joy . . . at the spectacle of so absolute a repudiation and so final a judgement of the kind of world which Mora leaves beneath her.' N. H. Reeve (ed.), *Henry James: The Shorter Fiction* (Basingstoke: Macmillan, 1997), p. 154.

4 BLUSHING IN THE DARK: LANGUAGE AND SEX IN *THE AMBASSADORS*

1 There are of course a number of readings of the novel which celebrate Strether's special responsiveness rather than diagnosing it as part of a problem. Nussbaum, for example, celebrates Strether's 'willingness to be passive, surrendering the invulnerable agency of the Kantian self'. Martha C. Nussbaum, *Love's Knowledge: Essays on Philosophy and Literature* (New York: Oxford University Press, 1990), p. 180. Ross Posnock describes Strether's 'realisation of freedom from the monadic ego' and calls his experience in the novel 'a hazardous venture that produces pleasure not in spite of but because it courts injury at every turn'. *The Trial of Curiosity: Henry James, William James, and the Challenge of Modernity* (New York: Oxford University Press, 1991), pp. 230, 231.

2 Robert Dawidoff insists upon how thoroughgoing a product of Woollett Strether is: 'If *The Ambassadors* was not provincial, Strether's intellectual habit was – at least at the start – characteristically so.' *The Genteel Tradition and the Sacred Rage: High Culture vs Democracy in Adams, James, and Santayana* (Chapel Hill: The University of Carolina Press, 1992), p. 76.

3 Ian Watt, 'The First Paragraph of *The Ambassadors:* An Explication'. *Essays in Criticism* 10 (1960), pp. 250–74.

4 Eric Haralson gives a sensitive account of why Strether does not marry Maria, placing his decision in the context of the particular history of a generation who could admire and be moved by the sexual, but not want it for themselves: they had 'a readily available ulterior discourse that could serve as a staging ground against the gathered forces of heteronormativity'. In Jonathan Freedman (ed.), *The Cambridge Companion to Henry James* (Cambridge University Press, 1998), p. 182.

5 Walter Benjamin, *Illuminations*, ed. Hannah Arendt, trans Harry Zohn (London: Fontana, 1992), p. 199.

6 'Guy de Maupassant' (1888), in *Henry James: Selected Literary Criticism*, ed. Morris Shapira (London: Heinemann, 1963), p. 93.

7 'Guy de Maupassant', p. 94.

8 *Within the Rim and Other Essays 1914–15* (London: n.pub., 1919), p. 91.

9 Sara Blair discusses the 'performative character' in James's work of 'racial and national identity'. Although she is primarily concerned with these issues of identity in relation to an emergent American culture, her formulations are useful for a consideration of how other 'national and racial' identities

perform themselves in the novels. 'James . . . is constructing a cultural position from which otherness can be more pleasurably and freely experienced,
and against which the limits of conventional filiations – of family, gender,
nation, culture, race – can be tested and contested . . . James unmoors the
ethnographic Gestalt from the projects of strenuous manhood and of Anglo-
Saxon renewal.' *Henry James and the Writing of Race and Nation* (Cambridge
University Press, 1996), pp. 5, 58.

10 'James's admiration for Balzac goes beyond a nostalgic taste for old French
pictures to real, though never humble or submissive, discipleship.' William
W. Stowe, *Balzac, James, and the Realist Novel* (Princeton University Press,
1983), p. xiv.

11 See Introduction, p. 11 above.

12 See Introduction, p. 7 above.

13 Ruth Bernard Yeazell, *Fictions of Modesty, Women and Courtship in the English
Novel* (Chicago University Press, 1991).

14 Yeazell, *Fictions of Modesty*, p. 78.

15 'The Story in It' (1902), in *The Complete Tales of Henry James*, ed. Leon Edel
(London: Rupert Hart-Davis, 1962–4), vol. XI.

16 Yeazell, *Fictions of Modesty*, p. 79.

17 'Guy de Maupassant', in Shapira (ed.), *Selected Literary Criticism*, p. 103.

18 Richard A. Hocks calls it 'Strether's ongoing dialectic of faith and suspi-
cion'. 'Multiple germs, metaphorical systems, and moral fluctuation in *The
Ambassadors*', in Gert Buelens (ed.), *Enacting History in Henry James: Narrative,
Power and Ethics* (Cambridge University Press, 1997), p. 53.

19 To Paul Bourget (1888). *Letters*, vol. III, p. 220. (Original in French: translation
from Georges Markow-Totevy, *Henry James*, London: Merlin Press, 1969.)
Subsequent quotations are from the same source.

20 Review of *Letters of R. L. Stevenson to his Family and Friends*, in *Essays on English
and American Writers*, ed. Leon Edel and Mark Wilson (New York: Viking and
Cambridge University Press, 1984), p. 1269.

21 'Instead of the central passion it gives the analogies or embodied likenesses
in which the mysterious passion itself is refracted.' Laurence B. Holland, *The
Expense of Vision: Essays on the Craft of Henry James* (Baltimore: Johns Hopkins
University Press, 1982), p. 314.

22 Martha Nussbaum makes the novel pivot upon the contrast and incompati-
bility between, on the one hand, Strether's 'perceptive equilibrium' and his
'receptive passivity', and on the other, the passion which 'asks for privacy'
and 'shuts out others'. 'Lovers see, at such times, only one another; and it
is not really deep if they *can* carefully see around and about them.' *Love's
Knowledge*, pp. 188–90.

23 '[*The Ambassadors*] is unique . . . among the late works in its focus upon middle
age (the "afternoon", the "twilight of life") rather than youth.' Sallie Sears,
The Negative Imagination: Form and Perspective in the Novels of Henry James
(Ithaca, N.Y.: Cornell University Press, 1963), p. 101.

24 Strether's exclusion, his ruefulness and his refusal of Maria are often read as
a part of a whole aesthetic of renunciation in the *oeuvre*. David McWhirter,

for example, contrasts the exceptional 'affirmation of love' in *The Golden Bowl* with 'thwarted and renounced passion' in *The Ambassadors* and *The Wings of the Dove*, and has Strether as 'a willing prisoner of his own infinite wanting'. *Desire and Love in Henry James* (Cambridge University Press, 1989), pp. 3, 8. It does seem possible, however, to give the novel a reading which makes Strether's exclusion as much contingent as chosen, and which does not write off the fulfilled passions of Mme de Vionnet and Chad just because they do not 'live happily ever after'. Ross Posnock resists the 'rhetoric' that portrays Strether as 'vicarious, renunciatory, prissy, fearful and ascetic', and argues that to label Strether's experience as vicarious 'ignores the fact that his complex mingling of past and present, concrete and abstract, mystery and reality challenges the binary assumptions built into the very concept of the vicarious – an opposition between mediated and unmediated experience . . . To oppose the actual to the vicarious, life to art, and active to passive is antithetical to the libidinal sublimation of James's psychic economy.' *Trial of Curiosity*, p. 231.

25 J. M. Coetzee, *Doubling the Point: Essays and Interviews*, ed. David Attwell (Cambridge, Mass.: Harvard University Press, 1992), p. 159. See Introduction, p. 5 above.

26 Quoted in Fred Kaplan, *Henry James: The Imagination of Genius* (London: Hodder and Stoughton, 1992), p. 514.

27 In *French Poets and Novelists* (London: Macmillan, 1878), p. 109.

28 Tony Tanner, *Adultery in the Novel* (Baltimore: Johns Hopkins University Press, 1979), p. 377.

29 '[Mrs Newsome's] vision of life appeals to [Strether] and stirs . . . his moral imagination . . . Behind her coldness and her blocklike hardness, Strether permits us to understand the deep sense of dignity that motivates her assault on life . . . It is because Mrs Newsome is no mere caricature, but a brilliantly comic rendering of some of the deepest features of Kantian morality, that the novel has the balance and power that it does.' Nussbaum, *Love's Knowledge*, pp. 176, 178–9.

30 'Surrender to a massive, unnurturing mother defines Lambert Strether's captive state at the start of *The Ambassadors*.' Posnock, *Trial of Curiosity*, p. 219.

31 McWhirter gives an opposite account of Woollett; he calls Woollett, 'though it is a society run by women . . . essentially a culture built on concepts rooted in paternal authority'; and describes its 'paternally-determined syntax' as 'speak[ing] in a direct, hurried, masculine voice' (as opposed to Strether's 'feminine, perhaps even . . . motherly strategy of expression'). McWhirter, *Desire and Love*, pp. 43, 47.

32 Benjamin, *Illuminations*, p. 210.

33 Quoted in André Maurois, *The Life of George Sand*, trans. Gerard Hopkins (London: Cape, 1953), p. 429.

34 David Gervais feels it is the other way round: Flaubert is serious about passion and James is afraid of it. In his comments on James's responses to the Flaubert/Sand correspondence, Gervais worries that James's attitude involves 'a kind of insurance against the tragic sense of life'. *Flaubert and Henry James* (London: Macmillan, 1978), p. 6.

5 POOR GIRLS WITH THEIR RENT TO PAY: CLASS
   IN 'IN THE CAGE' AND *THE WINGS OF THE DOVE*

1 John Goode (ed.), *The Air of Reality* (London: Methuen, 1972), pp. 265, 299.
2 The account of *The Ambassadors* in the last chapter was concerned with other
  issues and did not address this 'economic aspect' of the novel. For a very full
  account of how *The Ambassadors* 'as a whole works in tracing the suppressed
  connections between the worlds of culture and commerce' (153), see Richard
  Salmon's *Henry James and the Culture of Publicity* (Cambridge University Press,
  1997).
3 Walter Benjamin, *Illuminations*, ed. Hannah Arendt, trans. Harry Zohn
  (London: Fontana, 1992), p. 205.
4 Benjamin, *Illuminations*, p. 201.
5 Leon Edel, 'Introduction', in *The Princess Casamassima* (London: The Bodley
  Head, 1972), p. 6.
6 *Letters*, ed. Leon Edel (London: Macmillan, 1975–85), vol. II, p. 209.
7 'In the Cage' (1898), in *The Complete Tales* of Henry James, ed. Leon Edel
  (London: Rupert Hart-Davis, 1962–4), vol. X, p. 153.
8 Martha Nussbaum gives a fuller and more sympathetic account of the politics
  of *The Princess Casamassima* in *Love's Knowledge*: Essays on Philosophy and
  Literature (New York: Oxford University Press, 1990).
9 Goode calls it 'the most panoramic of the three international novels at the
  turn of the century'. 'The pervasive mystery of style: *The Wings of the Dove*',
  in Goode (ed.), *The Air of Reality*, p. 246.
10 Jonathan Freedman gives an extended and more troubling account of the
   Jewishness of the antiquarians in 'The Poetics of Cultural Decline: Degeneracy, Assimilation, and the Jew in James's *The Golden Bowl*'. *American Literary
   History* 7.3 (1995), 477–99. Freedman makes out a relationship between the
   'racial drama' played out in *The Golden Bowl* and a contemporary 'thematics
   of racial and cultural degeneration', in which the Jewish characters stand
   for the dangers of a refusal to assimilate to a 'new cultural amalgam'. His
   passages on the Damascene tiles are brilliantly illuminating, and he gives a
   powerfully persuasive account of the politics of empire in the novel. A reading which made James less than wholly sympathetic to Maggie's project of
   'assimilation', however, and which was less sure of the 'triumph' of the ending, might support a reading of James's attitude to the Jews' unassimilable
   qualities that made it less fearful and more tenderly appreciative.
11 Lawrence Holland writes at length analysing the differentiations of social
   status in *The Wings of the Dove* in his *The Expense of Vision: Essays on the Craft of
   Henry James* (Baltimore: Johns Hopkins University Press, 1982), pp. 298–300.
12 Michiel Heyns is not so sure that James always avoided condescension. In
   'The Bench of Desolation' in particular he feels he writes down to its lower
   middle-class characters: 'at best it aspires to a sort of lugubrious despon-
   dency'. 'The double narrative of *The Beast in the Jungle*', in Gert Buelens
   (ed.), *Enacting History in Henry James: Narrative, Power and Ethics* (Cambridge
   University Press, 1977), p. 123.

13 Nadine Gordimer, *A Soldier's Embrace* (Harmondsworth: Penguin, 1982).

14 *French Poets and Novelists* (London: Macmillan, 1878), p. 102.

15 René Girard, *To Double Business Bound* (London: The Athlone Press, 1988), p. 3.

16 Girard, *Double Business*, p. 49.

17 In Gard (ed.), *Henry James: The Critical Heritage* (London: Routledge and Kegan Paul, 1968), p. 349.

18 'The restraints of delicacy and tact usually reserved for sexual misadventures are here transferred to the marketplace. And once again a material transaction prompts and figures a social one.' Jean-Christophe Agnew, 'The Consuming Vision of Henry James', in R. W. Fox and T. J. Jackson Lears (eds.), *The Culture of Consumption: Critical Essays in American History* (New York: Pantheon Books, 1983), p. 95. (Agnew's reference here is actually to *The Golden Bowl*.)

19 Agnew writes about a world 'saturated with the imagery of the market, a world constructed and deconstructed by the appreciative vision.' Agnew, 'The Consuming Vision', p. 94.

20 Jonathan Freedman makes illuminating comparisons of the Bronzino portrait episode with Rossetti's poem 'The Portrait'. He also describes how 'Milly's power is generated by her ambiguous theatricality – her ability . . . to deploy the idiom of gesture and the language of dress to play for Kate, for Densher, even for Lord Mark, the roles they have cast her in without ever letting them (or the reader) know whether she has consciously adopted these parts'. *Professions of Taste: Henry James, British Aestheticism, and Commodity Culture* (Stanford University Press, 1990), pp. 211–12, 222.

21 Goode writes: 'by going to Venice and living and dying in a palace, Milly is adopting a style'. 'The pervasive mystery of style', in Goode (ed.), *The Air of Reality*, p. 281.

22 It is difficult to see where Hugh Stevens finds Kate's 'active resistance of the roles dictated to her by Victorian society'. *Henry James and Sexuality* (Cambridge University Press, 1998), p. 33.

23 *The Notebooks of Henry James*, ed. F. O. Matthiessen and Kenneth B. Murdock (New York: Oxford University Press), pp. 169–74.

24 David McWhirter's readings of Merton's and Milly's relationship are everywhere striking and subtle, especially his insisting on Milly's 'aggressiveness' in asking to visit Merton's room: 'an almost literal attempt to open a door into the loved one's solitude'. *Desire and Love in Henry James* (Cambridge University Press, 1989), p. 152.

25 McWhirter is very plausible on how this slightly dull and very innocent friendship develops into a relationship which threatens Kate: 'the intimacy which she and Densher are engaged in creating, through their words, their awkward silences, the myriad choices involved in their simply being there together, is already on the way to becoming a reality in which Kate Croy has no place'. His account of the failure of the relationship with Kate seems much more fair than those readings which simply make Merton discover

that Kate is 'bad': 'by postponing the enactment of their love, by failing to do what they "would" *when* they would, Kate and Densher have sacrificed the passion which motivated in the first place their flawed strategy of secrecy and delay'. *Desire and Love*, pp. 124, 132.

26 Nancy Armstrong warns against the kind of reading which, 'always with the Enlightenment motive of discovering truth and producing freedom', 'aims to discover forms of repression' or to 'perform acts of liberation'. *Desire and Domstic Fiction: A Political History of the Novel* (Oxford University Press, 1984), pp. 12, 23.

27 Carolyn Porter's remarks about *The Golden Bowl* seem apposite here: 'Everyone intends the best, everyone tries to act for the best, and no-one is really insincere. Yet at the same time, everyone is complicit in the construction of a social reality at the centre of which lies a flaw. It is a world which ought to be familiar to any modern reader . . . one in which something terrible has happened which no-one intended, but to which everyone has contributed, taking their cues from each other, reacting rather than initiating action, and, more often than not, attributing responsibility to the arrangement in which they are 'fixed'. *Seeing and Being: The Plight of the Participant Observer in Emerson, James, Adams, and Faulkner* (Middletown, Conn.: Wesleyan University Press, 1981), p. 137.

28 Milan Kundera, *Testaments Betrayed* (London: Faber and Faber, 1996), p. 91.

6 'A HOUSE OF QUIET': PRIVILEGES AND PLEASURES IN *THE GOLDEN BOWL*

1 Nicola Bradbury, *Henry James: The Late Novels* (Oxford: Clarendon Press, 1979), chap. 5. It is Maggie's own image too; their guests are 'a kind of renewed water supply for the tank in which, like a party of panting goldfish, they kept afloat' (494). Carolyn Porter writes: 'James's strategy here is not designed to represent the ordinary social interactions of ordinary people – however one defines the ordinary.' *Seeing and Being: The Plight of the Participant Observer in Emerson, James, Adams, and Faulkner* (Middletown, Conn.: Wesleyan University Press, 1981), pp. 154–5.

2 The concentration in this chapter is narrowly inwards upon James's own probing survey of a particular nexus of class, culture and economics in his small group of privileged trans-Atlantic subjects: he is interested in what binds together their particular arrangements for living, and what threatens to pressure those arrangements apart. Much work in James criticism recently, however, has been on building relationships outwards from James's constructions of class and nation to a wider history of class, race, and national identity around the turn of the century. In Patricia McKee's essay on *The Golden Bowl*, for example, she argues that 'Adam Verver's art collection . . . functions as a model for an American "race"', and further that 'this collectivity of persons is not . . . exactly identifiable as a race. It is a grouping that shares with other conceptions of the dominant, white population of the

United States the sense that only "others", only persons not fully American-
ised, are members of races.' Patricia McKee, *Producing American Races: Henry
James, William Faulkner, Toni Morrison* (Durham NC: Duke University Press,
1999), p. 64. Sara Blair describes a James who 'engages in sometimes tense
if fluent exchange with the shifting currency of nation and race, and who
variously and contextually works to construct a cultural subject unbound by
laws of Anglo-Saxon "nature"'. *Henry James and the Writing of Race and Nation*
(Cambridge University Press, 1996), p. 9. Jonathan Freedman takes much
further a reading which makes *The Golden Bowl* a 'racial drama'; he writes
about 'the translation of empire which it is this text's mission to celebrate',
and about James's 'desire to valorise a process of mutually modifying assimilation between Anglo-American and other "races" or nationalities'. 'The
Poetics of Cultural Decline: Degeneracy, Assimilation, and the Jew in James's
The Golden Bowl', *American Literary History* 7.3 (1995), 486, 494.
3 'This progressive abstraction of objects from their cultural and historical
contexts does not aim at their individualisation. Instead, objects become
pieces of a collection.' McKee, *Producing American Races*, p. 66.
4 W. B. Yeats, *Collected Poems* (London: Macmillan, 1973), p. 225. Lionel Trilling
also reads 'Ancestral Houses' alongside his James, in *The Liberal Imagination*
(New York: The Viking Press, 1950).
5 'Thus, when Charlotte gives him [the Prince] his cue, she calls upon him to
perform precisely the services for which his heritage has trained him.' Porter,
Seeing and Being, p. 157.
6 Is it at Gloucester that they sleep together for the first time – 'I've wanted everything', 'You shall have everything' (272) suggests it, as well as the superior
formal elegance for the novel of having this first specified opportunity be the
first actual opportunity? If so, then it is possible that in the whole novel they
only sleep together once, because it is on their return from Gloucester that
Maggie is alerted to their secret, after which we presume they have to be cir-
cumspect while they wait to see what she does. One does not want, of course,
to stumble into the (bourgeois!) vulgarity of being caught out counting, as the
Prince almost is when Maggie first confronts him with her 'proof', and he
queries '*two* relations?', misunderstanding her (429). Presuming Gloucester
is the first time further presumes (or does it?) that their love affair *before* their
marriages was unconsummated: the Colonel is sceptical about that (76).
7 '[The Prince] looks at things in a way that identifies "darkness" with European knowledge, sophistication, and aristocracy: marks of his distinction.'
McKee, *Producing American Races*, p. 98.
8 Judged harshly, it is possible to make James's Italian type come out like this:
'Prevarication, ambiguousness, an easy way with other people's emotions –
these are, as we have seen, qualities genetically encoded in the Prince's
Italianness.' Freedman, 'Poetics of Cultural Decline', p. 493. Martha Banta
writes: 'the Prince brings as his dowry a deep, dark, dense Old World record
of violence and magnificence'. In Freedman (ed.), *The Cambridge Companion
to Henry James* (Cambridge University Press, 1998), p. 36.

9 Jane Campion's film of *The Portrait of a Lady* made much effective play with these qualities of display and subjection in dress; Osmond literally tripped Isabel onto the floor in one scene by stepping on the train of a skirt that was wide at her ankles but tight around her knees.

10 Michiel Heyns, *Expulsion and the Nineteenth-century Novel: Scapegoats in English Fiction* (Cambridge University Press, 1984), p. 205. There is almost what amounts to a consensus of critical disapproval of (not to say animus towards) the lovers, and Charlotte in particular. Bradbury in *The Late Novels* writes about what she calls the 'elopement scene' at Matcham, 'the false tone of the operatic diction . . . depends on a complicity as tawdry in moral terms as the intellectually slipshod communication of the cliché'(149). Daniel Mark Fogel in *Henry James and the Structure of the Romantic Imagination* (Baton Rouge: Louisiana State University Press, 1981) says Charlotte's thoughts are 'consumed with self-display and self-justification, with perhaps as brazen an indulgence in vanity as is ever allowed a major James character', and he talks about 'the false equilibrium that Charlotte ought not to enjoy but to deplore' (129). The 'allowed' and the 'ought not to' are symptomatic of a certain kind of moralised reading: it is that punitive structuring again, which we saw at work in readings of *The Portrait of a Lady*, where critics seek to find what a character has done 'wrong' in order to justify James's 'punishing' them. In Manfred Mackenzie's *Communities of Honour and Love in Henry James* (Cambridge Mass.: Harvard University Press, 1976) the Prince and Charlotte 'would provide the official situation, the international marriage, with its poisoned or left-handed imitation' (174); Mackenzie even wonders whether Charlotte 'has in the first place broken off with Amerigo with a view to lying close and keeping herself for another go' (171)! There are of course more sympathetic voices: for instance, Carolyn Porter in *Seeing and Being*, who suggests that 'if Charlotte has misread her cues, and in turn miscues the Prince, she does so out of an apprehension of his value as an individual in whom public and private selves are unified, and out of a quality of devotion to that individual of which no-one else in the novel seems capable' (158).

11 That argument of Heyns's about James signalling his disapproval of the relationship by displaying in his writing a gap between 'bedizened description' and the moral reality of what is happening, is interestingly like Bradbury's argument that the whole 'uneasy narrative extravagance' of *The Golden Bowl* is a device intended to convey – to represent, presumably – 'the loss of a common basis of understanding', a sort of decay of integrity in the world of his characters; this even though Bradbury's fundamental argument, which has Maggie as eventually 'extricating' us from the 'confusion', is almost opposite to Heyns's. (Bradbury, *The Late Novels*, p. 135.) A distaste in these critics – and others – for the erotic, 'romance' content of the novel seems to produce a reading of James's late manner as a mere strategy of pastiche and self-irony (or perhaps the distaste is for the manner itself?).

12 It is interesting how James's spatial metaphor for the erotic sensation here is very like the model that has been used in previous chapters to describe that dialogue in his late novels between the intelligence that 'sees all round' a phenomenon and the imagination that acknowledges its bottomlessness.

13 Of course there are numerous exceptions to this pattern in both traditions. *Mill on the Floss*, for example, has the curve of tragedy, consequent on Maggie's bungled choice of the erotic, which she must be punished for without even having had her 'hour'. And although *Le Rouge et le Noir* appears to follow the European curve, that cannot be understood in terms of the erotic choice; if anything, it is Julien's 'choice' of 'linear' ambition, his obliviousness to the boundlessness of the erotic, that undoes him.

14 'The stealthy concussions around which the action revolves, in *The Ambassadors* and *The Wings of the Dove* and *The Golden Bowl*, these invariably yield winners and losers. The winners are the ones who realise that the silence is not and cannot be equally shared, and who can manipulate the silence to their own best advantage. And forgive themselves for doing so, should this prove necessary – ruthlessly.' Adrian Poole, 'James and the Shadow of the Roman Empire', in Gert Buelens (ed.), *Enacting History in Henry James: Narrative, Power and Ethics* (Cambridge University Press, 1997), p. 79. Freedman writes: 'the power that enables Maggie to enclose, enchain, and control is the combination of the possession of knowledge and the refusal to specify exactly what that knowledge might be'. *Professions of Taste: Henry James, British Aestheticism, and Commodity Culture* (Stanford University Press, 1990), p. 236.

15 Alfred Habegger, *Henry James and the 'Woman Business'* (Cambridge University Press, 1989), p. 151.

16 In Heyns's account, 'Charlotte is the scapegoat of Maggie's text, in that Maggie's fiction is "controlled by the effect of a scapegoat it does not acknowledge"; but *The Golden Bowl* "acknowledges the scapegoat effect which does not control it"'. *Expulsion and the Nineteenth-Century Novel*, p. 268.

17 The reference is to Dickinson's poem that opens 'Papa above! / Regard a Mouse / O'erpowered by the Cat!'. *The Complete Poems of Emily Dickinson*, ed. Thomas H. Johnson (Boston: Little, 1960), p. 32.

18 'This wish to be without flaw and this desire to remain her father's daughter – we suspect that they must be somehow connected.' Martha C. Nussbaum, *Love's Knowledge: Essays on Philosophy and Literature* (New York: Oxford University Press, 1990), p. 126.

19 Adam's assembling his collection for the ungrateful inhabitants of American City links interestingly with Freedman's account in his work on *The Golden Bowl* of 'high, self-privileging art-making', which mystified '"taste" and prescribed its display as a means of asserting and reproducing forms of class domination and social control'. *Professions of Taste*, p. 256.

20 *Autobiography*, ed. Frederick W. Dupee (Princeton University Press, 1983).

21 Nussbaum writes: 'we have a sense that bulwarks of ignorance are being erected against some threat that presses in from the world; that knowledge

of some truth is not simply absent, but is being actively refused for the sake of beatitude'. *Love's Knowledge*, p. 127.

22 As Tony Tanner puts it, 'a person involved may experience that anxiety of "unhappy consciousness" that is a result of feeling he or she is participating in two or more irreconcilable patterns, with no means of mediating them any longer.' Tony Tanner, *Adultery in the Novel* (Baltimore: Johns Hopkins University Press, 1979), p. 17.

23 'James presents us with a frightening image of the Oedipal fantasy hallucinated into fulfillment'. McWhirter, *Desire and Love in Henry James* (Cambridge University Press, 1989), p. 189.

24 According to Hugh Stevens, *'the* question is the sexual question'. *Henry James and Sexuality* (Cambridge University Press, 1998), p. 46.

25 Ian Watt, *The Rise of the Novel* (London: The Hogarth Press, 1987), p. 30. 'Le réel écrit' is from Flaubert.

Bibliography

JAMES'S WRITING

FICTIONS

All references to the full-length novels are to the Penguin editions (Harmondsworth, Middlesex), unless otherwise stated. The novels which are the main focus of the book are listed below. The original date of publication for each novel follows the title in brackets; then the date of the Penguin edition used; then an explanation of which text in each case the Penguin is based on.

The Portrait of a Lady (1881)	1981 (New York Edition)
What Maisie Knew (1897)	1985 (New York Edition)
The Awkward Age (1899)	1979 (New York Edition)
The Ambassadors (1903)	1986 (New York Edition, with misplacement of what is now chapter xii corrected)
The Wings of the Dove (1902)	1965 (First edition)
The Golden Bowl (1904)	1966 (First English edition, 1905)

Where I want to make references to differences between the New York Edition (1907–9) and the original 1881 edition of *The Portrait of a Lady*, I have used an original Macmillan text, London, 1881.

References to the shorter fictions, unless otherwise stated, are made to *The Complete Tales of Henry James*, ed. Leon Edel (London: Rupert Hart-Davis, 1962–4): this seems the best way of offering consistency. Edel's collection uses the original book form (not the magazine serialisation) in which the stories were first published. The dates of first book publication of the stories given significant treatment are as follows:

'The Turn of the Screw' (1898)
'In the Cage' (1898)
'The Bench of Desolation' (1910)

OTHER WRITING BY JAMES

Letters, 4 vols., ed. Leon Edel (London: Macmillan, 1975–85).
The Notebooks of Henry James, ed. F. O. Matthiessen and Kenneth B. Murdock (New York: Oxford University Press, 1947).
Autobiography, ed. Frederick W. Dupee (Princeton University Press, 1983).
French Poets and Novelists (London: Macmillan, 1878).
Essays in London and Elsewhere (London: Osgood, 1893).
Notes on Novelists (London: J. M. Dent, 1914).
Within the Rim and Other Essays 1914–5 (London, n.p., 1919).
Literary Reviews and Essays, ed. Albert Mordell (New York: Grove Press, 1957).
French Writers and American Women Essays, ed. Peter Buitenhaus (Branford Conn.: Compass, 1960).
Henry James: Selected Literary Criticism, ed. Morris Shapira (London: Heinemann, 1963).
Essays on English and American Writers, ed. Leon Edel and Mark Wilson (New York: Viking and Cambridge University Press, 1984).

STUDIES AND CRITICISM

Armstrong, Nancy, *Desire and Domestic Fiction: A Political History of the Novel* (Oxford University Press, 1987).
Bakhtin, M. M., *The Dialogic Imagination*, ed. Michael Holquist, trans. Caryl Emerson and Michael Holquist (Austin: Texas University Press, 1981).
Bell, Millicent, *Meaning in Henry James* (Cambridge, Mass.: Harvard University Press, 1991).
Benjamin, Walter, *Illuminations*, ed. Hannah Arendt, trans. Harry Zohn (London: Fontana, 1992).
Bersani, Leo, *A Future for Astyanax: Character and Desire in Literature* (London: Marion Boyars, 1978).
Blair, Sara, *Henry James and the Writing of Race and Nation* (Cambridge University Press, 1996).
Bradbury, Nicola, *Henry James: the late novels* (Oxford: Clarendon Press, 1979).
Brooks, Peter, *The Melodramatic Imagination* (New York: Columbia University Press, 1985).
Buelens, Gert, (ed.) *Enacting History in Henry James: Narrative, Power and Ethics* (Cambridge University Press, 1997).
Coetzee, J. M., *White Writing: On the Culture of Letters in South Africa* (Newhaven: Yale University Press, 1988).
  Doubling the Point: Essays and Interviews, ed. David Attwell (Cambridge, Mass.: Harvard University Press, 1992).
Cornwell, Neil and Maggie Malone (eds.), *New Casebooks: The Turn of the Screw and What Maisie Knew* (Basingstoke: Macmillan, 1998).
Dawidoff, Robert, *The Genteel Tradition and the Sacred Rage* (Chapel Hill: The University of North Carolina Press, 1992).

Edel, Leon, *The Life of Henry James* (Harmondsworth: Penguin, 1977).

Egan, Michael, *Henry James: The Ibsen years* (London: Vision Press, 1972).

Ermath, Elizabeth Deeds, *Realism and Consensus in the English Novel* (Princeton University Press, 1983).

Felman, Shoshana, *Writing and Madness*, trans. Martha Noel Evans and the author with the assistance of Brian Massumi (Ithaca, N. Y.: Cornell University Press, 1985).

Fitzgerald, Penelope, 'Reviewing the Struggle', *London Review of Books* 20. 12 (June 1998).

Fogel, Daniel Mark, *Henry James and the Structure of the Romantic Imagination* (Baton Rouge: Louisiana State University Press, 1981).

   Covert Relations: James Joyce, Virginia Woolf and Henry James (Charlottesville: University Press of Virginia, 1997).

Fox, Richard Wightman and T. J. Jackson Lears (eds.), *The Culture of Consumption: Critical Essays in American History 1880–1980* (New York: Pantheon Books, 1983).

Freedman, Jonathan, *Professions of Taste: Henry James, British Aestheticism, and Commodity Culture* (Stanford University Press, 1990).

   'The Poetics of Cultural Decline: Degeneracy, Assimilation, and the Jew in James's *The Golden Bowl*', *American Literary History* 7.3 (1995).

Freedman, Jonathan (ed.), *The Cambridge Companion to Henry James* (Cambridge University Press, 1998).

Gard, Roger, (ed.), *Henry James: The Critical Heritage* (London: Routledge and Kegan Paul, 1968).

Gervais, David, *Flaubert and Henry James* (London: Macmillan, 1978).

Girard, René, *To Double Business Bound* (London: The Athlone Press, 1988).

Goode, John (ed.), *The Air of Reality: New Essays on Henry James* (London: Methuen, 1972).

Gosse, Edmund (ed.), *Fantasia* by Mathilde Serao (Heinemann International Library, 1890).

Habegger, Alfred, *Henry James and the 'Woman Business'* (Cambridge University Press, 1989).

Heron, Bonnie L. 'Substantive Sexuality, Henry James constructs Isabel Archer as a complete woman in his revised version of *Portrait of a Lady*', *Henry James Review* 16.2 (1995).

Heyns, Michiel, *Expulsion and the Nineteenth-Century Novel: Scapegoats in English Fiction* (Cambridge University Press, 1984).

Holland, Laurence B., *The Expense of Vision: Essays on the Craft of Henry James* (Baltimore: Johns Hopkins University Press, 1982 [1964]).

Kaplan, Fred, *Henry James: The Imagination of Genius* (London: Hodder and Stoughton, 1992).

Kundera, Milan, *Testaments Betrayed* (London: Faber and Faber, 1996).

Leavis, F. R., *The Great Tradition* (London: Chatto and Windus, 1962).

Lebowitz, Naomi, *The Imagination of Loving: Henry James's Legacy to the Novel* (Detroit: Wayne State, 1965).

Lyon, Richard (ed.), *Santayana on America: Essays, Notes and Letters on American Life, Literature and Philosophy* (New York: Harcourt, 1968).

Mackenzie, Manfred, *Communities of Honour and Love in Henry James* (Cambridge Mass.: Harvard University Press, 1976).

Mann, Thomas, *Essays of Three Decades*, trans. H. T. Lowe-Porter (London: Secker and Warburg, n.d).

Markow-Totevy, Georges, *Henry James* (London: Merlin Press, 1969).

McKee, Patricia, *Producing American Races: Henry James, William Faulkner, Toni Morrison* (Durham, N. C.: Duke University Press, 1999).

McWhirter, David, *Desire and Love in Henry James* (Cambridge University Press, 1989).

Nussbaum, Martha C., *Love's Knowledge: Essays on Philosophy and Literature* (New York: Oxford University Press, 1990).

Pollak, Vivian R. (ed.), *New Essays on Daisy Miller and The Turn of the Screw* (Cambridge University Press, 1993).

Porter, Carolyn, *Seeing and Being: The Plight of the Participant Observer in Emerson, James, Adams, and Faulkner* (Middletown, Conn.: Wesleyan University Press, 1981).

Posnock, Ross, *The Trial of Curiosity: Henry James, William James, and the Challenge of Modernity* (New York: Oxford University Press, 1991).

Pound, Ezra, *Literary Essays*, ed. T. S. Eliot (London: Faber and Faber, 1974).

Reeve, N. H. (ed.), *Henry James: The Shorter Fiction* (Basingstoke: Macmillan, 1997).

Rowe, John Carlos, *The Theoretical Dimensions of Henry James* (London: Methuen, 1985).

Salmon, Richard, *Henry James and the Culture of Publicity* (Cambridge University Press, 1997).

Sears, Sallie, *The Negative Imagination: Form and Perspective in the Novels of Henry James* (Ithaca, N. Y.: Cornell University Press, 1963).

Sedgwick, Eve Kosofsky, *Epistemology of the Closet* (Stamford: University of California Press, 1990).

Stevens, Hugh, *Henry James and Sexuality* (Cambridge University Press, 1998).

Stone, Lawrence, *Road to Divorce* (Oxford University Press, 1992).

Stowe, William W., *Balzac, James, and the Realistic Novel* (Princeton University Press, 1983).

Tanner, Tony, *Adultery in the Novel* (Baltimore: Johns Hopkins University Press, 1979).

Tanner, Tony (ed.), *Modern Judgements: Henry James* (London: Macmillan, 1968).

Trilling, Lionel, *The Liberal Imagination* (New York: Doubleday and Co, 1953).

Walker, Pierre A., *Reading Henry James in French Cultural Contexts* (Northern Illinois University Press, 1995).

Watt, Ian, 'The First Paragraph of *The Ambassadors*: An Explication', *Essays in Criticism* 10 (1960), 250–74.

The Rise of the Novel (London: The Hogarth Press, 1987).

Yeazell, Ruth Bernard, *Language and Knowledge in the Late Novels of Henry James* (Chicago University Press, 1976).

Fictions of Modesty: Women and Courtship in the English Novel (Chicago University Press, 1991).

Yeazell, Ruth Bernard (ed.), *Henry James: A Collection of Critical Essays* (New Jersey: Prentice Hall, 1994).

OTHER LITERARY WORKS CITED

Chekhov, Anton, *Lady with a Lapdog and other stories*, trans. Magarshack (Harmondsworth: Penguin, 1964).

Dickinson, Emily, *The Complete Poems*, ed. Thomas H. Johnson (Boston: Little, 1960).

Gordimer, Nadine, *A Soldier's Embrace* (Harmondsworth: Penguin, 1982).

Stendhal, *Le Rouge et le Noir* (1830) (Paris: Garnier-Flammarion, 1964).

Tolstoy, Leo, *Anna Karenina* (1877), trans. Aylmer Maude (London: Oxford University Press, 1965).

Wharton, Edith, *Roman Fever* (London: Virago Modern Classics, 1983).

Yeats, W. B., *Collected Poems* (London: Macmillan, 1973).

Index